Pieter vanden Berch provisioneel secrets:
ende gesubstitueert fiscael vanden raedt
over fortresse de goede hoope —
den [illegible] ex officio —

Eijsch,

Contra

Joost vanden Laeck van Deventer —
Corporael vande soldaten over
begaene oppositie ende crimen lese
majestatis, jegens den E: Joan
van Riebeeck, opperkoopman
ende opperhooft der gemelde
fortresse &a. ged.e ende gevangen —

saeken [illegible] ende alle
de werelt notoir ende
inobedientie, oppositie
ende uitspoudie, welcke den
gedaegde offte gevangen aldaer opperhooft deser plaetse petulan-
opden 4en deser tot seer groote
cleijnachtinge ende violatie sijnder
E: respect ende authoriteijt heeft
begaen. —

Daer ter contrarie alle comp.s dienaeren volgens den [illegible] vanden generalen articulbrieff, ende ook des halven schuldigh sijn haere respective overigheden alle eer ende respect te be-wijsen ende deselver billicque bevelen sonder eenige con-tradictie te obedieren; ende wie ter contrarie doet ten hooghsten strafbaer is,

Soo weijnigh den gevangen sigh hier aen gelegen gelaten, ende deselve sijne schuldige plicht naergecomen heeft, blijckt ter contrarie uijt sijne begaene oppositie ende ongehoor-saemheden, op dato voorsz. petulanter tegen sijn E. voorsz. geperpetreert —.

Want soo als het opperhooft doende met sijn huijsvrouwe den schipper vant Jacht, ende [illegible] doe hij sijn huijs-vrouwe gegaen was omtrent een half quartier uurs buijten 't fort, is seecker bessen opde cant vande [illegible] met een soo vis die gevangen was, om sich wat te verfrissen ende verlustigen.

Soo

Our Legal Heritage

A project of *De Rebus – the South African Attorneys' Journal*, under the auspices of the Association of Law Societies of the Republic of South Africa

Our Legal Heritage

BUTTERWORTHS
Durban · Pretoria

ISBN: 0 409 04 084 3

THE BUTTERWORTH-GROUP

South Africa
BUTTERWORTH & CO (SA) (PTY) LTD
152-154 Gale Street Durban 4001

England
BUTTERWORTH & CO (PUBLISHERS) LTD
88 Kingsway London WC2B 6AB

Australia
BUTTERWORTHS PTY LTD
271–273 Lane Cove Road North Ryde NSW 2113

Canada
BUTTERWORTH & CO (CANADA) LTD
2265 Midland Avenue Scarborough Ontario MIP 4S1

New Zealand
BUTTERWORTHS OF NEW ZEALAND LTD
31–35 Cumberland Place Wellington

United States
BUTTERWORTHS PUBLISHERS INC
10 Tower Office Park Woburn Massachusetts 01801

Cover: Colin Bridgeford
Design and type-setting: Dieter Zimmermann (Pty) Ltd, Johannesburg
Printed in South Africa by Sigma Press (Pty) Ltd, Pretoria

Contributors

Co-editors: H F Mellet BA(Pret) LLB(SA), formerly editor of *De Rebus – the SA Attorneys' Journal*
Susan Scott BA LLB(Pret) LLD(SA), Associate Professor in Private Law, University of South Africa
Paul van Warmelo BA LLB(Pret) Doct Iur(Leyden) LLD hc(Cape Town), Temporary Senior Lecturer in Legal History, Comparative Law and Jurisprudence, University of South Africa; Honorary Professor in Law, University of the North

Editorial committee: J E Knoll BA LLB(Cape Town), chairman, R B Cleaver BA LLB(Stell), M L Benade BA(Stell) LLB(OFS) LLD(SA), R Sceales BCom(Witwatersrand) LLB(Stell), S W van der Merwe BA LLB(Pret)

Authors

Pieter Pauw BA LLB(RAU) LLD(Leyden)
Johan Scott BA(Hons) LLB(Pret) LLD(Leyden)
Paul van Warmelo BA LLB(Pret) Doct Iur (Leyden) LLD hc (Cape Town)
G E Devenish BSc(Witwatersrand) LLB(SA)
A N Oelofse BA LLB(Stell)
S N Roberts BA(Cantab) LLB(Natal)
J C Dugard BA LLB(Stell) LLB LLD(Cantab)
Ellison Kahn BCom LLB(Witwatersrand) LLM LLD(Natal) LLD hc (Cape Town)
J A van S d'Oliveira BIur(Pret) LLB LLD(SA)
D H Sampson BA(Hons) MA(Oxon)
G W Cook BA LLB(Witwatersrand)

Translation from Afrikaans of chapters 1, 2, 5, 7 and 10: Neville Botha BIur LLB(Pret), Senior Lecturer in Law, University of South Africa

Maps: Tienie du Plessis, Lecturer in Fine Arts, Technikon, Pretoria

Indexer: Marthie Boshoff BA(SA) HDipLib(Cape Town)

The Honourable F L H Rumpff, BA LLD hc (Pret) QC DVD, Chief Justice of the Republic of South Africa

FOREWORD

The Association of Law Societies of the Republic of South Africa is an association that not only looks after the interests of practising attorneys, or applies professional discipline whenever it is necessary, but also advances the interests of the law in a broader context. It has, for instance, made generous donations to the faculties of law at the universities of our country. The publication of *Our Legal Heritage* is further proof of the positive interest of the Association in the law in general. Through this publication the law student and the layman can now visually appreciate that the South African common law is mainly a rich cultural product of Western civilization. Its origin dates back to times before the birth of Christ and through the ages it has become essentially the product of cumulative individual juristic thought. Notwithstanding its age, it is a living system. Its continuous growth, neither rash nor irresponsible, causes basic principles to be developed and adapted in order to keep pace with the changing social conditions. The purpose is obvious: justice must not be dimmed by mould or rust but must be kept shining brightly.

Without a refined legal system a modern civilized state cannot exist and – with apologies to St Augustine – in regard to worldly welfare: *salus extra legem non est*. In my view, the common law of South Africa is unsurpassed by any other legal system. I sincerely hope that all who are interested in our law will cause this publication to be distributed to such an extent that many a reprint will be necessary.

F L H Rumpff
Chief Justice, March 1982

INTRODUCTION

The legal system of a country reflects to some extent the nature and the development of the community. In the same way every legal system has elements which give it a special character and which distinguish it from other systems. This is also true of the law of South Africa which is unique for several reasons:

- The law of South Africa consists of more than one system for the different peoples in the country. Apart from the common law of South Africa – usually referred to as the Roman-Dutch law – several systems of law apply under certain circumstances to the several Black peoples. There are today few communities where such is the case. However, in ancient times similar situations occurred. During the period of the early Roman Empire, Roman law applied to the Roman citizen – non-Roman subjects were considered as foreigners and the law of their country of origin applied to them. At a later stage tribes from beyond the Roman frontiers which settled within the Empire and the people of occupied territories were also allowed to maintain their own systems of law. In fact, in ancient Egypt no less than three systems of law applied – Egyptian, Greek and Roman!
- In South Africa, Roman-Dutch law was introduced from the provinces of Holland and Zeeland when the Dutch established a settlement at the Cape of Good Hope in 1652. Although in the Netherlands the law was codified early in the nineteenth century, Roman-Dutch law continued to develop in South Africa in a manner which distinguishes it markedly from other related legal systems. Firstly, it is still basically customary law – although vast fields of law have been created or re-enacted in statutory law. South African law is not a codified system as is the case with related systems in Europe. Secondly, it is one of the few remaining systems of customary law in which Roman law played a predominant role and in which that role has not yet been wholly discarded. Thirdly, the situation in South Africa, South West Africa (Namibia) and to a somewhat lesser degree in Zimbabwe, differs from other countries in which Roman-Dutch law is also customary law (Sri-Lanka, Botswana, Swaziland and Lesotho): Roman-Dutch law is not only being maintained in South Africa, but it is flourishing – South Africa is in fact the only place in the world where a truly uncodified system of civil law still exists.
- Modern Roman-Dutch law is a far cry from the system which was originally introduced in South Africa. Its growth has been influenced by a considerable number of factors. One of these factors is the fact that the Cape became a British colony towards the beginning of the previous century. As a result a legal system grew which was no longer wholly a civil system (based on Roman law) or a common-law system (based on English law). The system which developed is a symbiosis of the two systems. Much of the law of England was introduced by statute or by means of judicial decisions in courts which derived a great deal of their practice and procedure from English courts. Thus the legal atmosphere and methods of legal thinking and reasoning introduced from England also influenced South African law.

This book will attempt to give an account of the development and present state of South African law for the lawyer as well as for the non-lawyer. Therefore, some articles are more learned in nature than others. Care has been taken to illustrate important events in our legal history. In order to give due recognition to those men who have contributed to South African law, a large number of portraits with biographical and bibliographical notes have been added.

We have decided to review the main events in the origin and development of South African legal history. The repetition which occurs in some of the chapters can be explained by the fact that the subject-matter is discussed thematically.

Although the information in this book is based on research of primary and secondary sources, it has been decided to avoid inconveniencing the reader unnecessarily with footnotes. Also, only a limited number of cross-references have been used. Hopefully the index of names and places will provide the reader with the necessary references to persons, places and illustrations. The complete titles of references are given in the bibliography.

Finally, the editors would like to thank the many persons and institutions whose contributions made the publication of this book possible. First there is the editorial committee of *De Rebus – The SA Attorneys' Journal* who commissioned the project and who gave their wholehearted assistance to it. Secondly, the Association of Law Societies which provided the necessary finances for the development of the project. As a result of this it was possible to procure some extremely rare illustrations for the book. Thirdly, there are the contributors and writers who managed to fit the time-consuming research for the book into their already busy schedules.

A special word of thanks is due to Mr C T R Marais and Miss H J Visser of the audio-visual department of the University of Pretoria as well as Professor Johan Scott of the Law Faculty of the same university, for his help in obtaining many of the illustrations.

A personal word of thanks also to Mrs Madeline Parker, the assistant editor of *De Rebus – the SA Attorneys' Journal* and Mrs Sophie Grobler, secretary, who assisted the editors with a variety of tasks.

The editors

Contents

The Temple of Portunus is a small Ionic temple in the Italic style. It is one of the best preserved of the Roman buildings. Its original purpose is unknown, but it probably dates from the period of Sulla (138–78 BC).

Pieter Pauw BA LLB (RAU) LLD (Leyden) Advocate of the Supreme Court of South Africa

1

ROMAN LAW

Roman law is the oldest legal system still finding application in modern legal systems – notably that of South Africa. The concept of Roman law is subject to more than one interpretation. In this chapter, however, Roman law as the law of the Romans – the written law *(ius scriptum)* – will be discussed.

The Kingship

The legend of the establishment of Rome in 735 BC and of the twin brothers Romulus and Remus is known to all. The first period, up until 509 BC, during which seven kings ruled over Rome, is known as the Kingship.

Little is known of the law during this period. The populace was divided into a number of groups. There were three tribes (the Ramnes, Tities and Luceres). Each tribe was divided into ten *curiae* and each *curia* into ten *gentes* (agnatically related groups). These *gentes* consisted of *familiae*, each with a *paterfamilias* as head. The *familia* was a concept wider than the traditional family: a typical unit would, for example, be a great-grandfather together with all his descendants and their slaves. The populace was further divided into patricians (nobles) and plebs, as well as the *clientes* who may be equated with the serfs of the Middle Ages.

There were, during this period, also a number of popular assemblies. These were the *comitia tributa* (tribes), *comitia curiata (curiae), comitia calata* (*comitia curiata* assembled for religious purposes), and the *comitia centuriata* (for military purposes the populace was divided into groups of one hundred). In addition to these popular assemblies there was also the Senate: a council of wise elders who advised the king. These organs continued to function until the Principate (see page 00).

The community was basically agrarian and the law consequently unsophisticated. Scant distinction was drawn between law *(ius)* and religion *(fas)* which explains the prominent role of the priests in the administration of justice and the preservation of the *formulae* and the procedural law. Laws were, however, made during this period, the so-called *leges regiae*: directions for day-to-day existence drawn up with the co-operation of the popular assemblies.

The Republic

Tradition has it that the last king was banished, and the Republic established, in 509 BC. Although power was originally vested in the patricians, because of their uprisings, their assemblies *(concilium plebis)*, and their officials, the plebs gradually became a considerable force to be reckoned with. The Senate assumed new importance and new offices were created in the Republic. The most important of these were those of *consul* and *praetor*.

Times were troubled and the plebs struggled to acquire rights. Their struggle reached its climax in 286 BC when the *Lex Hortensia*, recognizing the *concilium plebis* as legislature, was adopted. *Plebiscita* were now to become *leges*.

As regards *leges*: there were many *leges* prior to this date, the most important probably being the *Lex duodecim Tabularum* (Law of Twelve Tables) of approximately 450 BC. This work may be regarded as a simple codification of the law then

An aerial view of Rome, showing the Palatine Hill with the ruins of the imperial palaces as seen from the north-east.

The Twelve Tables was a direct result of the struggle between the nobility and the plebeians who formed the bulk of the population. Law was originally administered by the patrician magistrates, and apparently even the knowledge of its contents was denied to the populace. In 451 BC, however, a code was set up in the market place on ten bronze tablets. Later a further two were added and these Twelve Tables served as a code and law book. This is an example of one of these tablets.

Marcus Tullius Cicero was one of the greatest Roman orators and writers. He was born in 106 BC and assassinated in 43 BC by the soldiers of Marcus Antonius. This versatile and eminent lawyer wrote profusely: his works range from treatises on oratory, rhetoric and philosophy to poetry and letters (the latter purposely written for later publication). He is an excellent example of the successful Roman orator.

existing in Rome. It embodies legislation, provisions regulating succession, the law of persons, delict, criminal law, procedure, etc. It was a positive step in the development of Roman law: for the first time an accessible code was available. It furthermore formed the basis of the *ius civile*, the law of the Roman citizen. This early law is characterized by its formalism.

Apart from *lex*, custom *(mos)* was also a source if the law.

Just as during the Kingship, during the Republic, too, the priests were for a considerable period in control of the administration of justice: law and religion were long still closely intertwined. Tradition has it that the monopoly of the priests was broken in 304 BC when one Cn Flavius disclosed the secret *formulae* – an act resulting in the administration of justice by laymen. This explanation is untenable for two reasons. In the first place the community had developed from largely agrarian to a community where trade and money assumed ever greater importance. This in turn, demanded a new dispensation. In the second, the Twelve Tables and the *praetor* played an important role in procedural law.

The praetor

The nature and development of Roman law is due largely to the office of the *praetor*. As an official he influenced the law in two ways. On the one hand he had *iurisdictio*. This does not mean that he was a judge, but rather that a claimant wishing to institute action, had first to approach the *praetor*. The *praetor* then considered the case and decided whether or not it was justiciable. If found justiciable, it was referred to a judge who was a layman. In deciding on the justiciability of a case, the *praetor* was not bound by existing law but could, if a specific case appeared fair and desirable, or was analogous to existing cases, declare it justiciable by granting an extended action – an *actio in factum* or *utilis*. In this way new law was created.

In another way, too, the *praetor* acted in a legally creative manner. In terms of his power to publish edicts *(ius edicendi)*, the *praetor* issued an edict *(edictum perpetuum)* at the outset of his annual term of office in which he advised what measures were envisaged during that period. In addition he could, during the course of the year, issue new edicts *(edicta repentina)* amending his original declaration or providing new measures. Subsequent *praetors* often took over the edicts of their predecessors – a practice which later became the rule *(edicta tralaticia)*. The *ius praetorium* was consequently born and this together with the law created by the officials, came to be known as the *ius honorarium*.

The *ius praetorium*, in particular, exerted an important influence on the *ius civile*. It was used to replace antiquated rules, to adapt the *ius civile* to meet the demands of practice, and to fill gaps. In this way it contributed greatly to temper the formalism of the *ius civile*. The relationship between the *ius civile* and the *ius honorarium* can be equated with that between common law and equity in England.

As the *ius civile* applied only to Roman citizens, the need for new provisions arose as an ever increasing number of non-Romans became involved in legal transactions. To this end two *praetors* were appointed: *urbanus* and *peregrinus*. The former was concerned solely with issues between Roman citizens; the latter with matters arising between foreigners or between a foreigner and a Roman citizen. In this way Roman law opened the door to concepts such as *ius naturale* (natural law) and *ius gentium* (the law common to all peoples). This resulted in a tremendous development – one thinks, for example, of consensual contracts which broke entirely with the formalism of the *ius civile*.

Portrait of a senator circa 330 AD. The Senate, which was constituted as a political organ during the Kingship, exercised considerable influence until the end of the Republican era, but this influence diminished during the Dominate, as an inevitable consequence of the emperor's dictatorial powers.

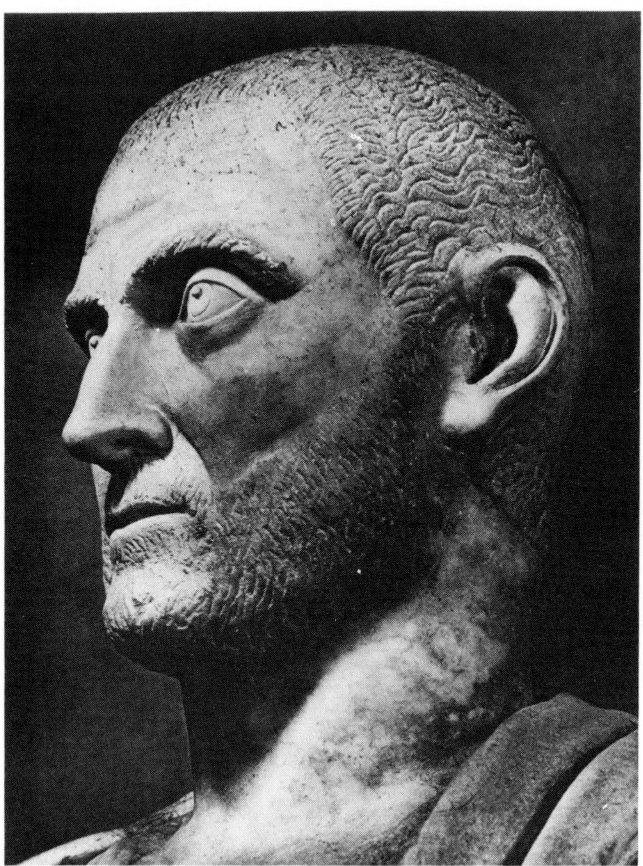

The jurists

A further factor destined to have a far-reaching effect on Roman law came into play during the Republic – viz jurists who were not priests. These jurists conducted legal cases for their clients, rendered advice and delivered legal opinions. They further interpreted and explained the *ius civile*. The jurist did not present his client's case. This was entrusted to an *orator* – someone like Cicero. Among the best known of the early jurists were S Aelus Paetus, P Mucius Scaevola, and M Iunius Brutus.

Although the popular assemblies continued to exist during the Republic, their legislative powers diminished. Despite the fact that the *Lex Hortensia* accorded *plebiscita* the force of *leges*, the legislative function was gradually usurped by the Senate. A major contributory factor in this process was that

Top: *Caius Julius Caesar was probably the most famous Roman of the Republic. He distinguished himself as general, orator, statesman and author. He was assassinated in 44 BC by Brutus and Cassius.*

Below: *Under the reign of the emperor Augustus (63 BC–14 AD) the Roman Empire attained unparalleled heights. Although the authority of the* comitia, *the Senate and the magistrates remained untouched, Augustus concentrated sufficient power in his own hands to control the entire administration of the State.*

by the end of the Republic, the *concilium plebis* was to a large extent manipulated by politicians while the Senate exhibited a large measure of continuity and was efficient.

Once Rome became a world power, the republican form of government based on the concept of a city state proved unsuitable for controlling so large a territory. Problems arose and the strongest leader with the strongest army could, in a seemingly legal manner, acquire dictatorial powers. This tendency, which manifested itself as early as Marius and Sulla, found full realization in Julius Caesar. The civil war following Caesar's death sounded the death knell for the Republic. The subsequent period, from 27 BC, with Augustus as *princeps* (caesar) is known as the Principate.

The Principate

While Caesar still accepted the republican form of government as basis, Augustus gradually introduced a new system. As *princeps* he controlled the entire machinery of state. This he manipulated very discreetly by still maintaining the republican institutions but ensuring that the real power was centered around his person. In this way the Principate was created, as it were, by convention. Augustus's successor, Tiberius, exercised power more directly and the Principate was thenceforth firmly established. Apart from the republican institutions retained during the Principate new offices were also created. Of particular importance in this regard are the *praefecti* – a factor also contributing to the vesting and entrenchment of central power in the emperor.

As far as Roman law is concerned, one may say that the office of *praetor* remained largely unaltered. As a result of annual repetition and extension, the praetorian law had evolved to such an extent during the Principate that there remained little scope for development. Consequently, in 130 AD the emperor Hadrian commanded the jurist Salvius Iuliaus to gather all the material under the title *Edictum Perpetuum*. This was a very important step in the development of Roman law as it afforded the jurists an opportunity to comment on the praetorian law and in this way to further its development.

In addition to the *Senatusconsulta* which still constituted an important source of private law, a new source of law in the person of the emperor arose during the Principate. As a result of the powers he had received by convention, the emperor also started issuing legal directives – the so-called *constitutiones*. The emperors made extensive use of these powers – particularly in the latter stages of the Principate.

The classical period

The most important source of law during the classical period was undoubtedly the works of the jurists, the *responsa prudentium*. Understandably so: the law was to a large extent fully developed and the *praetor's* activities had, after the *Edictum Perpetuum*, diminished and eventually died out altogether. The emperor and the Senate still created new law. There was consequently already a considerable volume and tradition; the time for processing and refining had dawned. It is for this reason that the period 0–250 AD is known as the classical period of Roman law; the period during which Roman law reached its zenith as a science.

Not only the scientific nature of the law, but also its eminent practicality exercised a strong influence. A factor contributing to this was the so-called *ius (publice) respondendi*: the right to give opinions. This was a privilege originally accorded eminent jurists by Augustus. In this way the opinions of the selected jurists came to bear great authority and it was almost automatic that a judge would, in the first instance, rely on these opinions.

The jurists further influenced practical law in that certain of them, for example Iulianus and later Ulpianus, Papinianus and Paulus, were in the service of the emperor. As the emperorship developed, a public service in which they were utilized came into being. It is thus not inconceivable that they were in a position to influence the emperor's *constitutiones*.

The jurists' greatest strength lay in their *responsa*. Because of the important role played by the

Top: *Marcus Aurelius (121–180 AD) was by nature a recluse and an introvert. Braced by his Stoic education, he spared himself neither at home nor in the battlefield.*

Below: *Title page of a seventeenth century edition of the* Corpus Iuris Civilis. *This edition includes commentaries, glosses, notes and correction on the original text. A photostatic reproduction of this edition, in six volumes, is nowadays freely obtainable.*

CORPVS
IVRIS CIVILIS
IVSTINIANEI,
CVM COMMENTARIIS ACCVRSII, SCHOLIIS CONTII, ET D. GOTHOFREDI LVCVBRATIONIBVS AD ACCVRSIVM, in quibus Glossæ obscuriores explicantur, similes & contrariæ afferuntur, vitiosæ notantur.

Accesserunt IACOBI CVIACII PARATITLA *in Pandectas & Codicem: eiusdémque* NOTÆ, OBSERVATIONES *&* EMENDATIONES *singulares in Pandectarum Libros* L. *Cod. Libros* XII. *Nouellas, Consuetudines Feudorum, & Iustiniani Institutiones.*

Item CHRONICI CANONES ab vniuerso Orbe condito vsque ad Vrbem conditam: ab Vrbe verò condita, FASTI Regij & Consulares vsque ad Iustiniani mortem, eodem CONTIO Auctore.

Præterea REMISSIONES PETRI BROSSEI, *quæ antea Sextum volumen efficiebant, opportuniùs vnicuique tomo subiectæ.*

Nunc verò Sextum volumen efficit INDEX locupletissimus à STEPHANO DAOYS Pampilonensi compilatus: Repertoriis omnibus, aut Thesauris hucusque editis vtilior & aptior.

Nouissimè accreuerunt TABVLÆ IVLI PACI *à Beriga, IC. celeberrimi; eiusdémque* INDICES *aliqui vtiliores: necnon* LOCI COMMVNES *ex rubricis titulorum.*

EDITIO SVPRA OMNEM OMNIVM ALIARVM CVRAM FIDA.

Ex HVGONIS A PORTA, & veterum exemplarium collatione à lacunis & mendis, quæ prioribus editionibus à quinquaginta annis inerant, repurgata, & perpetuis NOTIS illustrata.

Studio & operâ IOANNIS FEHI *Gaildorphensis IC.*

Tomus hic Primus Digestum Vetus continet.

LVGDVNI,

M. DC. XXVII.

The Roman Empire in 14 AD.

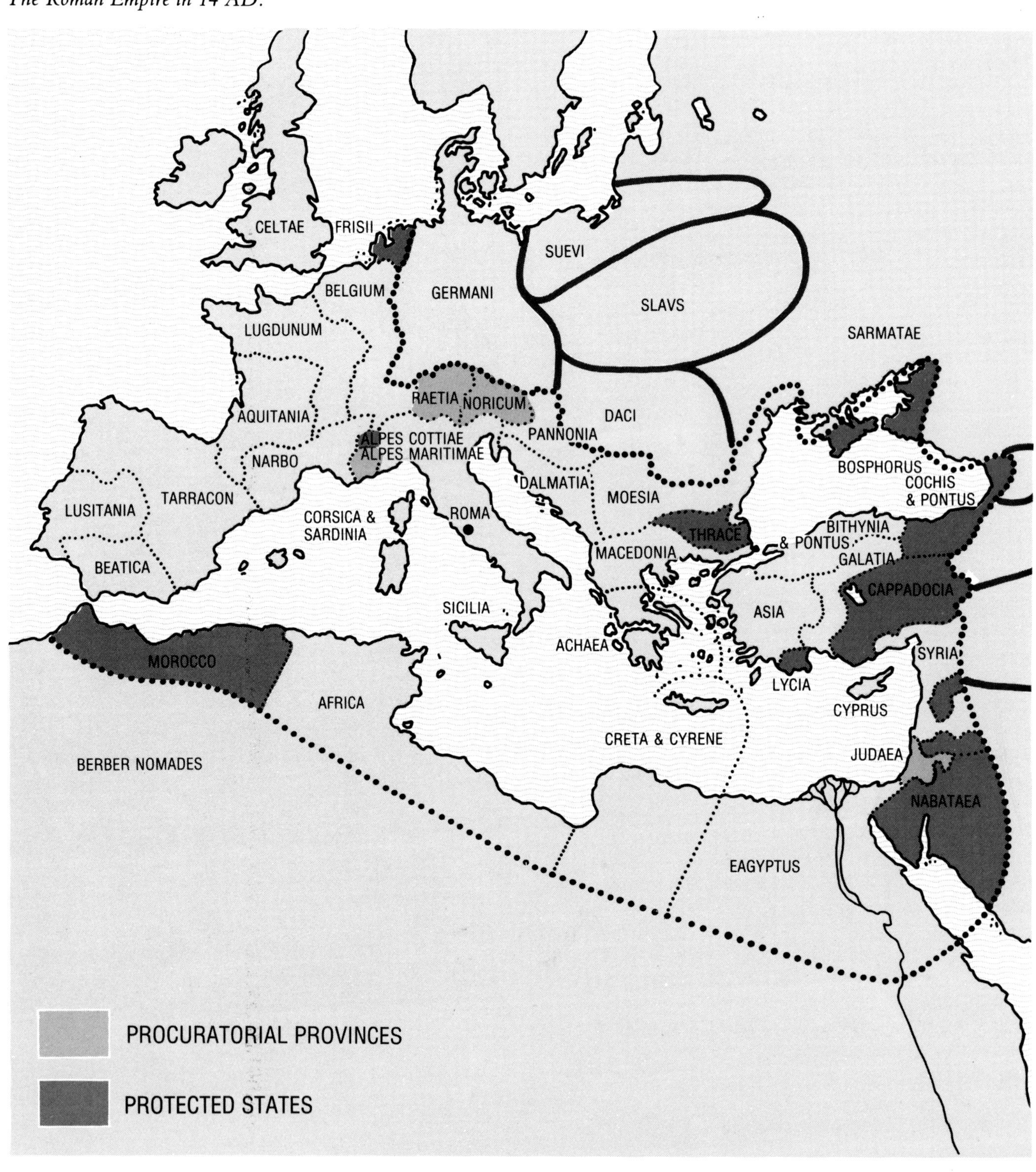

jurists, their options were regarded not as mere expositions of the law, but as the law itself. The possibility therefore existed that they could by their opinions create new law.

When we say that the jurists established a scientific system of law, we do not mean that they made use of involved theories and abstractions, as is the case today. The basis of the law of the jurists was an approach aimed at practice and was essentially casuistic. This emerges clearly if one examines the *Digesta*: no general rules are set, each case rather being approached individually. The works of the classical jurists evince a sense of reality centring around a problem case.

This should not, however, be interpreted to mean that the Roman jurists knew no theory. Certain norms had crystallized by this stage, and there were also various *leges, constitutiones* and *senatusconsulta*. As a result there were interpretations. There was, in addition, the *ius honorarium*.

The essence of the science of the classical jurist lay in interpretation. Their interpretations were based on logic. Definitions were formulated, particularly through use of the inductive method. This accentuates the fact that the jurists were concerned with concrete problems. Their interpretation was consequently wider than that which we today understand under the interpretation of statutes. They, for example, made frequent use of analogy and *argumenta e contrario*. Kaser has indicated that intuition, in other words a sense of justice, played an important role. The authority of great jurists of past eras *(veteres)* also influenced judgments. In short, there was no general formula for determining the law and a variety of methods was used to find a solution to a specific problem. It is further interesting to note that the jurists frequently gave no reasons for their findings. It is consequently difficult always to establish exactly why a specific jurist gave a specific solution to a problem with which he was faced.

To sum up, one could say that these *responsa prudentium* represented an elegant interpretation of the law. The supple methods avoided stagnation and ensured progress. The works of the jurists led to an amalgamation of the *ius civile* and the *ius*

Quintilian (first century AD), a jurist, was a famous teacher of rhetoric and advocacy, probably being the first rhetorician to receive a salary from the treasury. His famous work, the Institutio Oratoria, *is a treatise on the training of an orator, from infancy to adulthood.*

The Hagia Sophia in Constantinople (Istanbul). After the fall of the Roman Empire in the West in 476 AD, Constantinople became the capital of the Roman Empire. The empress Theodora, wife of Justinian, was an extremely religious woman and under her guidance the Hagia Sophia was built.

honorarium resulting in a single body of rules. The role of the *responsa* may be compared to that of the precedent system: rules which originated casuistically. The difference between the two lies in the fact that in the case of precedents authority is derived from a judgment, while in the case of *responsa* it was to be found in the opinions of the jurists.

Legal education also came to the fore during this period. The works of the jurists showed a greater degree of abstraction and systematizing than other works. This was aimed at making the material more easily digestible. The best-known teacher was Gaius (circa mid-second century AD).

The most renowned jurists of the classical period were, *inter alia,* Iulianus, Celsus *(filius),* Pomponius (high-classical period), and Ulpianus, Paulus, Papinianus, and Modestinus (late-classical period).

When Roman law was at its zenith, the Roman Empire was sinking into decline. At the outset of the third century AD problems arose and these increased gradually. Economic decline set in; internal problems and neighbouring uprisings against the empire led to continuing unrest.

The Imperial Period or Dominate

The official end of the Principate, when the crown was assumed by Diocletian, is set at 284 AD. The following period is known as the Dominate; the emperor was *dominus* and reigned as absolute ruler. The emperor and his public service was now extremely powerful. Diocletian divided the empire in two, east and west, for administrative purposes, but the power remained in the hands of the co-emperors.

In the atmosphere of unrest and decay the law lost its lustre. The emperor was to an ever increasing extent the sole source of law and the number of *constitutiones* increased markedly. The entire legal sphere declined and no jurists of note are encountered. Creative activities were limited and eventually ceased altogether. The post-classical productions were more often than not forgeries appearing under the name of a renowned jurist of earlier times – for example the *Epitome Gai*. The post-classical period reached its lowest ebb with the so-called Vulgate law. This was basically Roman law stripped of its high standard. Stagnation resulted in no further development. The quality of the jurists decreased and they were no longer able to appreciate and apply the finer points of law. In many areas the law became an amorphous mass.

The emperor Justinian (527–565 AD) was responsible for the codification of Roman law. This compilation later came to be known as the Corpus Iuris Civilis.

Attempts were made during this period to make the law accessible and to halt its deterioration. In the field of the emperor's *constitutiones* private collections, the *Codex Gregorianus* and *Hermogenianus*, were made. Theodosius II made an official collection, the *Codex Theodosianus*, which was accorded legal status in both the eastern and western empires in 439 AD. A number of citation laws were also issued during this period. These were laws in terms of which legal force was accorded to a specific work or to the works of a specific jurist. The most important of these laws was the *lex citationis* of 426 AD issued by Theodosius, in terms of which only the works of Gaius, Ulpianus, Papinianus, Paulus and Modestinus carried weight in litigation. The opinions of *veteres* cited by these jurists could also be used, provided that handwriting comparison ensured their authenticity. If a difference of opinion arose, the view of the majority prevailed. If there was a deadlock in voting, Papinianus's opinion was conclusive. This measure can to some extent be seen as a means by which the decline was halted. It, however, also advanced decline in the sense that as reliance was placed on a few jurists only, the door was closed on a great mass of valuable literature.

The Vandals invaded Rome in 455 AD, and in 476 AD the end of the Western Roman Empire finally dawned. The former Roman citizens, however, continued to live under their own legal system – at that stage Vulgate law. The barbarian leaders ordered the law of the different territories to be recorded. One consequently finds the *Lex Romana Visigothorum*, *Lex Romana Burgundionum* etc. Furthermore, the church continued to exist according to Roman law. These two factors promoted reception of scholarly law during the Middle Ages.

In the Eastern Roman Empire events took a different turn. After the fall of Rome, the concept of empire was transferred to Constantinople. Here it continued, subject to changes occasioned by Hellenic influence. Roman law did not decline to the same extent. Berytos (Beirut) was a strong Roman bastion and Roman law was taught at the university – the basis of classical law was preserved. It was, however, highly theoretical and a wide gap existed between theory and practice.

Justinian

When Justinian came to the throne in 527 AD the final peak of Roman law was reached. Tradition has it that the emperor cherished three ideals: to reconquer Italy, to extend Christianity, and to restore Roman law to its former glory. He realized all three, but only Roman law was permanent in that it was codified. In his task of codification, Justinian was assisted by committees under the guidance of Tribonianus, who could be termed his minister of justice.

The first area to be codified was that of the imperial *constitutiones (leges)*. The task was accomplished within a year and in 529 AD the *Codex (vetus)* saw the light of day. This work did not, however, prove satisfactory and in 534 AD a new *Codex*, the *Codex novus* or *repetitae praelectionis* came into being.

After the *Codex vetus* the law of the jurists *(ius)* fell to be considered. Differences of opinion among the jurists were settled and outdated concepts jettisoned. This mammoth work is the *Digesta* or *Pandectae* which is a collection of the opinions of the classical jurists. The work was commenced in 530 AD and was completed and received force of law three years later. The commission had to work through a staggering amount of material and the end result is embodied in fifty books divided into chapters, fragments and paragraphs. The jurists most extensively used were Ulpianus, Paulus, Papinianus, Modestinus and Gaius (eighty per cent).

Many interpolations, i e amendments to the original classical text, are to be found in the *Digesta*.

The *Institutiones* was also compiled (in 533 AD). Based on Gaius's work of the same name, this was intended as a textbook for students. Finally there were also the *Novellae*, new imperial *constitutiones* issued after the completion of the *Codex*.

The whole of Justinianus's codification is known as the *Corpus Iuris Civilis*. It formed the basis for the legal Renaissance of the Middle Ages and the reception of Roman laws.

Johan Scott BA (Hons) LLB (Pret) LLD (Leyden) Professor in Roman-Dutch Law and Private International Law University of Pretoria

2

MEDIEVAL LAW

The European legal scene from the sixth to the fifteenth centuries

The fall of Rome to the barbarians in 476 AD marked the onset of the decline of the once mighty Empire. Deterioration was not limited to the constitutional sphere; all symbols of civilization, including law, went into decline. The West-European continent was gradually split up into separate empires, as for example, that of the strongly Romanistic East-Goths, as well as that of the West-Goths, Vandals, Burgundians and Franks, each of which had its individual character. The fate of Roman culture – in the wide sense – depended largely on the extent to which it had earlier been assimilated in the various regions.

Statute books

The fact that the Germanic conquerors allowed their Roman subjects to live in terms of their own laws (the principle of personality, as opposed to territoriality of law) (cf p 9 above), formed the basis for the recording of the so-called *Leges Romanae*: records which had then to serve as statute books for their Roman subjects. This means of survival of Roman legal principles, in the midst of Germanic tribal law, is known as *infiltration*, as opposed to the later *reception*, that is, the influencing and transformation of local and tribal law by Roman legal principles. When compared to Justinian's subsequent monumental work, these works can scarcely be regarded as codifications in the true sense of the word – they are too basic and too incomplete. In this regard reference can be made to the *Lex Romana Visigothorum* (506 AD) of the West-Gothic ruler Alarik II and the *Lex Romana Burgundionum* (circa 517–534).

These statute books apart, the Germanic tribes later frequently recorded their own tribal law in statute books. Examples of such codifications are the *Lex Salica* (486–496) of the Salic Franks, and the *Lex Frisionum* (802–803). The Frankish Empire offers a striking example of the rise and development of the so-called monarchic law, that is rules derived from the legislative authority of the sovereign himself.

In the Eastern Roman Empire, Emperor Justinian (527–562) attempted to halt the decline of Roman law which had set in during the classical period, by commanding an extensive codification of Roman law – later known as the *Corpus Iuris Civilis*. Justinian hoped, hereby, to restore Roman law to the greatness reached during the classical period. The activities of the commission entrusted with this monumental task which was largely completed after approximately six years' uninterrupted labour, are described in chapter 1.

With the exception of a brief period during which Justinian's generals reconquered parts of Italy, the role of this codification was in the main limited to the Eastern Roman Empire. Only toward the close of the eleventh century a process of development was to begin, based on a revival of Roman law as embodied in the Justinianic codification.

The Roman law, which to a greater or lesser degree survived in Western Europe, is not literally based on the *Corpus Iuris Civilis*. This codification was known in compendiums such as the *Summa Perusina*, as regards the *Codex*, and the *Epitome Juliani*, as regards the *Novellae*. A considerable measure of interest was shown in Justinian's textbook, the *Institutiones*: an example of this is afforded by the Turin glosses or notations, the so-called *Codex Taurinensis*, which appeared during the tenth century, as well as by the *Brachylogus Iuris Civilis*, a textbook based on the Institutes, which was written two centuries later. For all practical purposes the Digest was completely neglected.

Survival of Roman law

There are a number of factors which explain why a scholarly interest in Roman law did not disappear entirely in Western Europe. Because the Franks regarded their Holy Roman Empire as a perpetuation of the earlier Roman Empire, there was a strong Roman tradition. The feeling was that, even if generally contradicted by reality, Roman law *should* survive. Furthermore, the emperors frequently applied those rules of Roman law which served their purposes, as, for example, the rule that the will of the emperor is law *(quod principi placuit, legis habet vigorem)*. A second possible factor lies in the *notarial practices* of the Middle

A page from the Codex Florentinus*: a manuscript of the Digest dating from the seventh century.*

The Mausoleum in Ravenna of Theodoric the Great, the Ostrogoth king who died in 526 AD. Theodoric superseded Odoacer as ruler of the Western Roman Empire in 493. Although he recognized the supremacy of the Eastern emperors, he ruled virtually independently in the West, retaining the Roman civil administration.

Ages. All notarial documents were, as a rule, drawn in Latin in accordance with Roman legal terminology. The "art of drawing documents" *(ars dictaminis)* consequently depended on the fact that the content of the terms was no longer understood or had been completely lost.

A further explanation for the survival of Roman legal principles is to be found in the idiom: *Ecclesia vivit secundum legem Romanam* – the Roman Catholic Church lives in accordance with Roman law. This meant that the legal relationships between the church and the outside world, on the one hand, and the church institutions, clergy and officials, on the other, were governed by Roman law – initially the *Codex Theodosianus*, to which were later added rules from numerous other sources, as, for example, the decisions of *concilia*, patristic writings, and Germanic tribal rules. In this way Canon law originated: a system strongly influenced by Roman law. Gradually both systems came to form components of what would later come to be known as the "scholarly" law.

Despite the gradual deterioration of Roman law, there remained a fine stream of legal wisdom running like a golden thread through this period. Available information tends to indicate that until the end of the eleventh century there was no large-scale scientific study of Roman law in Europe.

One of the earliest indications of a deeper interest in legal science was the appearance of the *Exceptiones Petri* in the south of France. It appears from the foreword to this work, which is based on the *Corpus Iuris Civilis*, that it was intended as a practical guide to judges, an aid to help them find their way through the maze of differing opinions of the jurists on various practical topics. The

Europe from 500 to 630 AD

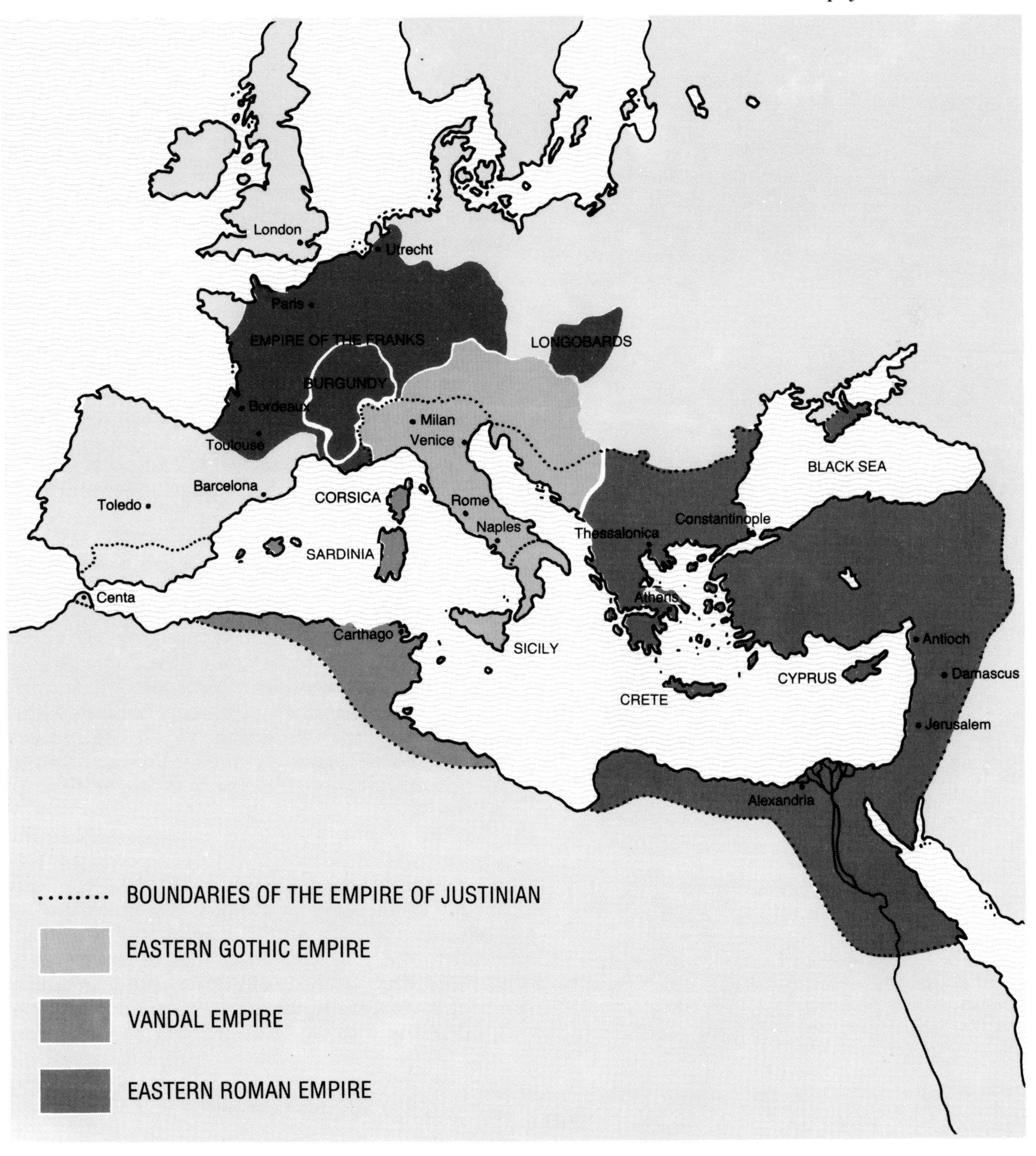

Charlemagne was crowned king of the Frankish Empire by Pope Leo III in 800 AD. This union between Church and State contributed to the spread of Canon law and thus, indirectly, the dissemination of Roman civil law throughout Western Europe.

writer does not scruple to extoll his own (Roman law orientated) theories – that which cannot stand up to the test of scientific analysis, should be trampled underfoot, is his motto.

In the Lombardian law schools the eleventh century showed signs of scientific activity too, indicative of a deeper interest in legal science. At these schools Lombardian law, based on the laws of the earlier Lombardian rulers such as Luitprand, Grimoald, Rothari and others, was developed into a scientific system by the local jurists. In this process lively differences of opinion arose between the jurists of Verona, Pavia and Nonantula, and Roman law was often relied upon in order to resolve the dispute. In essence, therefore, Roman law was supplementary to existing customary law.

Ravenna and Bologna

This period also saw a revival of interest in Roman law at the law school in Ravenna. We find polemics dating from the eleventh century, such as that of Petrus Crassus addressed to Pope Gregory VII, in which reliance is placed on the principles embodied in the *Corpus Iuris Civilis*. Opposition to this renewed interest in Roman law shown by the scholars of Ravenna is evident from Cardinal Damianus's pamphlet defending the Pope.

While the controversies represent but a small stream in the scientific study and practice of scholarly Roman law, the subsequent activities of the law school at Bologna symbolize the transition to the great river of the practical application of Roman law.

At this school, which had to counterbalance the ever-increasing influence of its counterpart in Ravenna, the famous tutor Irnerius made a start with the scientific study of Roman law based on the "rediscovered" *Corpus Iuris Civilis*, and more particularly the Digest, at the close of the eleventh century. Irnerius and his followers conducted their research principally through the medium of notations *(glossae)* to elucidate the text of the *Corpus Iuris Civilis* – thence their name of Glossators. By making the Justinianic Roman law available to practice, the Glossators ensured that Roman law immediately assumed a dominant role in the Euro-

Europe from 630 to 925 AD

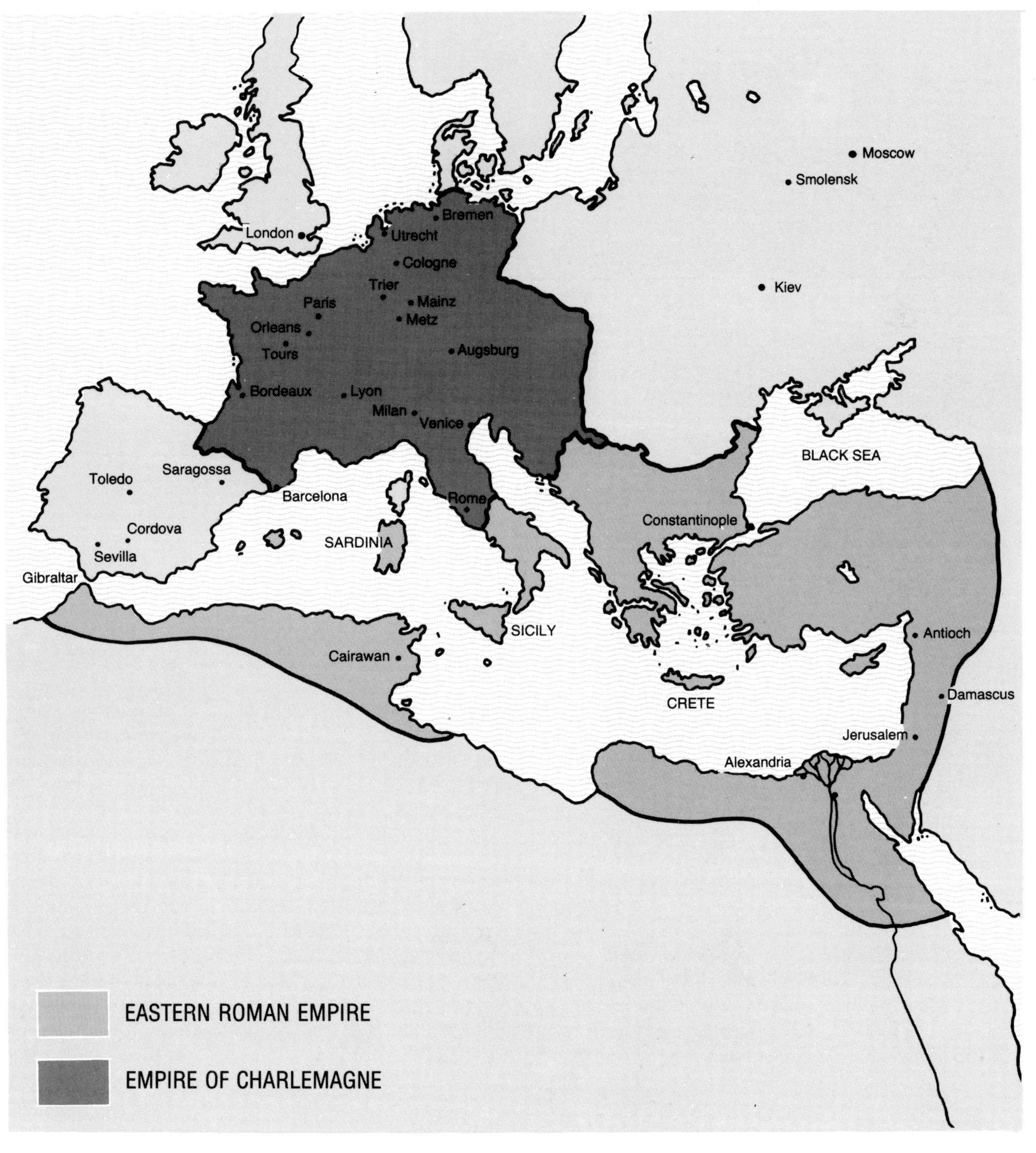

Bologna University. This university became the seat of the famous Glossatorial school after the rediscovery of the Corpus Iuris Civilis *in the eleventh century.*

pean legal scene. This was particularly so as the economic boom experienced in many cities at this time created the need for a scientific legal system capable of governing the complex legal relations which were becoming commonplace. To an ever-increasing extent Roman law was used to supplement the deficiencies existing in local legal systems. As so-called *ius commune*, a legal system shared by all Western European territories, Roman law on the one hand increasingly filled the role of a subsidiary legal system, while on the other it exerted a strong influence on existing legal institutions in that jurists tended to view their own rules through Roman lenses, so to speak, and thereby made their own systems more scientific. This latter process is most strikingly expressed by the term *reception*.

Reception

As South African common law is a product of reception, the term deserves brief explanation. One generally distinguishes between *early* reception (end twelfth to sixteenth centuries), and *total* reception (sixteenth century). Although the "rediscovered" Roman law had increased in importance since the period of the Glossators, the principal characteristic of the early period of reception must be seen as the increasing influence of Canon law. During this period the work of the so-called Canonists was of greater practical significance than that of the Roman law protagonists, namely the Legists. Canon law which was, as previously indicated, an off-shoot of Roman law, developed to such an extent through the influence of the Roman Catholic Church that it completely over-shad-

The title page of an edition of the Corpus Iuris Canonici *which was published in Basle, Switzerland, during the seventeenth century.*

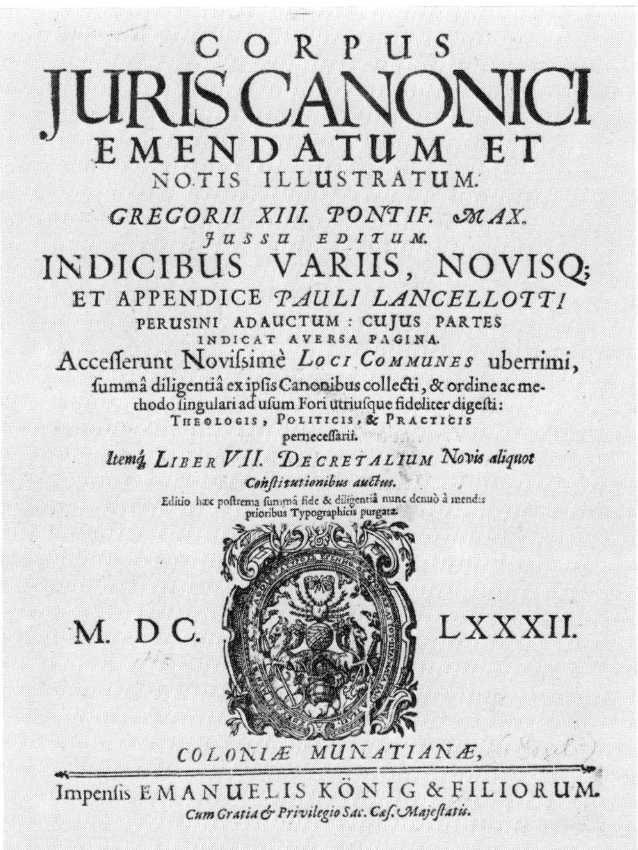

CORPUS
JURIS CANONICI
EMENDATUM ET
NOTIS ILLUSTRATUM.
GREGORII XIII. PONTIF. MAX.
JUSSU EDITUM.
INDICIBUS VARIIS, NOVISQ;
ET APPENDICE *PAULI LANCELLOTTI*
PERUSINI ADAUCTUM : CUJUS PARTES
INDICAT AVERSA PAGINA.
Accesserunt Novissimè *Loci Communes* uberrimi,
summâ diligentiâ ex ipsis Canonibus collecti, & ordine ac methodo singulari ad usum Fori utriusque fideliter digesti:
THEOLOGIS, POLITICIS, & PRACTICIS
pernecessarii.
Itemq; Liber VII. Decretalium Novis aliquot Constitutionibus auctus.
Editio hæc postrema summâ fide & diligentiâ nunc denuò à mendis prioribus Typographicis purgata.
M. DC. LXXXII.
COLONIÆ MUNATIANÆ,
Impensis EMANUELIS KÖNIG & FILIORUM.
Cum Gratia & Privilegio Sac. Cæs. Majestatis.

owed Roman law. In 1140 an unofficial collection of the sources of Canon law was made by the jurist monk Gratianus. This collection, known as the *Decretum Gratiani*, served both as source and as textbook. A second important source of Canon law came into being in 1234 after Pope Gregory IX had commanded that a collection of papal decrees *(Decretales)* be made. In this work the authority of the *Decretum Gratiani* is officially recognized with the result that this collection of *Decretales* is sometimes regarded as supplementary to the *Decretum* – hence its also being termed *Liber Extra*. Subsequent official additions were later incorporated under the title *Corpus Iuris Canonici*. Among the most important canonists were Cardinal Henricus de Segusia (circa mid-thirteenth century), also known as Hostiensis, Johannes Andreae (1270–1348), and Nicolaus de Tudeschis (1386–1445), also known as Panormitanus, whose extensive commentary on the *Corpus Iuris Canonici* may be regarded as the end of Canonism in the Middle Ages.

During the Post-Glossatorial period the influence of Canon law increased, partly because it was more modern than Roman law, but largely due to the direct influence of the church. Ecclesiastical courts enjoyed jurisdicition at almost every level: with regard to the person of a litigant *(ratione personae)*, that is in cases involving ecclesiastics or *personae miserabiles* (widows, orphans, the poor and crusaders); with regard to a specific cause of action or offence *(ratione materiae)*, for example, cases involving church property, wills, marriage and offences against religion, such as heresy or perjury; with regard to the sin committed *(ratione peccati)* – the church was of the opinion that as a subsidiary judiciary it was entitled to try each crime anew as a sin.

The basic principles of Roman law as embodied in the *Corpus Iuris Civilis*, however, remained intact and slowly but surely increased in stature until they eventually dominated the law of Europe – the process of total reception. A study of the European legal scene since the eleventh century is in essence a study of the rise of Roman law as *ius commune* for the Western European continent as a whole. This study of the scientific application of Roman law is simultaneously a study of the various legal schools which blossomed during this period. The most important of these, regarded chronologically until the fifteenth century, are the schools of the Glossators (twelfth to mid-thirteenth centuries), the Ultramontani (School of Orléans) (thirteenth to fourteenth centuries), and the Commentators (fourteenth to close of fifteenth century).

Irnerius aside, the most important Glossators were the so-called *quattuor doctores* (Bulgarus, Martinus Gosia, Hugo and Jacobus de porta Ravennate), Rogerius, Azo, Accursius and Odofredus. That the Glossators gained a definite impact on the practice of their time appears from phrases such as *Che non ha Azo non vade a Palazzo* (he who is not supported by the writings of Azo need not go to

Accursius (circa 1182–1263): a pupil of the famous Azo, he was one of the last great exponents of the Glossatorial school. Accursius compiled an exhaustive collection of glosses from the works of his predecessors. These Accursian glosses soon came to be regarded as the only authoritative commentary on the Corpus Iuris Civilis *and were soon added to all the standard texts of this work as* Glossa ordinaria.

Baldus (1327–1400): Baldus de Ubaldis may be regarded as one of the greatest Commentators or Post-Glossators. His commentaries on Roman and Canon law were held in high esteem and had a marked effect on the reception process of Roman law in Western Europe.

court) and *quidquid non agnoscit glossa, non agnoscit curia* (what is not recognized by the glosses, will not be recognized by the court).

In conclusion attention may be drawn to the activities of the Commentators or Post-Glossators. During the fourteenth century Italy was again the focal point of the theoretical study of "scholarly" law. Here a new research method was adopted, viz the writing of copious commentaries on all sections of the *Corpus Iuris Civilis*. It is difficult precisely to classify the methodology of the Commentators as their work can be regarded as an extension of the work of both the Glossators and the Ultramontani. The work of the Commentators is largely practice orientated and a striking characteristic is the systematic use of other sources in addition to the *Corpus Iuris Civilis*, in particular the *statuta* or local laws of the Italian cities and Canon law.

A number of jurists from this period have earned immortality, but surely the greatest exponent of the commentatorial period, and indeed of the European legal scene during the Middle Ages, must be Bartolus de Saxoferrato (1314–1357). It has been said of Bartolus that he symbolized all that is good as well as bad that was in later years said of legal science during the Middle Ages. His writings, in the form of commentaries, opinions and tracts, were disseminated throughout the length and breadth of Europe within a short period and exerted a tremendous influence on the theoretical study and practical application of legal sci-

Bartolus (1314–1357): Bartolus de Saxoferrato is undoubtedly the most illustrious member of the school of Commentators or Post-Glossators and certainly one of the greatest jurists of all time. So high was the regard for his abilities that, in Spain and Portugal, some of his works were (under certain circumstances) regarded as laying down binding law.

This is an example of a manuscript of the Digest with the glosses of Accursius. This manuscript, dating from the Middle Ages, was used by Van Bijnkershoek and is kept in the university library at Leyden.

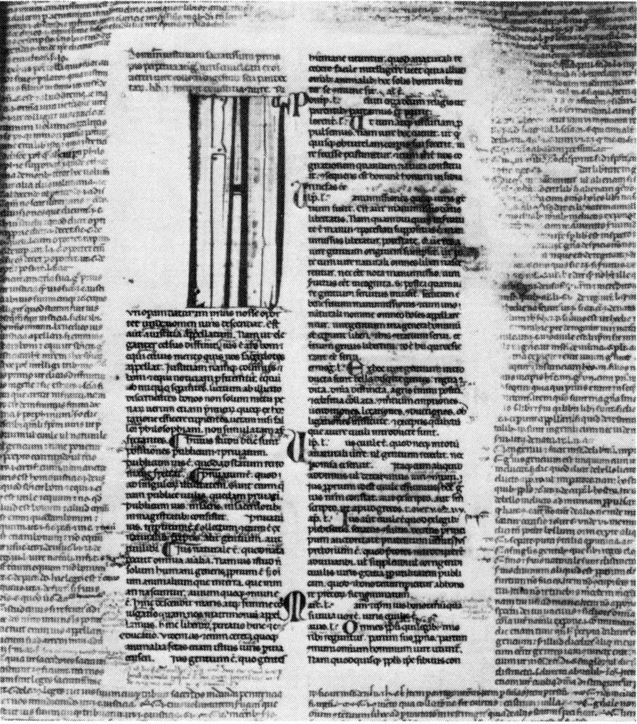

ence. A few other well-known Commentators were Cinus de Pistorio, Baldus de Ubaldis, Paulus de Castro, and Jason de Mayno.

It is the legal science as embodied in the works of the Commentators which during the fourteenth century spread beyond the borders of Italy to form a basis for legal development, particularly in Germany, but also in the present-day Netherlands. The influence of the jurists of the Middle Ages on the content of that which was later to form the basic material for reception makes it worth while for the historically orientated South African jurist to study this period.

Paul van Warmelo BA LLB (Pret) Doct Iur (Leyden) LLD hc (Cape Town)
Temporary Senior Lecturer in Legal History, Comparative Law and Jurisprudence University of South Africa;
Honorary Professor in Law University of the North

3

ROMAN-DUTCH LAW

When assessing Roman-Dutch law in its classical period which commenced in approximately 1600 and continued to the beginning of the nineteenth century, the Dutch (or Germanic) and Roman background must be borne in mind. It is during this period that Roman-Dutch law became a worthy comtemporary of any other system of law and to a great extent this was due to the influence of Roman law. The Low Countries entered a period of economic, financial and political importance and the law had to keep in step to meet the requirements of the times. The Germanic background was predominant in fields such as family and marriage law and also in the law of succession.

The law of these Germanic tribes and territories remained primitive in essence, although a process of development had begun when these tribes started to form new communities. At the same time, during the Middle Ages, the feudal system was established. The main implication of this dispensation was the fact that the relationship between feudal lords and serfs came into being. The lord was obliged to protect his bondsmen, and they had to reciprocate by maintaining an allegiance towards and rendering services to their lord. The result was that Europe disintegrated into a multitude of rather isolated communities, consisting of feudal lords and their serfs. A king regularly reigned over a conglomerate of such units, although his sovereignty was often more theoretical than real. The cities also developed into political entities, and thus Europe was basically divided into cities with their adjacent territories (where the citizens mainly dwelt) and regions in which a lord held sway over his vassals. These sections were all too often at loggerheads.

The law of that time was very localized, in the sense that each territory had its own law. These territories were sometimes extremely small – today one would be able to traverse it in one or two hours. Within a very limited period one would thus be able to set off on a journey in a territory which had its specific legal system, travel through a second territory to arrive promptly in a third, which had a totally different system of law. Of course, all these different systems had much in common, although major differences did occur. We have only to look at the systems of intestate succession, known as the *Aasdomsrecht* and *Schependomsrecht*, to realize how the law could vary within a relatively small territory. Although we may classify these systems as Germanic law, they are by no means of the same type as the Germanic law of the old primitive tribes. A development had occurred in the meantime and new systems of law were enfolded, which did not necessarily imply that all the ancient concepts had been rooted out. So, for instance, the *Aasdom* and *Schependom* systems had grown with the time, but their fundamental principles had remained unaltered since early Germanic times. It is even alleged that a principle like the one dictating that hereditary property should revert to its original owner (later formulated as *paterna paternis, materna maternis*) originated in a system dating back to the pre-Germanic period. The law was thus developed and adapted to meet the requirements of a specific group at a specific time. Major areas of the law were also put into writing, mainly in the period stretching from the fifth to the ninth century. Although we speak of the *Lex Salica*, *Leges Visigothorum*, *Lex Saxonum* and *Lex Frisionum*, these collections of laws are not accounts of early Germanic tribal law.

In this period some of the most typical institutions of what is generally described as Germanic law came into being and were further developed. Apart from the law of intestate succession (in Holland), the important family law institution of community of property originated and this in turn gave rise to the phenomenon of the antenuptial contract. Also of considerable importance was the feudal approach to the concept of ownership over immovable property, according to which private ownership was impossible. Accordingly the feudal lord (in England, the sovereign) was regarded as the owner of all real estate, which he granted to his bondsmen to hold in fee. So it has in principle remained in England up to this day. In Europe, again, the Roman law concept of ownership took root. Further concepts which may be mentioned in this context are the marital power of the husband

A work on the criminal law by a jurist of the South Netherlands, Joost de Damhouder (1507–1581), Practijcke in Criminele Saecken, *is unusual as it contains illustrations of the offences discussed. It is well known that the largest portion of this famous work by Damhouder was derived from the work of Philippus Wielant (1439-1519),* De Practycke Criminele.

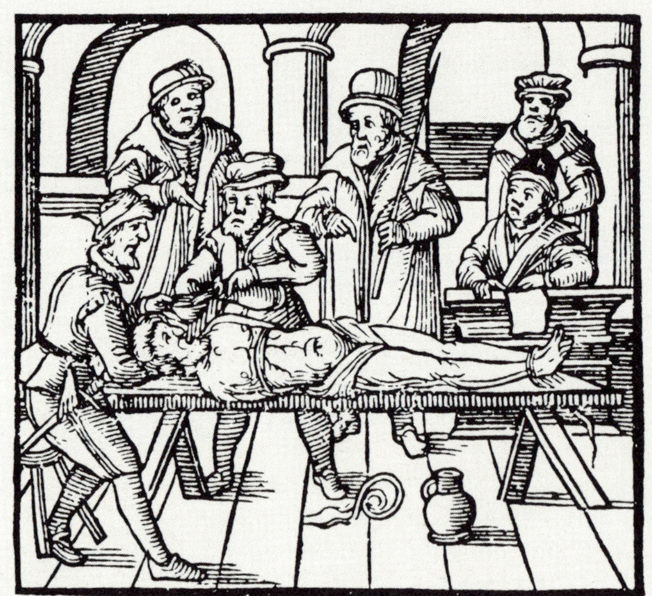

Torture

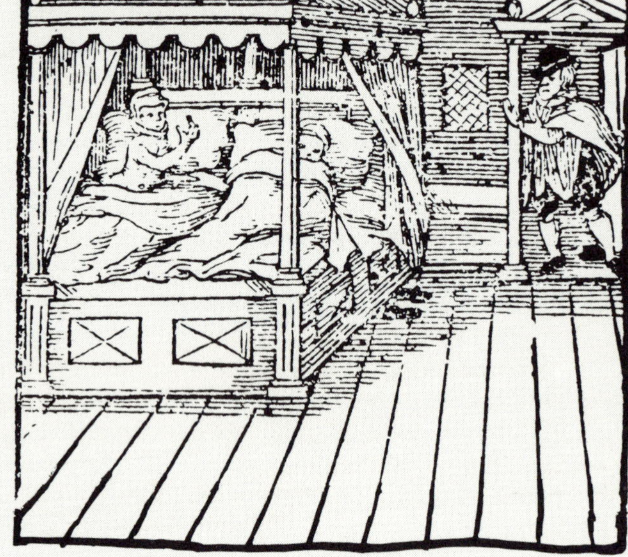

Adultery

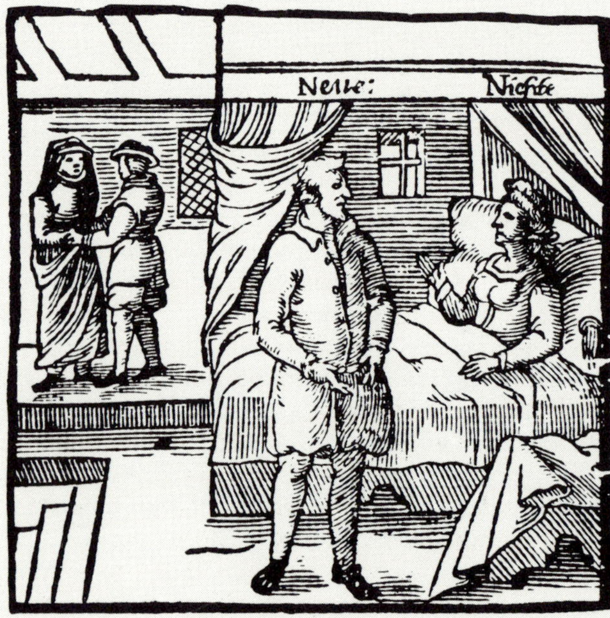

Incest

Theft from the house of a dead person

and the parental power of a father over his children, the latter being a further development of the early Germanic concept of *mundium*, viz a relationship of authority which corresponded in certain respects with the *patria potestas* of Roman law, although there were fundamentally major differences. Various other Germanic rules and concepts which developed had in a higher or lesser degree been evolved from ancient Germanic law.

Germanic law was thus by no means a homogeneous system of law. There were different systems with common characteristics, which applied or exerted an influence in larger or smaller territories. The influence of one system over another was also of some importance. Thus the influence of what may be called Frankish law was quite strong in the Netherlands, while the Saxon law from the East also exerted an influence. The gradual infiltration and reception of the highly developed Roman law (which was applied as a common system of law – the *ius commune*) effected a bigger homogeneity in the local systems of law which were in force in the various regions. We cannot, however, speak of a true unity within these different systems, in the period prior to the different codifications.

New branches of law developed (insurance, maritime law, negotiable instruments) and it is remarkable to what extent Roman law could be applied, not only in the Low Countries, but throughout the whole of Europe. It should be remembered that Roman law penetrated the law of the Low Countries at an early stage, but this influence becomes insignificant when one looks at its influence in the classical period presently under discussion. At the same time one should keep in mind that its influence was not always the same – the development of Roman law itself affected its influence at different periods.

It is interesting to note that the Roman-Dutch law of this period is characterized, on the one hand, by the work of theorists, but, on the other, by that of practitioners as well. For a knowledge of the law of this particular period it is necessary to rely mainly on the works of lawyers of the time. This does not mean that such writings date only from the seventeenth century onwards. Important

Joost Damhouder

works were published before. In fact, the development in the Low Countries moved from south to north. Before the seventeenth century the law had been developing strongly in the south and some outstanding lawyers had left their writings for posterity. In the north (in the territory of Roman-Dutch law) there were a number of well-known lawyers of whom Paulus Merula (1558–1607) is possibly the best known. *Manier van Procederen* is his best known work and it provides a detailed examination of procedure. There was also Jacob Coren (died in 1631) who published a volume of reports of court cases which is of considerable importance. Another who deserves mention is Cornelius Neostadius (1549–1606) who is mainly known for his collections of decided cases. It will

Hugo Grotius (1583–1645): Grotius is one of the most remarkable lawyers of all times. He started his law studies at the age of twelve years at the University of Leyden. Thereafter he practised as an advocate. Because of his participation in the religious disputes of his time he was gaoled in the Loevenstein castle, from which he escaped, concealed in a case of books which his wife had sent him. As an exile from the Netherlands he was appointed Swedish ambassador to the French court. Returning to the Netherlands from exile, his ship was wrecked and he died of pneumonia. He is

internationally known for his fundamental work on the law of the nations, De Iure Belli ac Pacis. *In South Africa his fame is primarily due to his excellent treatise on the prevailing law of Holland in his time,* Inleidinge tot de Hollandsche Rechts-Geleerdheid.

thus be seen that the practitioner left a valuable contribution for posterity, for all these writers and their works have to do with the practical application of law.

The seventeenth century, as a period in the history and development of Roman-Dutch law, begins with that most remarkable man, Hugo Grotius (1583-1645).

Grotius whose first major legal work, *Inleidinge tot de Hollandsche Rechts-Geleerdheid*, can be rated as a pioneering text-book of Roman-Dutch law, was

The Seven United Provinces of the Netherlands 1648.

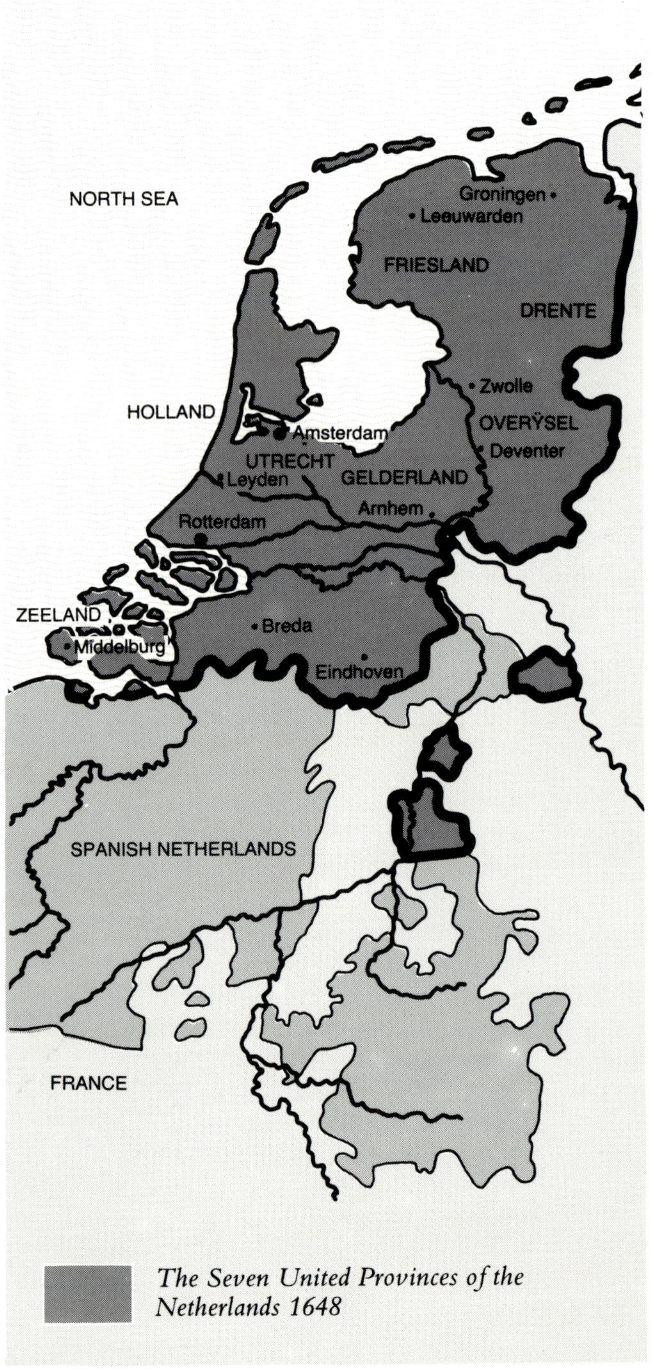

the first of a number of important writers on Roman-Dutch law. These writers were usually not practising lawyers, but were frequently teachers of law who expounded Roman-Dutch law theoretically – that is to say, they wrote on the law as such, and their point of departure was frequently Roman law. They set out Roman law as they understood it and for that purpose they relied on writings on Roman law, such as those of the Glossators and Commentators, and in particular of the writers of their own time. They were furthermore predominantly orientated towards the French Humanists. Even if they were not wholly devoted to Roman law and wrote mainly with an eye fixed on local conditions, they looked at Roman law, in the main, through the eyes of the Humanists. In fact, in the Low Countries a school of (Roman) lawyers came about which may be considered an offshoot of the French school and which is sometimes called the Dutch or Elegant school. They were of course not unaware of other approaches to law, and to Roman law in particular. It is a period in which the positive law of several countries received much more attention: reference may be made to the so-called *Usus modernus* of Roman law in Germany. In France the practitioners were also writing on the local laws and making full use of Roman law in their expositions and interpretations. It is not surprising, therefore, to see jurists in the Low Countries making use of the works of their contemporaries in Germany and France. It would seem, however, that Roman-Dutch law reached its highest level during this period, because of the particular use made of the writings of the Humanistic school.

The Roman method of legal thinking gave Roman-Dutch law a system, science and mental approach which sets it somewhat apart from other European systems of that time. In Roman-Dutch law, Roman law was subsidiary law. That is to say, in so far as the former failed to give an answer, the answer had (in principle) to be sought in Roman law.

It is impossible to discuss all the noteworthy Roman-Dutch lawyers since the time of Grotius. It is sufficient to mention some of them of whom

Paulus Merula (1558–1607): Merula is regarded as one of the outstanding Roman-Dutch jurists. He wrote a standard work on procedure, entitled Synopsis praxeos Civilis, Manier van Procederen in Hollandt, Zeelandt ende West Vriestlandt, belanghende Civile Saken.

Arnold Vinnius (1588–1657) may be the first. Another important writer was Simon van Groenewegen van der Made (1613–1652) who is worthy of mention because of his annotations on the abovementioned *Inleidinge* of Grotius. His important work was *De Legibus Abrogatis*, in which he discussed the law (i e primarily Roman law), meticulously pointing out which of the Roman laws had already been abolished in his time.

The next writer who cannot be passed by is Simon van Leeuwen (1626–1682). He is known mainly for two works, namely *Het Rooms-Hollandts-Recht* and *Censura Forensis*. The first work was written in the vernacular and he, so it seems, was the first to coin the name "Roman-Dutch

Influence of Roman law

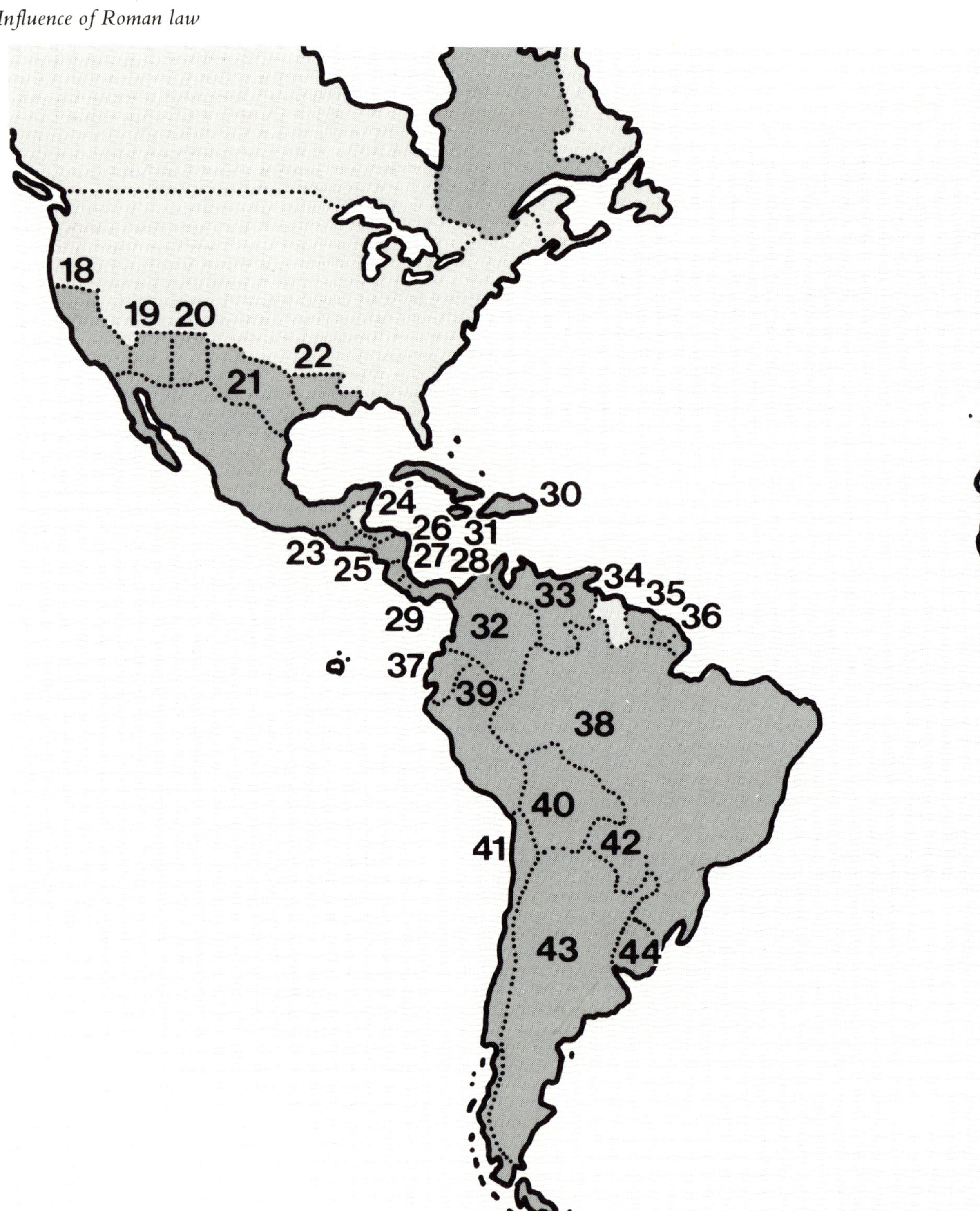

Jacobus Cuiacius (1522–1590): Cuiacius may be considered the founder of the school of the French Humanists. He was thoroughly versed in classic studies and in Roman law and was an outstanding jurist. The influence of the Humanists, and therefore of Cuiacius, on the jurists of the Low Countries was immense and most of the authoritative Roman-Dutch writers were followers of this school. Cuiacius wrote extensively on practically all branches of Roman law.

Gerhardus Noodt (1647–1725): Noodt was professor at several universities of the Northern Low Countries. He was a scholar of European fame, regarded particularly as an authority on Roman law. Noodt was a leading member of the Elegant school and a follower of the French or Humanistic school.

law". There were many other writers, some of whom wrote general works, while others wrote monographs. Some were outstanding lawyers, others less so. Furthermore, the period was one in which there were not only important writers on Roman-Dutch law, but also writers on the law of the several provinces of the Low Countries. There was, for instance, Ulrich Huber (1636–1694), one of the outstanding lawyers of his time, who wrote on Roman law and the law of Friesland (which had much in common with Roman-Dutch law, but was even more Roman law orientated). From the province of Utrecht there was Gerard van Wassenaer (circa 1664) who wrote mainly on procedure. Also from Utrecht was Antonius Matthaeus II (1601–1654) whose most important work was a treatise on criminal law *(De Criminibus)*, which dealt with Roman criminal law. It is worthy of note that this work must be considered as serving the purpose of expounding Roman-Dutch law as well, the reason being that criminal law and procedure was mainly derived from Roman law, although it was strongly influenced in the Low Countries by Germanic law.

Apart from Grotius, certainly the best known jurist of Roman-Dutch law is Johannes Voet (1647–1713). His *Commentarius ad Pandectas* supplies a good example of the method followed by some Roman-Dutch writers.

Voet brings us to the eighteenth century and in this period another of the great Roman-Dutch lawyers made his appearance. He was Cornelis van

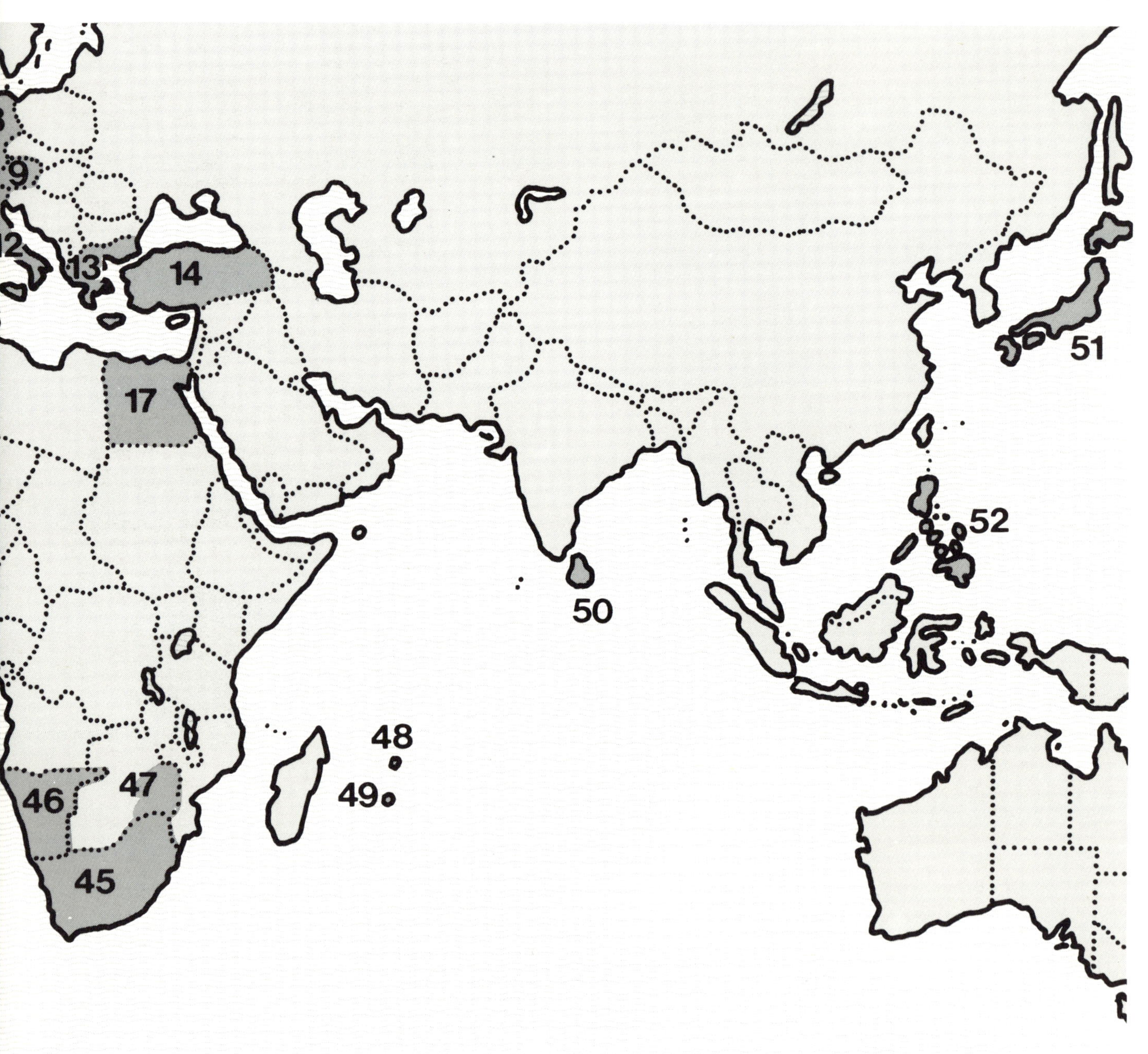
9
12
13
14
17
46
47
45
48
49
50
51
52

13. *Greece:* The Greek code which came into operation in 1946 was influenced largely by Byzantine law. 14. *Turkey:* A code which amounted to the adoption of the Swiss *Zivilgesetzbuch* and the *Obligationenrecht*, was adopted in 1926. 15. *Morocco:* The *Code des Obligations et des Contrats* (1913) was influenced largely by the French *Code Civil*. 16. *Tunisia:* In 1906 they also adopted the *Code des Obligations et des Contrats* which is based mainly on the French code. 17. *Egypt:* The *Nouveau Code Civil* of 1948 was based on the French code to a large extent. 18. *California:* Minor Roman law influences. 19. *Arizona:* Minor Roman law influences. 20. *New Mexico:* Minor Roman law influences. 21. *Texas:* Minor Roman law influences. 22. *Louisiana:* A *Civil Code* based on the French *Code Civil* was adopted in 1825. 23. *Guatemala:* The *Codigo Civil* of 1877 was amended in terms of the French code in 1882 and was replaced in 1932 by a code influenced largely by Spanish law. 24. *Belise:* English influence. 25. *El Salvador:* The *Codigo Civil* of 1880 was influenced by the French *Code Civil*. 26. *Honduras:* The *Codigo Civil* of 1891 was influenced by the French code. 27. *Nicaragua:* The *Codigo Civil* was adopted in 1867 and amended in 1904 under the influence of the French code. 28. *Costa Rica:* The *Codigo Civil* of 1865 was influenced by the French code. 29. *Panama:* The *Codigo Civil* of 1917 was influenced by the French *Code Civil*. 30. *Dominican Republic:* The *Codigo Civil* of 1884 is a translation of the French *Code Civil*. 31. *Haiti:* The *Codigo Civil* of 1826 shows Spanish influence. 32. *Columbia: Codigo Civil* of 1877. 33. *Venezuela:* The *Codigo Civil* of 1863 was influenced by the French *Code Civil*. 34. *British Guiana:* Roman law obtained until 1917. 35. *Surinam and the Dutch Antilles:* Adapted Dutch private law. 36. *French Guiana:* Adapted French law. 37. *Ecuador:* The *Codigo Civil* of 1861 was influenced by the French code. 38. *Brazil:* The civilian code of 1917 was influenced by the French *Code Civil* and Portuguese law. 39. *Peru:* The *Codigo Civil* of 1852 was influenced by the French code, but the code of 1936 was influenced by Portuguese law. 40. *Bolivia:* The *Codigo Civil* of 1845 was a Spanish translation of the French code. 41. *Chile:* The *Codigo Civil* of 1857 was influenced by the French code. 42. *Paraguay:* The Argentinian code was adopted in 1889. 43. *Argentine:* The *Codigo Civil* of 1871 was influenced by the French *Code Civil*. 44. *Uruguay:* The *Codigo Civil* of 1868 was influenced by the French code. 45. *Republic of South Africa:* The common law of South Africa is Roman-Dutch law which, in the narrow sense, is the law of the Province of Holland after the reception of Roman law and, in the broad sense, is the law as recorded by Dutch authors of the seventeenth and eighteenth centuries. 46. *South West Africa – Namibia:* Roman-Dutch law. 47. *Zimbabwe:* Roman-Dutch law with English influence. 48. *Seychelles:* French *Code Civil*. 49. *Mauritius:* French *Code Civil*. 50. *Sri Lanka:* Roman-Dutch law going back to the seventeenth century. 51. *Japan:* Code of 1898 influenced by Windscheid's draft for the German *Bürgerliches Gesetzbuch*. 52. *Philippines:* Spanish private law.

THE INFLUENCE OF ROMAN LAW

1. *Scotland:* Modern Scottish law shows clear signs of having been influenced by Roman law. This is as a result of a process of reception which started during the thirteenth and fourteenth centuries when Scotland and England were involved in a struggle against each other and the Scots turned to France where they came into contact with the French and other European legal systems. Especially in the seventeenth and eighteenth centuries many of the Scottish students attended Dutch universities where they made a thorough study of Roman law. After the *Treaty of Union* in 1707 when England and Scotland were united, the influence of Roman law decreased considerably. 2. *The Netherlands:* There had been an infiltration of Roman law in the Netherlands long before the twelfth century, while an early reception took place from the twelfth to the middle of the fifteenth centuries and a "complete" reception took place from the middle of the fifteenth century to the eighteenth century. The codification movement which became very popular in Europe during the eighteenth century also made an appearance in the Netherlands. The *Wetboek Napoleon ingerigt voor het koningrijk Holland* (an adaptation of the French *Code Civil* in Holland) obtained in Holland as a code for the period 1809–1811. After that the *Code Civil* obtained in Holland until the *Burgerlijk Wetboek* was eventually adopted in 1838. The *Burgerlijk Wetboek* was strongly influenced by the French code and therefore had a Roman law orientation, while customary law had limited influence. 3. *Belgium:* The French *Code Civil* obtained in Belgium after it became a part of France. An amended form of the *Code Civil* was later retained. 4. *Luxembourg:* French *Code Civil.* 5. *France:* The *Code Civil* was compiled in 1804 and amended and added to later. This code was largely influenced by Roman law, but also by Natural law and French customary law. 6. *Spain:* The Spanish *Codigo Civil* of 1867 was influenced by the French *Code Civil* to a large extent. 7. *Portugal:* The Portuguese *Codigo Civil* of 1867 was influenced by the French code to a large extent. 8. *Germany:* Here codification took place far later than in France and Holland, namely in 1900. As far as content and technique are concerned, the German *Bürgerliches Gesetzbuch* has strong romanistic characteristics while the system followed was influenced by the Pandectists. Consequently, it has much in common with the French *Code Civil.* 9. *Austria:* In Austria the *Allgemeines Bürgerliches Gesetzbuch* was adopted in 1810. It was amended in 1912 and became operative in 1918. This code was greatly influenced by Natural law. 10. *Switzerland:* The Swiss *Zivilgesetzbuch* became operative in 1912 and the revised *Obligationenrecht* in 1911. The Roman influence is far less than in the German code. 11. *Monaco:* The *Code Civil* was adopted in 1875. It is an improved version of the French code. 12. *Italy:* The *Codice Civile* was adopted in 1866 and was renewed in 1940. It was influenced to a large extent by the French code.

Johan van den Sande (1568–1638): Sande is well known in South Africa, probably on account of English translations of two of his important works, viz, *a treatise on the law of cession,* Commentarius de actionum cessione, *and one on the law upon restraints against alienation of property,* Commentarius de prohibita rerum alienatione. *Both these works are mainly treatises on Roman law.*

Desiderius Erasmus (circa 1467–1536): he was a brilliant man who became the most famous Humanist of the Northern Renaissance and who led the Humanist reform in theology, education, rhetoric and classical studies. The Humanistic approach had a profound influence on the development of legal studies.

Bijnkershoek (1673–1743), a remarkable lawyer who made his mark on different areas of the law. He was a Roman legal authority (in the tradition of the Humanists and the Elegant school) of considerable repute. He also wrote on Roman-Dutch law, but his work consisted mainly of monographs. His most important contribution to the development of Roman-Dutch literature was, however, as a lawyer in the Court of Holland.

Something also needs to be mentioned of the higher courts in the Low Countries. Going back to 1428, the most important court in the northern provinces of the Low Countries was the Court of Holland which attained, at a somewhat later stage, the status of an appeal court. In 1473 a further court, situated in the south, was created. This was the Grand Council of Malines, which had appeal jurisdiction, and cases from the North were also dealt with there. This changed when in 1581 a Hooge Raad van Holland en Zeeland was established as a supreme court and the highest court of appeal. It lasted until the Napoleonic period.

An important practitioner who should also be mentioned is Willem Pauw (1712–1787). He became a councillor of the *Hooge Raad* in 1740, afterwards attaining the distinction of being appointed its president towards the end of his life. Like Van Bijnkershoek he also published reports on the cases heard by him.

Two lawyers who lived at the turn of the eighteenth century are worthy of mention. The first is DG van der Keessel (1738–1816) who was a re-

1 *Johannes Voet (1647–1713): Johannes Voet needs no introduction to the South African legal profession. His main work,* Commentarius ad Pandectas, *is held in esteem in South African courts and by South African writers. It is an exhaustive commentary on the* Digest of Justinian. *Basically Voet discusses Roman law and then explains the influence of customary and local law on it. This method adopted by Voet renders the* Commentarius *invaluable as a work on Roman-Dutch law.*

2 *Zacharias Huber (1669–1732): he was the son of the famous jurist, Ulrich Huber. Like his father, he wrote on Roman law and the law of Friesland. He is best known for his collection of decisions of the supreme court of Friesland, under the title* Decisiones Frisicae sive Observationes rerum Forensium ac Notabilium in Suprema Frisiorum Curia Iudicatarum.

3 *Jacobus Voorda (1698–1768): he was the father of Bavius Voorda. Jacobus Voorda studied at Franeker and lectured there as well as at Utrecht. His best known work is the* Interpretatio iuris Romani. *Some of his works are only available in manuscript form.*

1

3

2

4

4 *Simon van Leeuwen (1626–1682): Van Leeuwen practised as an advocate at The Hague. He is considered to be one of the leading Roman-Dutch authorities, in particular distinguishing himself as the first author to employ the term "Roman-Dutch law".*

5 *Gerlach Scheltinga (1708–1765): Scheltinga was a professor of law at the University of Leyden, where he lectured on Roman-Dutch law, using Grotius'* Inleidinge *as a guide.*

6 *Dionysius Godefridus van der Keessel (1738–1816): Van der Keessel was professor of law at Groningen and Leyden. He was one of the last of the Roman-Dutch authorities. Apart from his works on Roman law, he wrote* Theses Selectae *which are excerpts from a more comprehensive work,* Praelectiones ad ius hodiernum. *The* Praelectiones *is a fairly extensive commentary on the* Inleidinge *of Grotius. His* Praelectiones ad ius criminale *being a commentary on books 47 and 48 of Justinian's* Digest, *is an extensive exposition of the criminal law as applied in the courts of Holland in his time.*

5

7

6

7 *Cornelis van Bijnkershoek (1673-1743): Van Bijnkershoek ranks as a jurist of world fame. His regard as a jurist of international status is due mainly to his contribution in the field of international law. On the other hand, his works on Roman and Roman-Dutch law are equally famous and of the same high standard. He wrote treatises on procedure, on Roman-Dutch law* (Quaestiones Iuris Privati *and* Quaestiones Iuris Publici) *and on Roman law* (Quaestiones Iuris Romani). *He also reported a vast number of cases heard before the* Hooge Raad: Observationes Tumultuariae. *He was a member of this tribunal from 1704 until he was appointed its president in 1724 – an office which he held until his death.*

Robert Joseph Pothier (1699–1772): Pothier was a member of the French court of appeal and was held in high esteem as judge and as a teacher of law. He rearranged the Digest *of Justinian in a work entitled* Pandectae Justinianeae, in novam ordinem digestae. *He also wrote extensively on French law, including treatises on the law of obligations and specific contracts. His works had a considerable influence on the French* Code Civil. *Van der Linden, the well-known Roman-Dutch jurist, was greatly influenced by Pothier and this may, possibly, be one of the reasons why Pothier is frequently referred to by South African courts.*

markable writer on the law of his time. He was a teacher of law, first at Groningen and later at Leyden. He published his *Theses Selectae*, containing a number of notes (derived from his lectures to his students) serving as comments on the *Inleidinge* of Grotius. But he was also an expert on Roman law and his lectures on this system (which have been published only in part) show him to have been a worthy member of the Elegant school. However, he was also a lecturer on criminal law, who, like Matthaeus II, followed the trend of criminal law as expounded in the Digest of Justinian. It is noticeable that he worked at a time when great changes were coming about in various legal systems.

Finally there is Johannes van der Linden (1756–1853). He is best known for his *Koopmans-Handboek*. It is not his most meritorious work, but it has achieved popularity in modern times. In this work and in others, Van der Linden showed himself to be a lawyer worthy to be reckoned as one of the foremost writers on Roman-Dutch law. He already lived, however, in the period in which the drive for codification of the law was predominant. The French *Code Civil* came about during his lifetime. The work of the French jurist, Pothier (1699–1772) was of the utmost importance in this code and it is, therefore, not surprising that in his *Koopmans-Handboek* Van der Linden refers frequently to Pothier. Van der Linden also prepared a code of civil law for the Netherlands (which was, however, not adopted) in which he attempted to codify Roman-Dutch law.

It was a sign of the times that he attempted to do so. With the beginning of the nineteenth century Roman-Dutch law was to disappear as the law of the land in its country of origin. It was, however, to have a new lease of life in southern Africa.

G E Devenish BSc (Witwatersrand) LLB(SA) Associate Professor in Constitutional Law
University of Bophuthatswana

4

THE CAPE OF GOOD HOPE 1652–1909

In 1620 Andrew Schillinge and Humphrey Fitzherbert took possession of the Cape of Good Hope on behalf of King James of England. This act was never ratified and in 1652 Jan van Riebeeck, an employee of the *Vereenigde Geoctroyeerde Oost-Indische Compagnie* (VOC) established a refreshment station on behalf of his employer at the Cape. The VOC was a subject of the *Republiek der Vereenigde Nederlanden*, which was at the apogee of its influence and power as the leading mercantile nation of Europe.

Top: *Portrait of Prince William I of Orange-Nassau by Adziaen Thomas Key. After a stormy political career the Prince of Orange became the hereditary sovereign of Holland and Zeeland in 1582, but before the preliminaries had been completed he was assassinated by Balthazar Gérard.*

Below: *Seat of the Dutch-East-India Company: East-India House in Amsterdam where most of the meetings of the Council of Seventeen* (Here Sewentien) *were held.*

The early constitutional position and subsequent development

Overseas settlements of the Netherlands were the concern of all the member states of the confederation which had as its central organ the Estates-General. The latter had by virtue of the *Octrooi* of 1602 delegated power to the VOC. This included the maintenance of law and order and even the right of keeping an army in those settlements. Executive control of the company vested in the Council of Seventeen (*Here Sewentien*), the directorate of which had its seat in Amsterdam.

Directly under the VOC stood the Governor-General-in-Council in Batavia, and under him in turn, the local Governor-in-Council at the Cape, which was one of the *buitencomptoiren,* i e a foreign station of the VOC's head station in Batavia.

The settlement, like other dependencies of the VOC, was governed by a *Raad van Politie* (Council of Policy) which in essence was a modified form of the broad council which operated on the ships of the company, consisting of the commander and his senior officers. The *artyckelbrief* set out the regulations governing the service of overseas employees of the VOC. The council ensured that the commander or governor of a dependency exercised his powers in accordance with the interests of the VOC. The overriding interests of the company were commercial: the government of the settlement was of secondary importance.

During the first five years of the embryonic settlement and before the advent of the free burghers legal relationships were regulated primarily on an employer-employee basis. Only after the rec-

Map showing influence of VOC.

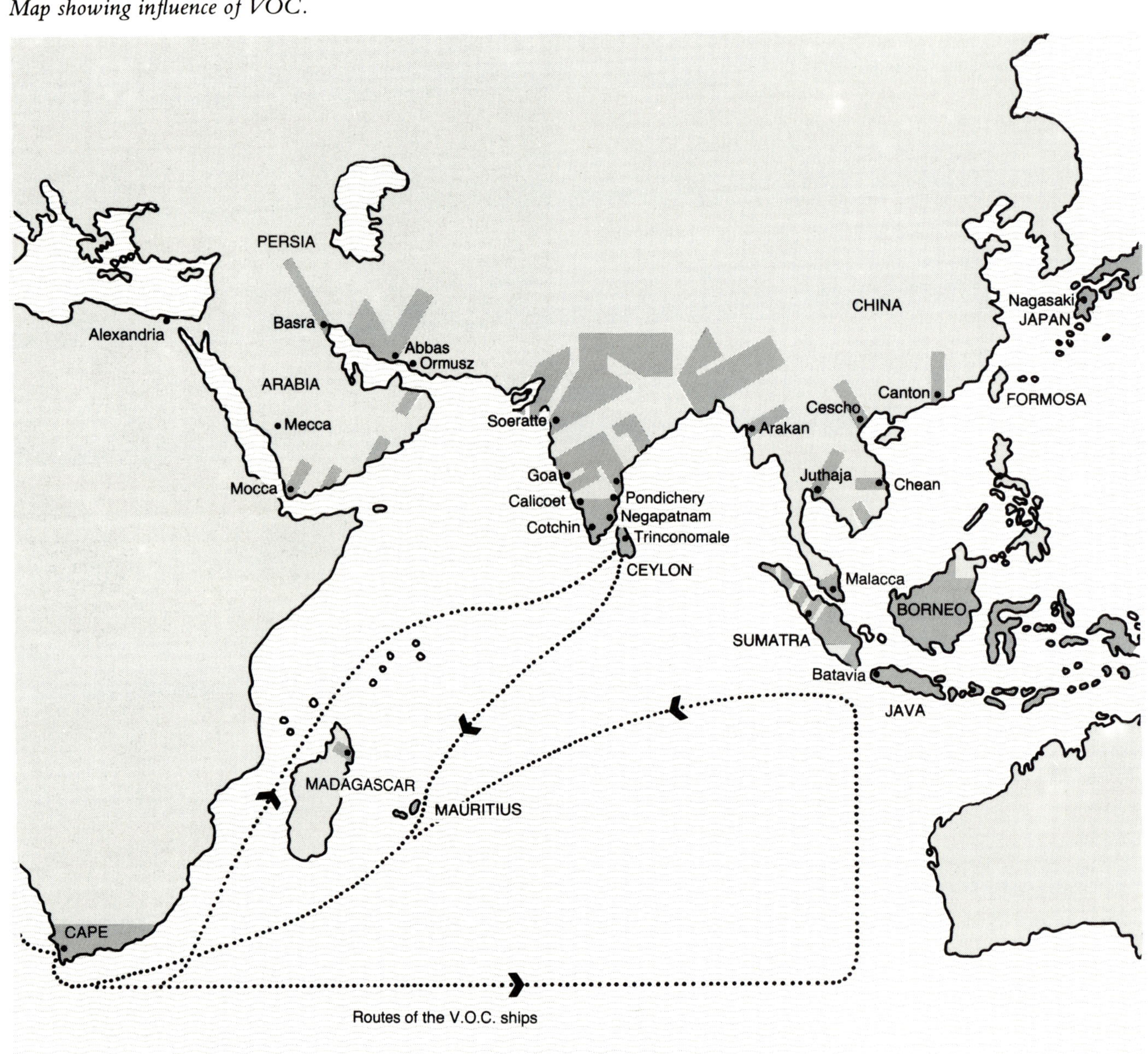

ognition of the first free burghers in 1657 did the VOC in addition assume the role of constitutional authority and begin to legislate for employees, burghers, liberated slaves, free Blacks and slaves. Initially the indigenous Khoikhoi ("Hottentot") and San ("Bushman") people who became assimilated into the settler community were subject to the laws of the Cape settlement. In the eighteenth century all indigenous persons residing within the boundaries of the settlement were under the jurisdiction of the Cape government which directed that Hottentot servants should receive wages and redress for ill-treatment, and the Cape courts even judged cases in which Khoikhoi had injured one another.

Although the Cape governors never attempted to dispense with their councils, their authority was very great and virtually autocratic since they usually obtained the co-operation of their councils by persuasion and where this was not forthcoming, they did have the power to overrule objections although this was seldom done. Governors were subjected to instructions from the Council of Seventeen in distant Amsterdam and to instructions from the council of Batavia which sometimes contradicted the instructions from the chamber. The vast distances involved and the slow and inadequate means of communication lessened the control exerted over the governors and facilitated autocratic behaviour.

Initially government at the Cape vested in a commander and after 1691 in a governor, who was assisted by his *secunde* or second-in-command and his council, consisting of the governor, the *secunde* and six senior officials.

The Cape council levied taxes and controlled all commercial enterprises. Under the company rule transfers and mortgages of land were originally passed before two commissioners of the Council of Policy and countersigned by the secretary. After 1718 mortgage bonds and transfers were executed before commissioners of the court of justice. Of great significance is the fact that records of the title deeds were kept. The burghers did not enjoy representation in the Council of Policy and therefore did not participate directly in legislating or the

Top: *The auctioneer: an etching by Rembrandt depicting the auctioneer Pieter Haaringh who sold Rembrandt's possessions in execution. The Roman-Dutch law of insolvency thus attained very real dimensions for this later world-renowned artist.*

Below: *Frederik Russouw, a typical free burgher at the turn of the seventeenth century.*

Portrait of the members of the Steelmasters' Guild by Rembrandt.

imposition of taxation. The burghers were, however, involved in the administration of justice since burgher councillors assisted in trying cases involving burghers. The burgher councillors were consulted on all matters affecting the burgher population.

A burgher council, later designated the burgher senate, was constituted by those burghers selected to attend the Council of Justice but it had merely *de facto* recognition and fulfilled the function of a modern town council.

From 1657, when the first burgher was appointed to the Council of Justice, to 1778, there was virtually no progress towards democracy in the central executive and legislative government "and there was a visible list towards anarchy and contempt for the law in the *platteland*".[1] The free burghers displayed a stern determination to protect and maintain their economic interests and their civil liberties against company restrictions and authoritarianism. The conduct of the colourful and cultured Adam Tas personified this determination. Tas came into conflict with Governor W A

1 Wilson and Thompson *The Oxford History of South Africa* 214.

Slaves working in the early Cape – busy threshing wheat.

Portrait of Speelman, a Hottentot. The Hottentots were the direct cause of the introduction of the first pass legislation in the history of South Africa.

van der Stel, who manifestly abused his position for the sake of private profit. Tas was the ringleader of a group of burghers who had secretly smuggled a petition to the directors in Amsterdam. His uncle, Henning Hüsing and three others were exiled. Tas was imprisoned in the Castle for thirteen months. The exiles sought the ear of the directors and informed them of the torture and the irregular trial to which they had been subjected. The governor was consequently recalled and dismissed after an inquiry. Tas was released from the Castle. From the day of his release Tas renamed his farm Libertas. This was a skilful play on words, reflecting both his name and his newfound freedom. The *Kaapse Patriotte* movement from 1779–1791 in which the burgher councillors were actively involved, was a manifestation of greater political awareness. In 1779 this movement made demands for equal representation of burghers with officials on both the Councils of Justice and Policy, by means of free elections, subject to the approval of the governor and sitting burgher members. In 1791 they demanded *de iure* recognition for the burgher council. These demands were only partly met: in 1783 the Council of Justice was reorganized and constituted of six burghers and six

Abraham van Riebeeck (1653–1713), the third son of Jan van Riebeeck, was born in the old fort in Table Bay. He graduated in law from Leyden and was the only South African ever to serve as governor-general of Dutch East India.

officials. Recognition was granted to the burgher council in 1793 and a commission of three burghers and three officials was created in 1785 to determine official prices for agricultural produce. In regard to the central legislative and executive government the "narrow official oligarchy"[2] was maintained.

The Council of Justice

For the first four years of the settlement the commander's council exercised judicial, legislative and executive functions. However, in 1656 the council was divided into two parts, viz the Political Council *(Raad van Politie)* and the Council of Justice *(Raad van Justitie)*. The former was charged with legislating and the execution of policy, the latter with the administration of justice.

In 1657 an important change occurred in the composition of the Council of Justice when a burgher, Van Goens, was appointed to the council.[3] In June 1658 another burgher was appointed to the Council of Justice. With the passing of the years the Council of Justice became increasingly representative of the burghers culminating in 1783 with an equal representation for burghers and officials. Although the political structure at the Cape during the VOC rule was virtually autocratic, the administration of justice did involve burgher representation and participation in accordance with the time-honoured principle that the people themselves should have a share in determining law.

Until the end of the seventeenth century the Council of Justice was not composed of lawyers but of laymen. Only in the twilight period of the company rule was a manifestation found of the influence of qualified persons practising before the Bar of the council or serving as judges thereon.

The Council of Justice was the colony's highest court of justice which not only heard cases in the first instance but also fulfilled an appellate role in regard to all the lower courts at the Cape. The judgments of the council were given on a collegiate basis and appeal lay to the High Court of Justice in distant Batavia which inevitably entailed expense and delay.

The council had both civil and criminal jurisdiction. However, "no sentence was carried out until it had received the governor's *fiat* and when confirmed had to be executed without delay".[4] Even after the separation of the Council of Policy from the Council of Justice the latter continued with manifold executive functions. In 1685 Commander Van Rheede pronounced the *de iure* separation of the two councils. In practice there was not a clear demarcation between the functions of the two councils since they were largely composed of the same people and the vital distinction between

2 Op cit 217.

3 Visagie *Regspleging en Reg aan die Kaap van 1652 tot 1806* 42.

4 Botha 1915 *SALJ* 319 323.

Two pages from the record of a civil case heard by the Council of Justice.

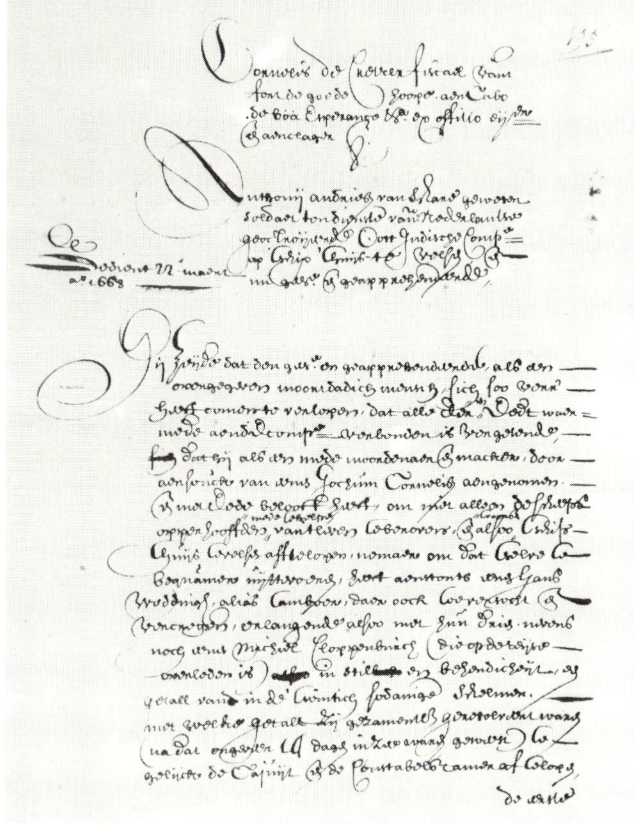

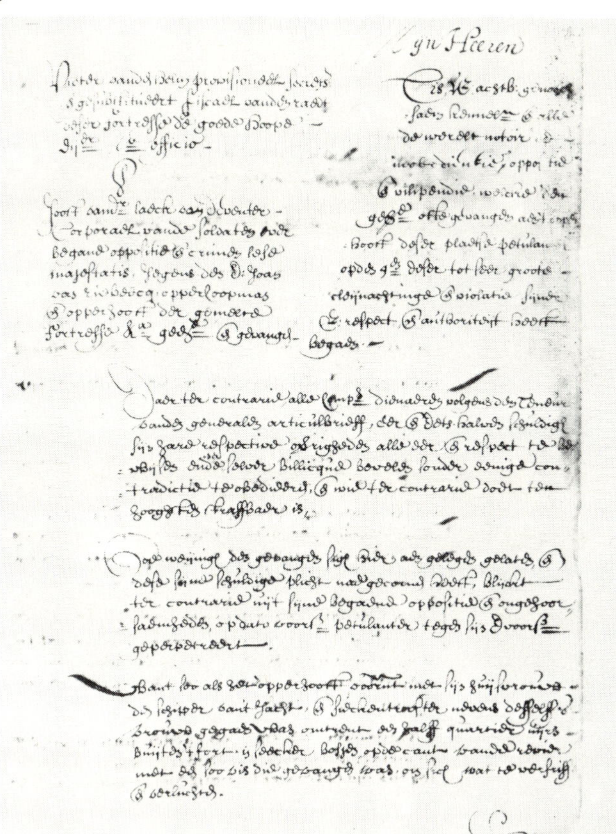

legislative and judicial power as known today did not exist.

In 1691 the commander was replaced by a governor who presided over the Council of Justice until 1734 when the governor was excluded and the *secunde* took the chair. The governor was still required to approve penalties imposed by the council. This change was in accordance with instructions from the Council of Seventeen in 1732 forbidding senior officials from participating in the administration of justice. However, it was only in 1783 when equal representation of burghers and officials in the Council of Justice was authorized that a true differentiation between the two councils occurred. Initially the judiciary was completely untrained and although burgher judges were permanently appointed they received no remuneration and they sat only in those matters concerning their peers and were appointed and dismissed at the governor's pleasure.

Over the years and from a very modest start (in 1739 the Council of Justice had only ten lawbooks) a reasonably well-equipped library, including the works of authoritative Dutch writers as well as the works of jurists from other provinces of the Netherlands and adjoining countries, was built up by the council.[5]

The fiscal

The functions of the fiscal were to act as a watchdog over the interests of the company, to exercise summary jurisdiction in petty cases and to investigate alleged crimes. The Council of Justice, how-

5 Visagie 75.

The "Burgerwacht" House was completed in 1755 to serve as the headquarters of the burghers entrusted with the maintenance of law and order in Cape Town.

ever, determined whether a prosecution should occur.

In 1688 the first fiscal who was directly responsible to the Council of Seventeen was appointed. He was a member of the council and in addition to his salary received a share (usually a third) of all fines and punitive confiscations, a practice which promoted a sadistic zeal to his prosecutions and which made him the most reprehensible official in the company's employ. "The fiscals, who should have ensured honest administration, were so hated and feared by the burghers that the predatory butcher-bird was called 'fiskaal' in Afrikaans."[6]

The powers of the fiscal were so considerable that he had authority to report even the governor to the Chamber of Seventeen or the authorities in Batavia.

> "But the only official whose power approached that of the governor was the independent fiscal who in addition to acting as public prosecutor in criminal trials, preventing smuggling, and controlling the police, was in 1688 given vast powers to punish officials for dereliction of duty, including the right to report the governor to the Seventeen, with whom he corresponded directly."[7]

In addition he was given the right of *preventie* (prevention or intervention) regarding prosecutions in the lower courts. The great measure of freedom enjoyed by this official led to complaints so that in 1793 his position was made subordinate to the governor.

Legal practitioners

The legal fraternity was constituted by advocates *(advocaten)*, attorneys *(procureurs)* and notaries *(notarissen)*.

In Roman-Dutch law the attorney assisted and instructed the advocate who exclusively had a right of audience in the higher courts. However, since there was a dearth of practising advocates during the period of the company's rule, attorneys appeared before all the courts.

The notary did much of the work of a modern attorney and practitioners very often combined this office with a practice at the Bar of the Council of Justice.

6 Wilson and Thompson 218.
7 Op cit 217.

Hendrik Adriaan van Rheede tot Drakenstein (1637–1691) visited the Cape in 1685. He wrote a comprehensive report on local conditions and laid down detailed regulations covering a variety of matters. It was he who gave the Constantia estate to Governor Simon van der Stel.

The Council of Justice admitted attorneys after the prescribed oath had been taken but no professional qualifications were necessary for admission. In 1781 the Governor-in-Council resolved to empower the Court of Justice to admit only a certain number of attorneys. A *placaat* in the statutes of Batavia (Van Diemen's Code) of 1642 contains the earliest rules of conduct. In 1791, however, a detailed code of instructions was drawn up to regulate the functions and professional conduct of attorneys as a result of a complaint of the council that legal practitioners were indifferent and ignorant.

From time to time a tariff of fees for attorneys was laid down. Certain irregularities occurred in 1793 which resulted in the commissioners of the Court of Justice preparing a draft tariff for submission to the authorities, which increased charges

The very first deed for a piece of land which Jan van Riebeeck granted to a free burgher, Jacob Cloete, in 1657.

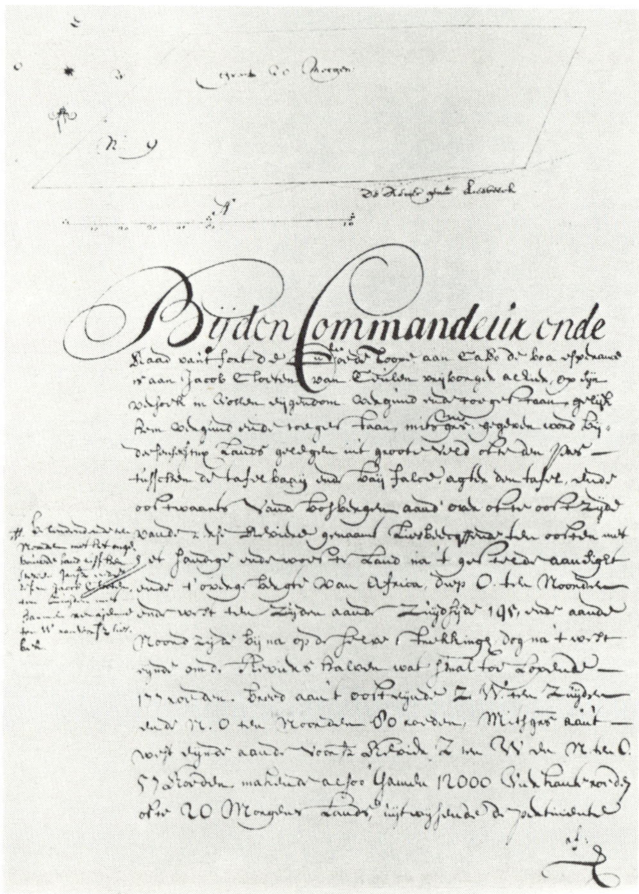

slightly and suggested that 500 rixdollars should be furnished by attorneys as security.

Persons born in the colony, or who had a right of residence and who had graduated as doctors of law at one of the universities of Holland could be admitted as advocates of the Court of Justice. Advocates were required to sign all pleadings, petitions etc. The court could appoint advocates to act *pro Deo* for indigent persons who had a just claim. A tariff regulated the charges of advocates. Until the abolition of the Court of Justice in 1827 advocates handed in written statements of their arguments in addition to the verbal addresses they made to the court.

Notaries were admitted by the government and if they were adequately qualified they were entitled to practise as advocates as well. However, a notary as such "had no *locus standi* before any of the Cape courts, in fact by his instructions he was expressly forbidden to act as an attorney-at-law and no-one was permitted to employ any legal assistance before the court unless he was a duly admitted advocate or attorney".[8] In the early years of the settlement notarial work was performed by the secretaries of the two councils. A code of instructions for notaries was drawn up in 1793. Notaries were required to give security. There was a biennial inspection of their protocols and registers by commissioners of the Court of Justice and in outlying districts by the *landdrost* and *heemraden*.

8 Botha 1924 *SALJ* 255 261.

The Drostdy *in Stellenbosch which was completed in 1687.*

The lower courts

Court of petty cases

In 1682 the *Collegie van Commissarissen van Kleine Zaken* was created to relieve the Council of Justice of relatively trivial matters. It had jurisdiction to try disputes the subject-matter of which did not exceed three hundred guilders. It was constituted of two company employees, two burghers and a secretary and operated under the supervision of the Council of Justice. In 1795 it had a president (company official), a vice-president (burgher) and four other members. Litigation was extremely costly and costs could amount to as much as the sum sued for. It sat at least once a week and in 1711 it fused with the matrimonial court.

The courts of landdrost *and* heemraden

As the country districts became more populated it became necessary to create district courts to decide cases in which small amounts were involved. In country districts courts of the *landdrost* (magistrate) were established, whereas in Cape Town the court of petty cases catered for a similar need.

These courts were modelled on the court of *baljuw en mannen* of the Netherlands. Each district was under the control of a *landdrost*, who was assisted by a board of *heemraden* over which he presided.

In 1682 a *Kollege van Heemraden* (board of *heemraden*) was established for Stellenbosch and three years later a *landdrost* was appointed there. These courts acted as administrative and judicial bodies.

The Drostdy *in Graaff-Reinet in 1811. Commissioner De Mist commissioned the renowned architect L Thibault to design the building in 1804.*

In 1797 there were three *drostdys* (districts over which *landdrosts* had jurisdiction), namely Stellenbosch, Swellendam and Graaff-Reinet. By 1804 there were five such *drostdys*, Uitenhage and Tulbagh being the new additions. Initially the Stellenbosch court had jurisdiction to try civil cases in which the disputed amount did not exceed 50 rixdollars. In 1793 this was raised to 100 rixdollars. On account of its considerable distance from the capital Graaff-Reinet had jurisdiction to try civil cases up to 1 000 guilders.

Initially all crimes had to be prosecuted before the Court of Justice subject to the fiscal's "Right of Prevention"[9] or intervention. Such prosecutions occurred according to the Cape laws and the Criminal Ordinance of 9 July 1570.

In regard to civil matters the procedure was simple. Parties appeared in person and stated their case without any formality. Where disputes concerned inter alia the use of roads, water courses or the borders of farms, a reconciliation was always attempted. Inspections *in loco* by the *heemraden* were also carried out.

Collegie van Commissarissen van Huwelyk Zaken (matrimonial court)

In 1676 the Council of Policy resolved to establish at the Cape a matrimonial court according to the custom of India. It was constituted of two officials and two burghers. It operated under the supervision of the Council of Justice and a president (Martinus van Banchem) and a secretary (Andries de Man) were duly appointed. By the custom of India was meant the statutes of Batavia, which were observed at the Cape. The laws it applied were based on the Political Ordinance of 1580.

It was responsible for issuing a certificate of non-impediment to a proposed marriage, which was essential for the publication of the banns and subsequent church ceremony. In 1711 the matrimonial court and the court of petty cases amalgamated.

9 Botha 1921 *SALJ* 409.

The Drostdy *in Somerset-East.*

The Weeskamer

The *Weeskamer* (orphan chamber) was founded in 1675. This was an institution that was well known in both the Netherlands and the Dutch East Indies. Initially it was composed of a president appointed by the commander and two officials and two burghers.

In 1699 its composition was amended to include a vice-president. It exercised control over the estates of deceased persons and minors and administered intestate estates. The orphan chamber's work was supervised by the Council of Justice.

From 1746 executors testamentary were required to lodge inventories with the chamber and wills had to be registered with it from 1711.

Sources of law

It is perplexing that neither the Charter *(Octrooi)* of 1602 nor the *artyckelbrief* specified which system of law had to apply in the settlements of the company. There still is controversy as to whether the Governor-General-in-Council at Batavia and the Governor-in-Council at the Cape had formal authority to legislate. However, from the inception of the settlement local laws were made and applied at the Cape, although these *placaats* may have been *ultra vires.* Indeed there was a plethora of local *placaats.* During the company's rule consolidation of these local laws was never attempted. In 1862 a commission was appointed to investigate these *placaats;* it was decided to retain nine of them and to discard the balance. Apparently none is in force today.

Promulgation occurred by oral announcement from the court-house and by posting up the *placaat* in a public place. The *placaats* came into operation immediately but the authorities in Batavia and Holland had a veto power. Normally these *placaats* were effective only while they were displayed. Consequently it was necessary to "promulgate and re-promulgate from time to time"[10] *generaale pla-*

10 Hahlo and Kahn *The Union of South Africa: The Development of its Laws and Constitution* 16.

The Drostdy *in Worcester, completed in 1824, represents the best surviving example of Regency architecture in South Africa today.*

caaten which contained a collection of local regulations.

The jurisprudential and legal significance of these *placaats* is negligible, but they do give a vivid insight into life at the Cape in the days of the VOC.

The placaats *of the Governor-General-in-Council at Batavia*

There is some doubt as to whether *placaats* issued by the Batavian governor-general were *proprio vigore* valid. There is, however, no doubt that the statutes of Batavia (Van Diemen's Code) were applied by the Council of Justice. These comprised the laws in operation in the Dutch East Indies issued by Antonio van Diemen, governor-general in 1642. The code's application was never ratified by the Estates-General and hence there is controversy as to its validity.

In 1715 the Governor-in-Council at the Cape resolved formally that the statutes of Batavia should be taken as the basis of the law together with Roman law and modern law, and without derogating from the statutes issued at the Cape.

The Groot Placaet Boeck, *a collection of legislation of the Netherlands with emphasis on ordinances and* placaaten *of the States General, Holland, Zeeland and West Friesland, published in ten volumes between 1658 and 1797. Important legislation in the field of intestate succession, such as the Perpetual Edict, Political Ordinance and the Charter (*"Octrooi"*) of 1661, is to be found here. The illustration shows the title page of the sixth volume of this work followed by an extract from a* placaat *dealing with the office of attorney.*

Art. I V.

Dat meede de Procureurs na advenant de jaaren dat ſyluiden zyn geimmatriculeert, haarluider plaats ſullen neemen op de Procureurs Sitbanken, van vooren af van het Buffet, en ſoo vervolgens na agteren toe, en gehouden ſullen weeſen alhier in den Hage, en geſont weeſende, geduurende de Audientie in de Rolle preſent te zyn, en te blyven, ten minſten by haar abſentie, haarluider Opperclercquen, om haar Meeſters ſaaken waar te neemen, wel geinſtrueert aldaar te ſenden en laaten blyven. En ſullen de Procureurs en haarluider Opperclercquen haarluiden in alle modeſtie draagen, en buiten haarluider termyn nog by de Edele Heeren Commiſſariſſen, nog by het Buffet begeeven, op pœne en executie als vooren, ſonder dat'er in de Binneaudientie en reſpective Ingangen van dien eenige andere van de Clercquen ſullen moogen koomen, ten waare om haar eenige advertentie te doen, in welken gevalle, de advertentie gedaan zynde, deſelve gehouden ſullen zyn daatelijk buiten de voorſchreeve Audientie te gaan, waar toe den Officier van den Hove, en eerſte Deurwaarders geauthoriſeert werden de voorſchreeve Clercquen als vooren te doen vertrekken.

In 1766 Van der Parra, governor-general of Batavia, drafted a revised code. There is no certainty whether the Van der Parra code applied at the Cape. Both these codes contained very little substantive law.

The statutes of Holland

There has been controversy as to whether the statutes of Holland were valid for the Cape. These were general statutes of Holland which prior to 1652 had become an integral part of the common law.

The Estates-General

This was the ultimate authority over all overseas settlements and consequently enjoyed legislative powers over the refreshment station established at the Cape.

Important examples of the exercise of this legislative power are:

(i) the *artyckelbrief* which was a *placaat* dealing with the maintenance of order and discipline applicable to all company employees;
(ii) the *Octrooi* of 10 January 1661 which regulated

The First British Occupation of the Cape: a painting depicting three battleships of the Netherlands which visited Simon's Bay harbour in 1795. The Cape fell into British hands for the first time shortly after the completion of this picture by C de Jong, captain of one of the ships.

the law of intestate succession (this has survived to the present time);

(iii) the *placaat* of 1778 which abolished the confiscation of property of a condemned criminal.

The common law

In the *Octrooi* of 1602 there is no indication of the system of law to be applied at the Cape. It was accepted that the law of the province of Holland, as the most powerful and influential of the provinces of the United Netherlands, would apply.

During the embryonic period of the Dutch settlement at the Cape the administration of justice was rudimentary.

The separation of the Council of Justice from the Council of Policy, the appointment of an independent fiscal, the restriction on the number of practising attorneys and the requirement of the annual renewal of admission by practitioners must have led to greater efficiency and sophistication in the administration of justice and practice of law. Also there was a gradual increase in the number of persons who received their legal training abroad.

It is not possible to assess the nature and quality of law practised by the Council of Justice since proceedings of this court were *foribus clausis* (behind closed doors) and the court did not deliver judgments in the modern sense of the word, i e the grounds for its decisions were not disclosed. The doctrine of *stare decisis* did not apply during this period. Direct evidence of the substantive law applied by the Council of Justice during the VOC rule of the Cape is therefore absent.

It is apparent from the records available in the archives that the great institutional writers of Holland were quoted and examined in the courts. In addition, Roman law and the works of jurists of the other adjoining provinces of the Netherlands were used as a supplementary source of the common law. For instance, it is known that the Council of Justice possessed a copy of the *Corpus Iuris Civilis*.

During the entire period of company rule, the general administration of justice and the practice of law left much to be desired. Firstly, corruption was endemic to the whole VOC service, since

Top: *Prisoners and their warder.*
Below: *The old gaol in Cape Town.*

The Drostdy *in Tulbagh built in 1804.*

officials were deliberately underpaid. This corruption must have influenced the administration of justice. Most of the legal practitioners had little formal training until well into the eighteenth century and the courts were staffed by untrained laymen. In addition the Council of Justice never received fixed instructions to guide it.

Commissioner Verburg described the laws at the Cape as "too minute, and in some respects rather too rigid, and if acted upon to the letter without connivance the inhabitants would be subject to constant penalties so severe as often to produce their ruin".[11]

The burghers also became dissatisfied because there was no compilation of the existing statutes and this led to uncertainty.

However, although the administration of justice was inept, rudimentary and at times amateurish, there is no doubt that Roman-Dutch law had taken root in the Cape soil.

The era of codification brought an end to the great tradition and practice of Roman-Dutch law in the Netherlands. "Thus the *Code Civil* wrote finis to Roman-Dutch law in its country of origin."[12] By some strange quirk of history Roman-Dutch law was to survive as a result of the cession of the Cape to Great Britain.

11 Wilson and Thompson 221.

12 Hahlo and Kahn *The South African Legal System and its Background* 564.

The First British Occupation

Article 7 of the Articles of Capitulation of 1795 permitted the colonists to "retain all the privileges which they now enjoy". After a brief interlude the Council of Justice was re-established and continued to administer justice in accordance with extant "laws, statutes and customs". The Political Council was, however, abolished. The Council of Justice was reduced from thirteen to eight and each member received a remuneration. A civil court of appeal in cases where the amount in dispute exceeded £200 was constituted by the governor and lieutenant-governor, with the theoretical prospect of appeal to the Privy Council. The civil jurisdiction of the courts of *landdrost* and *heemraden* was increased. McCartney, the British governor, abolished the obnoxious and medieval use of torture to extract confessions in criminal trials. "The instruments of death and torture were the gibbet, flogging and strangling posts, the cross upon which limbs were broken and branding irons for castigations, ropes' ends, split rattans, twigs of quince trees, leather traces and the sjambok are used."[13] Barbarous methods of execution and punishment were abolished. Before the death sentence could be passed, it was necessary that the accused should confess his crime. In order, therefore, to obtain his confession in a case where proof of his guilt was sufficient, but he would not acknowledge it, he was subject to torture and the early Cape records show that not only the rack, but also the thumbscrew were used for this purpose. The degree of torture seems to have varied.

The Batavian interlude

As a result of the Treaty of Amiens of 1802, the Cape of Good Hope was restored to the Netherlands. Commissioner-general De Mist was appointed. He recognized the need for improvements and reform in regard to the administration of justice. Although this interlude was of short duration it is of considerable legal and judicial interest. De Mist's report clearly sets out the inadequacy and decadence which prevailed. De Mist

Portrait of Napoleon I (1769–1821) by Ingres.

was a young lawyer with liberal and republican views who effected sweeping judicial and constitutional reforms. The Council of Justice was transformed from a primarily commercial management board into a more political and constitutional instrument of government. The burgher senate was given a more democratic character and renamed the *Raad van Gemeente*.

All districts were subdivided into wards, each under a field cornet, and a weekly post was introduced between the *drostdys*. A free trade policy was introduced.

The *Raad van Justitie* was expressly declared independent and was constituted of a president and six councillors, three of whom were qualified Dutch lawyers and three burghers who had a

13 Botha 1915 *SALJ* 324.

Sir Andries Stockenström (1792–1864), officer and politician who as magistrate of Graaff-Reinet gained notoriety for his part in the suppression of the Slagtersnek Rebellion (1815).

knowledge of the administration of justice. The *Hoogs Geregshof* at The Hague was to act as the appeal court for the Cape. An attorney-general replaced the detested fiscal. The courts of the *landdrost* and *heemraden* were furnished with a code of instructions and two new districts, Tulbagh and Uitenhage, were constituted.

Only graduates in law from Dutch universities were permitted to be advocates and persons wishing to be admitted were required to pass examinations administered by the courts' commissioners. Tariffs were prescribed for legal practitioners. In 1803 a *desolate boedelkamer* was created for the administration of insolvent estates and the execution of civil judgments.

De Mist's enlightened judicial reforms together with modern ideas on economic matters, trade and religious freedom were destined to be of short duration. The Treaty of Amiens brought about a temporary cessation of hostilities only and within a year Europe was once again engulfed in war, with the Batavian Republic a subservient ally of Napoleon.

The Second British Occupation

In 1806 the British repossessed the Cape. Article 8 of the Articles of Capitulation expressly provided that "the burghers and inhabitants shall preserve all their rights and privileges which they have enjoyed hitherto". The significance and meaning of this provision has been a matter of controversy. Fortunately the system of Roman-Dutch law was not replaced but De Mist's enlightened reforms were terminated. Once again the Council of Justice was composed of colonists appointed by the governor, "all save the chief justice holding office *durante bene placito* (at the governor's pleasure)".[14] This meant that the court was not independent and that the judges were appointed as a mark of favour and simultaneously continued with their other occupations. A civil court of appeal was constituted of the governor and/or lieutenant-governor, whereas in criminal matters appeals lay to the governor sitting with two nominated assessors. The vice-admiralty court was resurrected and the hated fiscal reinstituted.

Initially the British government did not interfere with burgher representation on the judicial bodies.

Gradually reforms were effected during the early years of the Second British Occupation. In 1811 circuit courts composed of two members of the Council of Justice were created which gave relief to both litigants and prisoners. In 1813 all court proceedings were opened to the public. Between 1817 and 1819 the courts of *landdrost* and *heemraden* were expressly vested with criminal jurisdiction. In terms of Ordinance 18 of 1826 a permanent commissioner sat in a court for petty cases in Cape Town.

Although British forces occupied the Cape for the second time in 1806, formal cession to Great Britain occurred only in 1814. From 1820 onwards with the arrival of the British settlers an increased tempo of judicial and legal reform was discernible

14 Hahlo and Kahn *The Union of South Africa* 204.

Second British Occupation of the Cape: in January 1806 Sir David Baird in command of 6 000 men conquered the army of General Janssens thereby finally placing the Cape under British control.

together with a policy of assimilation and anglicization.

A new criminal procedure code was introduced in 1819 which showed innovations of English origin. In terms of Ordinances 1 of 1825 and 27 of 1826 English replaced Dutch as the official language of the courts.

The First and Second Charters of Justice and their consequences

In 1823 Commissioners Bigge and Colebrook were appointed by the British government to enquire into and report on the Cape's affairs, inter alia the existing legal system. After a comprehensive investigation they formulated the recommendations they deemed necessary. Largely as a result of these recommendations the First Charter of Justice (1827) was issued thereby initiating a new judicial and legal dispensation for the Cape.

The charter confirmed an earlier decision to retain the Roman-Dutch common law.

Both the First and Second (1832) Charters, however, effected fundamental changes in the administration of justice. The old Council of Justice was abolished and replaced by the Cape Supreme Court, constituted of a chief justice, two puisne judges and a vice-admiralty court judge. The judges were to hold office *quamdiu se bene gesserint* (provided they behave themselves) and to be appointed solely from the ranks of the advocates, thereby establishing an independent and competent judiciary with an unimpeachable record of integrity and impartiality which continues to the present time. In contrast the judges of the council were appointed and removed at the governor's pleasure. The British government refused to impose the English dual judicature (i e the separation between legal and equitable jurisdiction).

To the profound dismay of the colonists the

A sketch of the Elim mission town.

burgher senate and inferior courts of the *landdrost* and *heemraden* were dispensed with and the latter were replaced by resident magistrates. The officers of these inferior courts had been drawn from the ranks of the Dutch colonists in accordance with a time-honoured principle that had its genesis in Germanic practice that the people should participate in the determination of the law. Since 1822 English had been the colony's official language and in 1827 and 1832 English became the sole language of the superior and inferior courts respectively.

"What little popular representation the Cape-Dutch had exercised like the official use of their language was eliminated."[15]

These matters could possibly have been justified by a desire for the efficient administration of justice but unfortunately like so many other measures of this period they left posterity with a legacy of acrimony and recrimination.

The profession was to be "divided". Advocates had to be United Kingdom barristers or doctors of law of Oxford, Cambridge or Dublin. Attorneys had to be qualified practitioners from Great Britain or instructed in law by a Cape advocate or attorney.

New judicial posts modelled on English count-

15 Hosten, Edwards, Nathan and Bosman *Introduction to South African Law and Legal Theory* 198.

From 1820 the Eastern Province developed rapidly and as new towns were established and trade expanded, Grahamstown to an ever increasing extent came to be regarded as the centre of the region. Agitation throughout the territory persuaded the governor, Sir Philip Wodehouse, to agree to a session of the colonial parliament being held in the town in 1864. This session is depicted here.

erparts were also created: a registrar; a master of the supreme court who replaced the *weeskamer* and the *desolate boedelkamer;* a sheriff and in the place of the fiscal an attorney-general who was to act as prosecutor, government draftsman and legal adviser.

The Supreme Court sat with open doors, a practice dating back to 1813, and had both full original and review jurisdiction. There had to be at least two circuits annually. Civil appeals lay to the Privy Council in matters where the amount in dispute was above £500, but otherwise only by special leave of the council. Executive *fiat* was required for criminal sentences of banishment, transportation or death.

Roman-Dutch law was officially retained as the common law of the Cape but the English-modelled institutions would lead to an adoption and infiltration of English law. Legislation was used as a potent weapon for English law penetration resulting in inter alia the introduction of the British accusatorial criminal procedure code, the law of evidence conforming to the practice of the courts of record at Westminster and the administration of estates.

Statutes on company law, negotiable instruments and insolvency were based on the British counterparts. The entire field of commercial laws: insurance, patents, trade marks and copyright, was adopted from English law. This did not imply

In 1848 Lord Grey, the British Colonial Secretary, launched a project in terms of which the Cape would become a penal colony to which convicted prisoners and those who had served their sentences would be sent. The Cape residents protested so hotly that the whole idea was abandoned. The painting shows a protest meeting held on the Parade in Cape Town on 4 July 1849.

that Roman-Dutch law was inherently incapable of developing a viable mercantile law. Unfortunately the essential instrument for legal development, namely a university with a civil law tradition, was absent at the Cape in the formative period of our law. Menzies, the learned, virile and capable Scottish lawyer and early Cape judge, commented favourably on and upheld the Roman-Dutch institution of *namptissement,* which has in the guise of provisional sentence endured to the present time.

In terms of Ordinance 69 of 1828 the office of registrar of deeds was created. This legislation stipulated that in future all deeds of transfer of bonded property, mortgages and other similar acts and instruments should be certified and registered before and signed by the registrar of deeds. The various deeds were prepared and drawn up in the deeds registry office. In 1844 Ordinance 14 brought about important changes. Transfer deeds and deeds of hypothecation could now be prepared or drawn up by an advocate of the Supreme Court or a duly authorized conveyancer. From 1 July 1844 a proper register of deeds was kept. This system was subsequently adopted by other South African territories.

The gravest threat to Roman-Dutch law was not the direct adoption of English statutes but rather the influence of English law by way of a kind of osmosis. The early judges were schooled in English law, they had to apply an unacquainted

The hall in which the Cape Legislative Assembly met from 1854–1884.

legal system and they were thus inclined to seek solutions in the more accessible English judgments and English legal textbooks.

Constitutional development

A significant constitutional evolution occurred in the Cape in the nineteenth century. The British settlers arrived in 1820 and the British government wished to convert the Cape into a British colony in government, law and spirit. The leaders of the British settlers were aware of the reform movements and liberal thinking in the United Kingdom during the Industrial Revolution.

The government of the colony was autocratic and administered by a virtually all-powerful governor subject only to the restraint of the Colonial Secretary, a ninety days' sail away. By proclamation he legislated at his will, subject only to orders in council, letters patent and royal instructions. Thomas Pringle, John Fairbairn and the printer George Grey played a decisive role in the struggle for press freedom against the dictatorial governor, Lord Charles Somerset. Ordinance 60 of 1829 established the freedom of the press.

Other civil liberties have their origin in this period. Ordinance 68 of 1830 partially removed disabilities imposed on Roman Catholics. The last disabilities imposed on persons or bodies for religious reasons were removed in 1868.

The Cape liberal non-racial policy had its gene-

Cape Districts under the Batavian Republic.

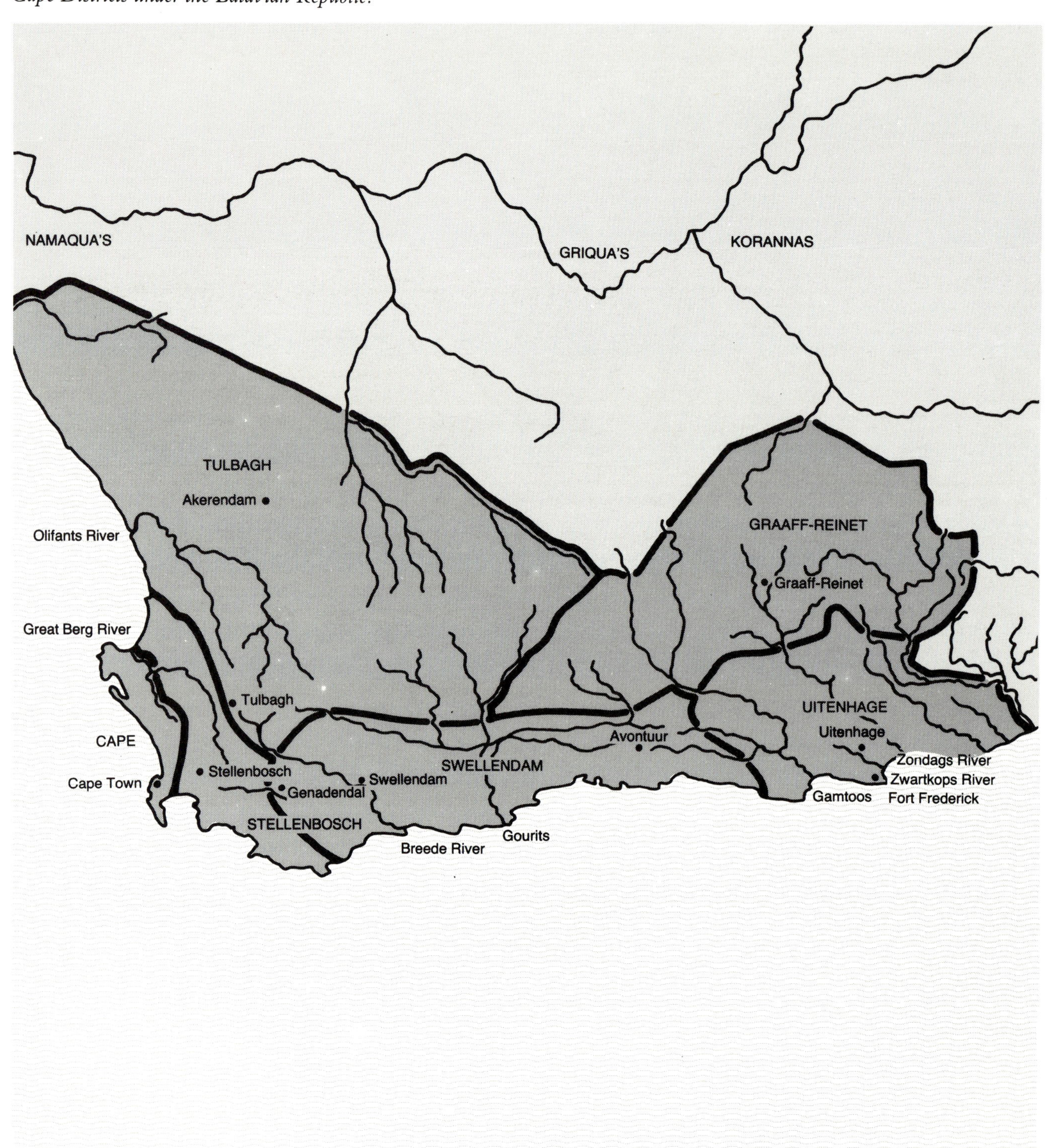

Prominent Cape officials.

sis in this period. Ordinance 50 of 1828 repealed the restrictive Hottentot laws of 1809–1819 and gave Hottentots, Bushmen and free Coloured persons full civic rights including the right to buy land on the same terms as Europeans.

The Slavery Abolition Act passed by the British Parliament through the efforts of the legendary William Wilberforce abolished slavery at the Cape from 1 December 1834.

The press freedom struggle was of significance for the development of independent thought which presaged the reform of central government with the advent firstly of representative and subsequently responsible government. The successful conclusion of the press struggle brought public policy within the scope of general debate.

Representative government had its origin in local government with the establishment of representative municipal boards from 1837, elected by householders on a non-racial property qualification. These boards were empowered to enact regulations subject to executive approval.

The colony received a new constitution in 1834 in terms of which the executive council was to be composed of the governor who presided, four senior officials, who together with the attorney-general and from five to seven unofficial nominees, sat in the legislative council. In theory the governor's rights were curtailed, in practice they were enormous.

Although the legislative council was regarded with opprobium, it nevertheless did subsequently after an initial protest allow freedom of debate and opened its doors to the public.

A new and vital era in the history of South Africa began with the Great Trek in 1835. Parties of Boers (farmers) formed themselves into organized groups and trekked into the wild and unexplored northern hinterland. The disgruntled Boers were disturbed by the grant of equal civil rights to Coloured people, by the slave emancipation and its consequences, they were fearful of anglicization and resentful of an alien government that dealt with the endemic instability on the eastern frontier with vacillation and a lack of firmness. The incessant frontier wars with the indigenous Black people were a constant source of concern to the government and the people of the colony during this period. The Voortrekkers left their farms and homesteads behind and trekked in covered wagons to the untamed lands beyond the Orange and Vaal Rivers and established a new way of life.

The famous *Durham Report*, published in 1839, paved the way for a new and enlightened British colonial policy which was to make evolutionary constitutional development possible. Durham pointed out that the Americans had rebelled because their freedom was inhibited and that the lesson to be learnt was that greater freedom and responsibility would enhance loyalty and respect for the Crown. He recommended that Canada should be given full responsible government. Within ten years this recommendation was realized for Canada and within twenty years for New Zealand, Tasmania and most of the Australian colonies.

In the Cape there were serious obstacles in the way of democratic institutions: the loss of White people to the hinterland, racial antagonism, the incessant frontier wars and the devolution sentiments of the colonists in the eastern districts. Ordinance 15 of 1848 established freedom of public meetings which is an essential precondition for representative government.

By virtue of Ordinance 2 of 1852 representative government materialized in 1853. A parliament was established for the Cape, constituted of three parts: the governor, an upper house (Legislative Council) and a lower house (House of Assembly). There was to be a qualified non-racial franchise, fixed at a low level on the explicit insistence of the British government. "The movement, under the blessing of Downing Street, towards equality before the law based on civilization and not colour had reached its apogee."[16]

The crown colonial period had ended and the first parliament met in May 1854. Westminster-model government with its exemplary parliamentary traditions had commenced and the colonial parliament based its internal rules on the parliament of Westminster.

Although responsible government merely required an amendment to s 79 of the constitution, this only materialized after nearly twenty years in 1872 when the so-called "responsibles" under Molteno were able to command sufficient support in both houses to secure the passage of the necessary bill.

In 1909, the year preceding the advent of Union, 14,8 per cent of the voters on the roll were non-Whites. This meant that the non-White vote was certainly not insignificant.

In 1892 the secret ballot was introduced for parliamentary elections. In 1883 the Powers and Privileges of Parliament Act was passed, thereby facilitating the functioning of the colonial parliament. This legislation was based on the corresponding Act applicable to the imperial parliament. Since 1882 Dutch had become a permissible language for parliamentary debates.

As the boundaries of the colony increased the prospect of indigenous tribal people qualifying as voters provoked Rhodes to raise the franchise qualifications. Communal land tenure became insufficient by virtue of legislation in 1887. Subsequently the property occupation test was increased from £25 to £75 and the £25 salary together with board and lodging qualification repealed.

> "The stranger who once had been within the gate was thus excluded from the roll but at the cost of concurrent exclusion of the backveld and the illiterate White."[17]

The Cape colonial period ended with the unification of South Africa in 1910. The decision of the national convention to adopt a unitary as opposed to a federal form of government was of decisive importance for the future of South Africa. Whether a federal form of government would have been more advantageous than a unitary one is a matter of considerable dispute.

The judiciary

The vast territorial expansion of the colony necessitated the founding of the Eastern Districts Court (EDC) at Grahamstown in 1864 and the High Court of Griqualand (HCG) in 1880 in addition to the Supreme Court situated in Cape Town.

Judicial appointments were initially made from the three United Kingdom Bars. However, after 1873 all appointments were made from the ranks of the local advocates.

There were lean years for Roman-Dutch law during the period when judicial posts were usually occupied by overseas incumbents who were often "mediocre"[18] and unschooled in the works of the institutionalized writers.

In 1873 Henry de Villiers, a native of the Cape who was only thirty-one years of age, was ap-

16 Hahlo and Kahn *The Union of South Africa* 54.

17 Op cit 58.

18 Op cit 208.

William Henry Somerset Bell. *Born at Fort Hare in 1856, died in Johannesburg in 1939. He was an attorney in Grahamstown and Johannesburg and published several works. He was the founder in 1884 of the* Cape Law Journal *of which he was also the editor.*

Jonathan Ayliff. *Frontier member of the Legislative Assembly, Cape Parliament 1865.*

pointed chief justice, a post he was to fill with great distinction for more than forty years. De Villiers was not the greatest South African jurist of the nineteenth century, but he was probably the greatest judge of the colonial period.

A separate Court of Appeal was established in 1879 composed of the chief justice, two puisne judges sitting at Cape Town and the judge-president of the EDC. Its lifespan was short since it was abolished in 1886.

The highest court of appeal was the Privy Council situated in London. It was seldom resorted to. It was subject to the criticism that it was both tardy and sometimes ignorant of the principles of Roman-Dutch law.

The jurisdiction of magistrates' courts was increased gradually until 1885. However, the Resident Magistrate's Court Act 43 of 1885 created "a tangle of inconsistencies and anomalies".[19] This unsatisfactory situation remained until the advent of Union.

Punitive criminal jurisdiction was increased by Act 20 of 1865 to a moderate level. The magistracy was largely untrained and fulfilled numerous administrative functions. This led to complaints and demands for reform.

The legal profession

The legal profession continued in its divided form. The Bar was a small cohesive group with most of its members being English trained. A local qualification as an advocate was introduced in 1858 with the establishment of a Board of Public Examiners whose functions were subsequently assumed by the University of the Cape of Good Hope in 1873.

By virtue of Rule of Court 149, promulgated on 4 September 1829, attorneys were entitled to qualify by serving five years of articles. However, from 1877 a practical examination became a prerequisite for aspirant attorneys. Matriculation and

19 1885 *Cape Law Journal* 283.

a second-class pass of the board (later the university) entitled an aspirant attorney to two years' remission. From 1883 local entry by simply serving five years' articles was abolished.

Notaries were initially simply admitted by the government. This proved undesirable and subsequently from 1858 notaries were required to serve four years' articles and had to satisfy court-appointed examiners or be qualified attorneys. From 1903 only attorneys could be appointed as notaries.

Deeds of transfer and mortgage bonds were initially drawn up exclusively by advocates and government-appointed conveyancers. From 1858 an examination had to be written by aspirant conveyancers. Admission as conveyancers was limited to attorneys from 1903.

In 1883 the Incorporated Law Society was established to ensure and facilitate professional integrity, uniform practice, and to superintend training and administer disciplinary measures. Such measures had become essential as the attorney's profession was almost exclusively home trained and lacked the traditions of the Bar. Act 20 of 1856 permitted so-called law agents who were "persons of full age and good fame and character" simply on payment of a £10 fee and admission by a magistrate's court to practice. The dearth of attorneys in the sparsely populated rural districts resulted in an uneasy toleration of these untrained "practitioners". From 1885 no future admission was permitted where a district had two attorneys, a measure which inevitably led to the decline and unlamented demise of law agents.

Although English law could have totally usurped Roman-Dutch law as the common law, the latter withstood the onslaught. Fortunately "there was always one judge to keep the lamp of Roman-Dutch learning alight".[20]

Firstly there was the Scot, Menzies, who probably made the most abiding mark on our judicial system in the early colonial period through his reports. Then came the native-born Cloete who had been a pupil of Van der Keessel and subsequently the brilliant Watermeyer, of German descent but native born whose untimely death was a great loss to the bench.

Conclusion

The nineteenth century was a formative period for South African law. During this period English law exerted a profound influence on the development and evolution of our law and the administration of justice.

The extent to which this influence has been detrimental or beneficial is a matter of considerable controversy. Even the most ardent exponents of Roman-Dutch law are prepared to concede that the influence of English law has not been entirely detrimental.

The influence of English law was greatest during the period 1860–1910 when the British Empire and its influence reached its zenith.

Roman-Dutch law in its original form was principally constituted primarily from two sources: Roman law and local Dutch law, but it had also been infused and enriched by French, Spanish and Italian legal conceptions and ideas. The ancient Roman law element gave Roman-Dutch law a catholic basis and character which was further enhanced by the reception of civilian components derived from other legal systems besides the basic Dutch component with its strong Germanic element. The fusion of these different components produced "one of the world's great legal systems".[21] In principle therefore where English law supplemented Roman-Dutch law and infused it with new ideas its influence was not unprecedented and should not be considered to be inherently detrimental to the character of Roman-Dutch law. Where, however, it supplanted fundamental and sound Roman-Dutch law principles its influence was regrettable.

The system of law applicable in a country is inextricably bound up with the nature and quality of the administration of justice. In regard to the latter the British influence has been of inestimable value since "the rule of law did not exist at the

20 Hahlo and Kahn *The South African Legal System* 208.

21 Op cit 596.

Cape during the company period".[22] The rule of law and everything that it entails, i e the independence of the judiciary, equality before the courts, the absence of arbitrary executive power and discretion and the maintenance of procedural and human rights found in our common law is a great legacy inherited from British law and government.

22 Wilson and Thompson 297.

The Cape colonial legal tradition synthesized two basic components: firstly, the Roman-Dutch common law originating from the early Dutch connection and influence and, secondly, the rule of law which was the product of the British colonial period. With the unification of the four colonies, the erstwhile Union of South Africa and its successor the Republic of South Africa became the custodian of this great legal heritage.

The Great Trek (1835 to 1848)

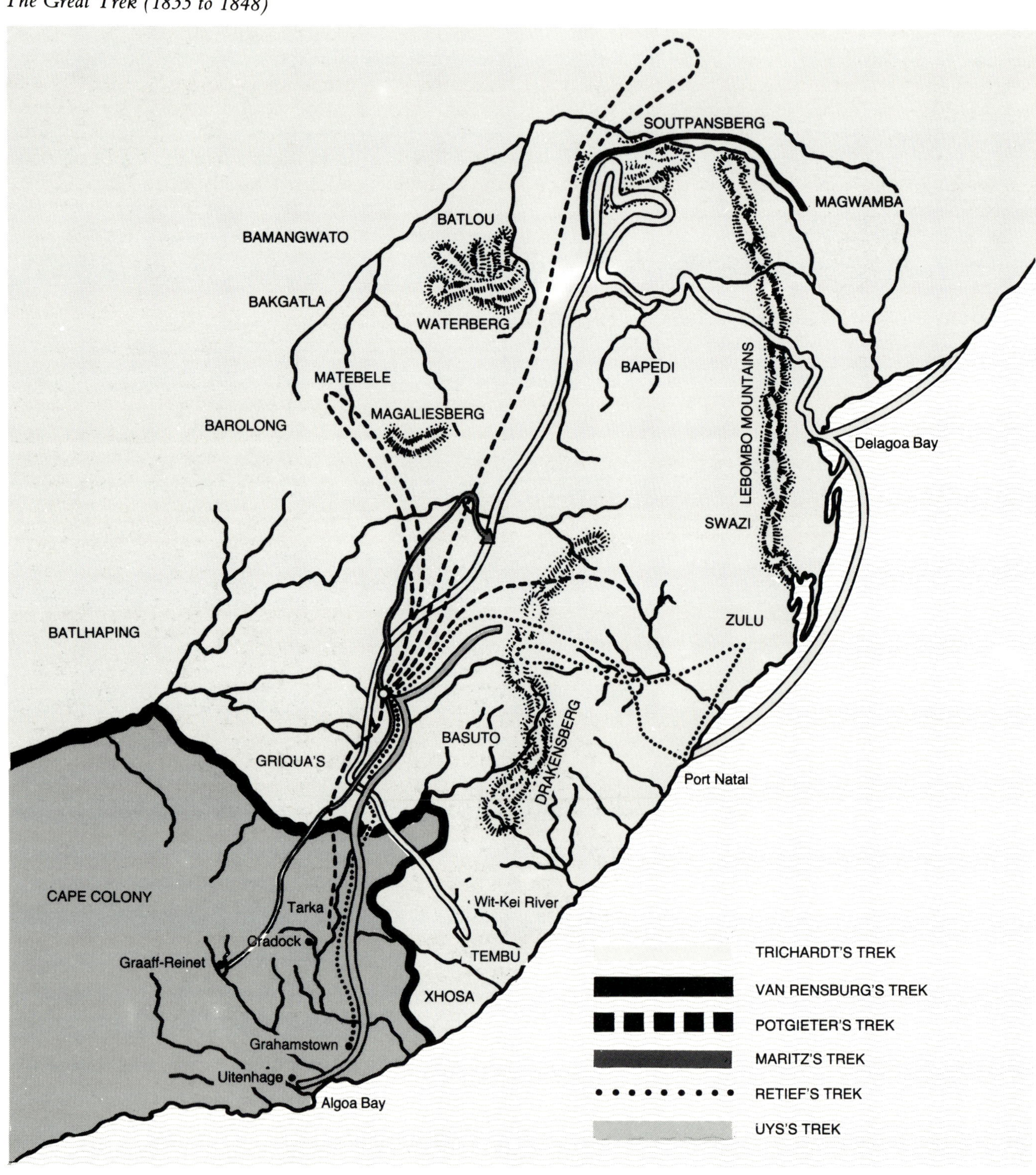

A N Oelofse BA LLB (Stell) Senior Lecturer in Mercantile Law University of South Africa

5

THE ORANGE FREE STATE 1843–1909

The period before 1854[1]

By the end of 1836 the exodus of White Trekkers from the Cape Colony had more or less reached saturation point.

In 1843 the Free State Trekkers obtained a legislative body of their own – although its decisions remained subject to confirmation by the Natal council.[2] After the British occupation of Port Natal in 1842 this scheme was, of course, of little practical significance. The British occupation also led the Trekkers north of the Vaal to sever all ties with Natal. A new and independent republic maintaining loose ties with the territory north of the Orange River was established north of the Vaal River. The British recognized the independence of the territory north of the Vaal at the Sand River Convention of 1852. As had formerly been the case in the Free State, provision was made in the so-called Thirty-three Articles for a judiciary with legislative powers.

In the interim, the governor of the Cape Colony, Sir Harry Smith, proclaimed the territory between the Orange and Vaal Rivers as British territory on 3 February 1848.

A proclamation of 14 March 1849 provided that the applicable legal system would be Roman-Dutch law "as received and administered in the courts of the Cape Colony . . ." The magistrates' jurisdiction was defined. Criminal cases falling outside the jurisdiction of a magistrate were heard by a circuit court of four magistrates. Where the Cape of Good Hope Punishment Act applied, the circuit court could not impose a fine exceeding 1 000 *riksdaalders* (rixdollars). A term of imprisonment (not exceeding two years) could be imposed. The practical effect of this was that serious crimes were referred to the Cape court for decision.

The British administration was eventually forced to change its views – largely as a result of the tremendous financial burden resulting from protection against Basuto invasions. The independence of the territory bordered by the Orange, the Vaal and the Drakensberg was recognized at the Bloemfontein Convention of 23 February 1854. The Trekkers in this area were again left to their own resources.

1 This section is based largely on Hahlo and Kahn *The Union of South Africa: The Development of its Laws and Constitution* 59 *et seq*.

2 Cf further chapter 4 on British action with regard to the "escape" of the Trekkers from the Cape and the constitutional arrangements regarding the Trekkers.

The period 1854–1876[3]

At the conclusion of the Bloemfontein Convention, a Volksraad (House of Assembly) was immediately summoned to draw up a constitution for the Orange Free State. Legislative power was to be in the hands of the Volksraad elected by enfranchised burghers. The executive power fell to the president assisted by an advisory council. As regards the law to be applied in the new republic, the constitution provided: "Het Romeinsch-Hollandsch recht zal de hoofwet van dezen staat sijn alwaar geen andere wet door den Volksraad gemaakt is" (Roman-Dutch law will be the law of the land where no other laws have been made by the Volksraad).

Roman-Dutch law was further defined in the constitution as the principles found in the textbooks of Voet, Van der Linden, Van der Keessel and the authorities there cited. As Chief Justice Rumpff correctly noted in his address delivered at the centenary celebrations of the Free State Supreme Court on 17 August 1974, the last five words of this definition incorporated the entire legacy of the Roman-Dutch legal history into the law of the Free State.

A number of attempts were made to alter the law applicable in the Free State – apparently because when faced with a practical problem, the existing provision left many practitioners wandering in a maze of confusion. Only one of these attempts almost succeeded. During the 1863 session of the Volksraad, a commission was appointed to revise the constitution and propose amendments. Section 56 of the draft amendment

3 Cf in this regard Hahlo and Kahn *op cit* 72 *et seq;* Scholtz *Die Geskiedenis van die Regspleging in die Oranje-Vrystaat 1854–1876.*

Signatories of the Bloemfontein Convention, 3 February 1854.

to the constitution proposed by the commission, freely translated, read as follows:

> "The constitution together with the laws made by the Volksraad will be the constitution of the state; however, where the Volksraad has made no statutory provision, guidance will be sought from the following Roman-Dutch works: Hugo de Groot, Van Leeuwen, and Van der Linden, and no reference to or quotations from other works will be permitted."

Fortunately, this amendment was not accepted. Subsequent judgments by the Free State Supreme Court clearly indicate that the judges did not consider themselves limited to only certain Roman-Dutch authors. Reference was frequently made to Cape and even English and Scottish decisions. In 1877 Sir Henry de Villiers (then chief justice of the Cape Supreme Court) wrote in a letter to Barkly that the Cape judgments carried as much weight in the Free State and Transvaal as the latter two courts' own decisions. It cannot thus be said that "pure" Roman-Dutch law was applied – it was rather Roman-Dutch law as it was applied in the Cape Colony.

A strong Cape influence can be discerned in the legislative sphere as well. For example, chapter 104 of the Free State Statute Book (which dealt with insolvent estates) was based largely on Cape Ordinance 6 of 1843, while both Ordinance 28 of 1902 (bills of exchange) and the Cape Act 19 of 1893 were based on the 1882 British Bills of Exchange Act. English law was, on occasion, even directly introduced, as e g in section 1 of Ordinance 5 of 1902 which was in turn based on Cape Act 8 of 1879. Legislative influence was, however, really strongly felt only after 1876.

Now we must return to the structure of the courts and their development during the period 1854–1876.

The court structure

When the Free State attained independence in 1854, the territory was divided into five districts, viz, Bloemfontein, Smithfield, Winburg, Harrismith and Fauresmith. There was a magistrate for each of these districts. The jurisdiction of the magistrates' and circuit courts (the Court of Combined Magistrates) has already been mentioned.

The 1854 constitution provided for two types of *landdrost* courts with lower court status. In the first place there was the regular *landdrost* court with civil jurisdiction to an amount of £37-10 and criminal jurisdiction of three months' imprisonment. On the first Wednesday of every month the *landdrost* sat with two *heemraden*. His civil jurisdiction was then £75 and his criminal jurisdiction limited to four months' imprisonment. The *heemraden* and the *landdrost* had equal say. Nothing was said of

The magistrate's office, Smithfield.

fines. Ordinance 5 of 1857 extended the criminal jurisdiction of these courts in that it empowered a *landdrost* to impose a fine of £5 and 25 strokes with a cane. The corresponding extended jurisdiction of the *landdrost* and *heemraden* was £10 and 39 strokes. This same ordinance provided a further remedy, viz "borgstelling tot bewaring der rust" (bail for the maintenance of peace) to an amount of £100 for a period of six months. The maximum bail in the case of the *landdrost* and *heemraden* was £200. This institution is today still to be found in our law. It is extensively provided for in section 384 of the old Criminal Procedure Act 56 of 1955. This is one of the two sections in the old Criminal Procedure Act which have not been repealed by the Criminal Procedure Act now in force (Act 51 of 1977).

When Ordinance 5 of 1857 was considered by the Volksraad it met with heated opposition from certain quarters because of the possibility of corporal punishment being inflicted on a White. President Boshof, however, pointed out the necessity of persuading White recidivists to new insights by this means. The ordinance was accepted without amendment.

Jacobus Nicolaas Boshof (1808–1881). After taking up the presidency in 1855, Boshof set about placing the public service, financial institutions and judicature on a sound footing, a task in which he largely succeeded. Problems with the Basuto and with his own people over union with the Transvaal (he favoured federation with the Cape Colony) led him to resign in 1859 after which he settled in Natal.

The Circuit Court of Combined Landdrosts

The Court of Combined Landdrosts (magistrates) was in essence a continuation of the Combined Magistrates' Court dating from the Orange River Sovereignty. On 18 April 1854 the Volksraad resolved that the Court of Combined Landdrosts should sit twice a year in each district, provided that there were at least six cases to be heard. The constitution provided that three *landdrosts* sit in this court. An 1856 ordinance further provided that the *landdrost* in whose district the session was held should act as chairman. The fact that all five *landdrosts* of the five districts were not required to sit was an improvement on the Combined Magistrates Court. A further advantage was that there was no possibility of a deadlock in voting. The great drawback, however, was that the *landdrost* before whom the case had originally served, also served on the Court of Combined Landdrosts. This meant that for that *landdrost* a detached approach to appeal cases was impossible. The court sat for the first time on 28 June 1854 in Smithfield. The *landdrosts* were Lowen from Bloemfontein, Ford from Smithfield and Visser from Fauresmith.

In terms of Ordinance 1 of 1856 the Court of Combined Landdrosts enjoyed unlimited civil jurisdiction. The ordinance also provided for unlimited criminal jurisdiction. The crime must, however, have been committed within the district in which the court sat. It was further required that a jury assist in every criminal case and no conviction could be made without the concurrence of the jury. Ordinance 9 of 1856 extended the court's jurisdiction to cover crimes committed by Free State citizens in the neighbouring native territories.

The Court of Combined Landdrosts was not merely a court of first instance for cases exceeding the *landdrost* or *landdrost* and *heemraden's* jurisdiction. In terms of Ordinance 1 of 1856 it was also an appeal court hearing appeals against the decisions of a single *landdrost* or a *landdrost* and *heemraden*. This was, however, a strange type of appeal as the case could be heard *de novo* by the Court of Combined Landdrosts. Any party was entitled to present fresh evidence.

It must be understood that the *landdrosts* could by no stretch of the imagination be classed as jurists, and it was largely this that precipitated moves towards the establishment of an independent and professional supreme court.

The executive as court of appeal

The constitution made no provision in the court hierarchy for a court of appeal superior to the Court of Combined Landdrosts. To fill the gap the Volksraad resolved on 8 September 1854 that until such time as alternative arrangements could be made the executive under the chairmanship of the president would act as court of appeal from the decisions of the Court of Combined Landdrosts. None of the members of the executive was a jurist until J H Brand who had previously practised in the Cape as an advocate, took over the presidency. Brand's legal experience was, however, no more than coincidental and there was still no provision for the administration of justice in the highest court of the land to be in the hands of professional jurists.

There were, moreover, serious objections to the Executive Council's acting as court of appeal. Pressure of work forced the Executive Council to interrupt alternately its judicial and administrative duties; there was no effective system of reporting judgments which could then have served as guidelines for the other courts; and finally the unification of the highest executive and judicial powers in a single body definitely did nothing to promote respect for the highest legal body in the country – an unsuccessful appellant could easily claim that his case was lost on political bias. The necessity for the separation of executive and judicial authority – a prerequisite for any democratic system – began to emerge for the first time.

Initially an appellant wishing to appeal to the Executive Council was required to pay five pounds. When this provision was abolished in 1856 there was such a flood of appeals that it was necessary to reintroduce it in 1872. This provision did not apply in criminal cases but on 10 June 1874 the Volksraad provided that an accused wishing to appeal to the Executive Council was required to pay three pounds to the State. Other than was the case in appeals to the Court of Combined Landdrosts, no new evidence was permitted before the Executive Council.

The role of the Executive Council as a legal institution was never of great significance. Few cases went as far as the Executive Council, and where they did, the judgments of the Court of Combined Landdrosts were by and large upheld. The council sat as an appeal court for the last time on 29 August 1872. The movement towards an independent professional court had, however, started considerably earlier – viz in 1856. Before we briefly consider this lengthy developmental path, it is first necessary to touch upon the judicial role of the Volksraad.

Christoffel Cornelius Froneman, special magistrate for the Ladybrand district circa *1899–1900.*

The Volksraad as court of law

In addition to its obvious legislative function, the Volksraad also fulfilled a few judicial functions. The most important of these was the power conferred by section 17 of the Constitution to try the president and other public officers on charges of high treason, bribery, and other serious crimes. The Volksraad was empowered to dismiss the official concerned and to prohibit him from again holding public office. The courts, however, reserved the power to impose the normal criminal penalties. This power was exercised only once as

Johannes Henricus (Jan) Brand (1823–1888). In 1864 at the age of forty, Jan Brand became the fourth president of the Orange Free State. During his twenty-five-year term of office Brand succeeded, in the midst of the turmoil of the Basuto wars, uprisings among the Griqua and the discovery of diamonds, in transforming the Free State from a struggling community into a "model state". He died suddenly on 14 July on the eve of yet another term of office.

Josias Philip Hoffman (1807–1879), the first president of the Orange Free State. He held office for one year only but managed during this time to live in peace with the Basuto.

regards a president, viz in 1855 when President Hoffman was accused of high treason for giving a barrel of gunpowder to the Basuto Chief Moshesh. The result of the case was the resignation of President Hoffman. The Volksraad also sat as court of appeal against the decisions of the Executive Council in land commission cases. This function did not last long, however, as in 1861 (Ordinance 1 of 1861) the Volksraad was abolished as a court of appeal.

Progression towards an independent Supreme Court

One Hamelberg, a Hollander who had practised as an attorney in Bloemfontein since 1856, was the first person to suggest (in a letter to *The Friend* of 9 January 1858) that the highest court should be presided over by a competent jurist. The greatest problem was the salary of the new chief justice. The Volksraad was reluctant to offer a high salary, particularly because the Basuto wars were causing financial headaches. The merit of the creation of the new court was generally never doubted.

It was President Brand who finally got things moving. He assumed office as president in 1864. On 7 May 1866 he recommended to the Volksraad that a judge be appointed. The Volksraad expressed its approval by requesting Brand to draw up a draft ordinance for discussion at its next session. Brand proposed that a judge be appointed by the state president. This judge would replace the Court of Combined Landdrosts. No qualifications were specified for the new office and the

The so-called "Blue Black" (1865). An example of paper currency in use in the Orange Free State.

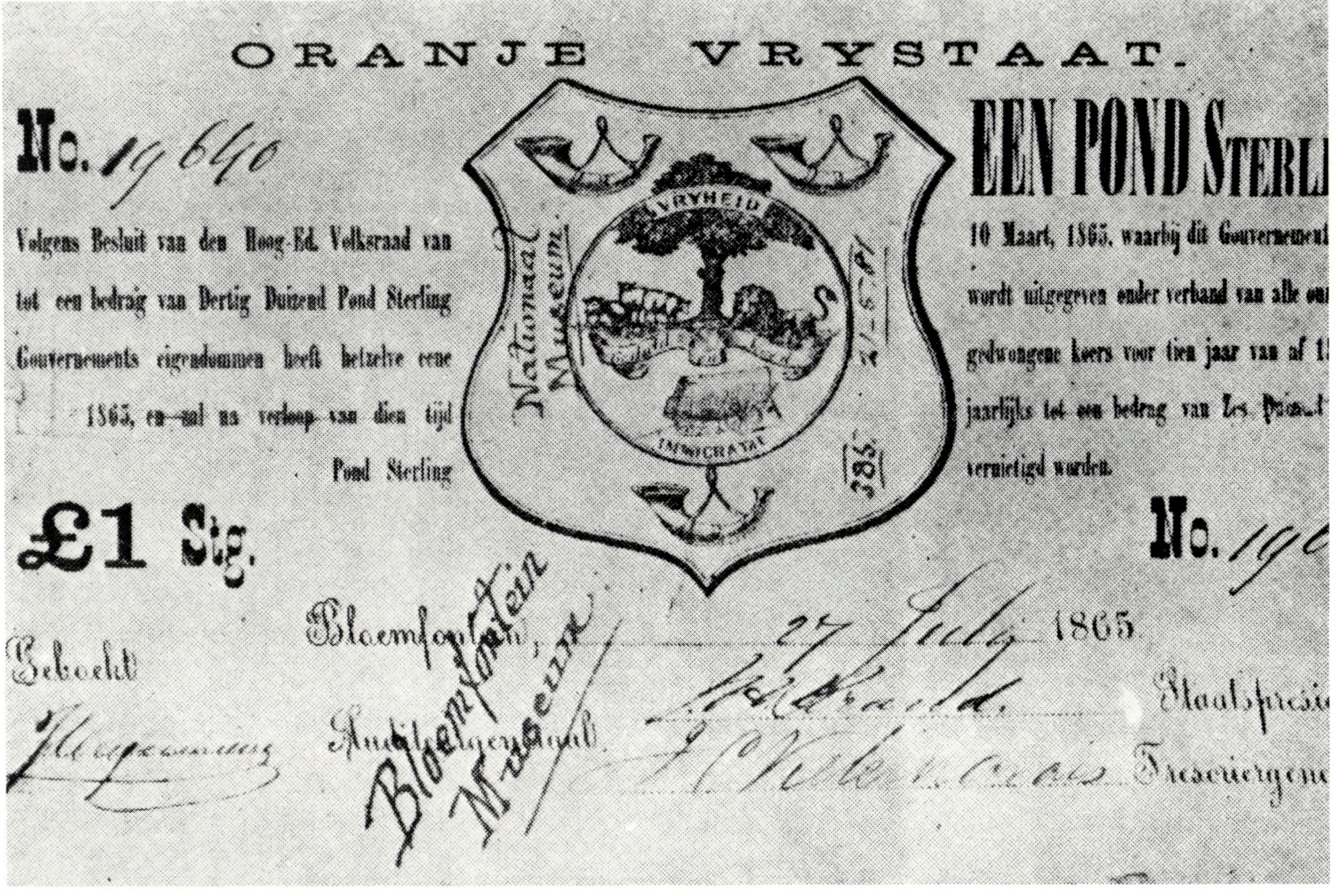

determination of salary was left to the Volksraad. The Executive Council would continue to function as court of appeal. As no qualifications were set (as opposed to Brand's 1862 proposal) it is doubtful whether these proposals would have brought about any real improvement. Brand himself later realized that his proposals lacked substance and during the course of the next few years formulated various new proposals.

On 3 April 1872 Brand proposed that an appeal court to hear all appeals from the Court of Combined Landdrosts be established. During October 1873 he succeeded in persuading the Volksraad to authorize him to appoint a practising advocate, F W Reitz (who was later to become state president), as judge. At the same meeting a commission of inquiry into the administration of justice under the chairmanship of Brand was established. All this was to lead to the establishment of the independent and professional Orange Free State Supreme Court in 1875.

With Reitz's appointment as judge, the Executive Council as court of appeal faded from the scene. Appeals from the Court of Combined Landdrosts would now serve before the highest court of appeal consisting of Reitz as chief justice and W W Collins and C W Hutton as assessors. Although the Free State now had an appeal court with a legal expert at the helm, all the courts of first instance remained in the hands of amateurs. Reitz's two assessors had no legal training either. This was, however, soon to change. The highest

Judge and assessors of the first Supreme Court, 1873. From left to right: F W Reitz, W W Collins and C W Hutton.

court of appeal sat for the first time on 17 August 1874 in a building which at that stage still served as the city hall.

In 1875 the Court of Combined Landdrosts was abolished by Ordinance 2 of 1875 and replaced by a single-judge circuit court which took over all the functions of the Court of Combined Landdrosts. It consequently heard cases falling outside the jurisdiction of the *landdrost* and *landdrost* and *heemraden* as well as appeals from these courts. Provision was also made for a Supreme Court consisting of a chief justice and one other judge. Appeals against the decisions of the circuit court could be lodged with the Supreme Court. If the parties consented, civil cases could be heard by the Supreme Court as court of first instance. The Supreme Court had its seat in Bloemfontein. The ordinance further provided that when the Supreme Court heard an appeal against the decision of the circuit court, the judge who had presided over the Circuit Court could not also serve on the Supreme Court. That this should be so, goes without saying. This of course meant that three judges were required to man the newly established courts. Reitz was appointed chief justice with James Buchanan and the renowned Melius de Villiers as judges. Melius de Villiers, brother to Sir Henry de Villiers (chief justice of the Cape) played a prominent role in later developments. One of his greatest distinctions was that he was the first South African to be appointed a professor of law at Leyden University.

The period 1876–1900

The twenty-four-year period from 1876–1900 was a time of peace and tranquility in which, in the juridical sphere too, nothing of particular note occurred. A few highlights may be mentioned:

- Justice Buchanan resigned in 1880 after a difference of opinion as regards pension benefits. Justice R Gregorowski filled his post. After the death of President Brand, Chief Justice Reitz became state president. This led to Melius de Villiers being appointed as the Free State's second chief justice of the Supreme Court in 1889. M T Steyn who was also later to become state president, filled De Villiers's place. The following persons also served as judges in the period before the British occupation of Bloemfontein in 1900: A J McGregor, J B M Hertzog, A E J Krause, L J Jacobsz and H Stuart.
- In 1890 there was a serious conflict between Chief Justice Melius de Villiers and the Volksraad. This dispute clearly shows the independence of the judiciary – an independence fiercely guarded throughout its existence. Melius de Villiers himself later had the following to say of the incident:

> "According to the Orange Free State Constitution which could be altered or amended only in a certain prescribed manner and not by ordinary legislation, ju-

dicial power was vested in the Courts of Law exclusively. A certain Hollander named De Vries had in the press grossly insulted the Volksraad and its members in their capacity as such and this gave occasion to an Ordinance being passed by the Volksraad for the protection of its privilege as defined therein. In terms of this Ordinance persons adjudged by the Volksraad to have transgressed the provisions of this Ordinance were rendered liable to fine or to imprisonment for a considerable period or to both fine and imprisonment. At the Circuit Court held at Boshof, in thanking the jury for the services they had rendered, I took the opportunity of addressing them on this subject, maintaining that the Ordinance was unconstitutional, and that in case a person who had actually been imprisoned by virtue of a sentence of the Volksraad applied to the court for his release, there would be no other course open for the court than to order his release. Somewhat unexpectedly these remarks led to much agitation throughout the state, in which extreme indignation was expressed at the course which the Volksraad had adopted. Very sensibly the obnoxious Ordinance was therefore repealed."

That the Supreme Court indeed had the power to test Volksraad legislation against the principles of the constitution, appears from the judgment in *Cassim and Solomon v The State* (delivered in November 1891). This case concerned the question whether a prohibition on entry into the country by Asians conflicted with section 58 of the constitution which provided that all were equal before the law. The court found that section 58 of the constitution had not been violated. This piece of legislation was later incorporated into chapter 33 of the Orange Free State Statute Book and today still forms part of the law of the Orange Free State.

In 1891 all existing ordinances were collected in a logical whole, viz the Statute Book of the Orange Free State. The Statute Book consisted of 146 chapters and was the fruit of the labours of a commission headed by Melius de Villiers.

The Supreme Court did not have a building of its own during this period. The court used the Volksraad's council chamber when the Volksraad was not in session. During Volksraad sessions the court had to move to the city hall. The council hall was at the top of Maitland Street. It was destroyed by fire in 1908 but was rebuilt on the same site and today houses the National Afrikaans Literary Museum. In 1893 a new council hall was built for the Volksraad and until the end of the South African War (1899–1902) the court occupied the old council hall. The new "Raadsaal" (council hall) is in President Brand Street directly opposite the appeal court and is now used for sessions of the provincial council.

When the British occupied Bloemfontein in 1900, Justices Hertzog and Stuart were away on commando with the burghers. Chief Justice Melius de Villiers had received orders to remain in Bloemfontein. With the arrival of Lord Roberts in Bloemfontein the doors of the court building were locked by the military authorities. For all practical purposes, the Supreme Court of the Orange Free State had ceased to function.

Francis William Reitz (1844–1934). After the death of Brand, Reitz assumed the presidency in 1889. Before accepting this office he served as chief justice of the Orange Free State. In contrast to his predecessor, he strove for greater co-operation with the Transvaal. Poor health forced Reitz to resign in 1895.

James Buchanan (1841–1893). After a successful career as an advocate at the Cape Bar, Buchanan entered politics in 1872. He was appointed state attorney of the Transvaal Republic in 1873 and was at the same time a member of the Transvaal Executive Council. He was appointed a judge of the Free State Supreme Court under Chief Justice Reitz in 1876, and in 1879 was appointed in Griqualand West. A brilliant student, Buchanan was one of the first judges to have received

all his training in South Africa. While practising at the Cape Bar he was the first editor of the South African Law Reports *(1868–1870) and co-editor of the* Cape Appeal Court Reports. *He also published the following works:* Precedents in Pleading *(1878),* Decisions in Insolvency *(1879), and a three-volume translation of Voet's* Commentarius ad Pandectas *(1880, 1881 and 1883).*

The period 1900–1910

Between 1900 and 1902 the Free State was ruled by military authorities and a high commissioner. In 1902 the territory (then known as the Orange River Colony) was granted a crown colony government. Responsible government followed in 1907.

The *landdrosts* were replaced by resident magistrates whose jurisdiction in both civil and criminal cases was fully defined in the Magistrates' Court Ordinance 7 of 1902. Ordinance 6 of 1902 conferred very limited criminal jurisdiction on resident justices of the peace.

The High Court of the Orange River Colony replaced the Supreme Court. The High Court initially consisted of two judges but as from 1904 it consisted of a chief justice (Sir Andries Maasdorp), and two judges (AW Fawkes and D Ward). The High Court exercised unlimited jurisdiction over the entire territory.

From 1904 one judge constituted a quorum in criminal cases, while in civil cases the number was two. Provision was also made for a circuit court consisting of a single judge with jurisdiction concurrent with that of the High Court in the district over which he presided. Both the circuit court and the High Court could hear appeals against magistrates' judgments. The highest court of appeal for criminal cases was the High Court (the Transvaal Supreme Court before 1904). In civil cases appeal from the circuit court lay to the High Court and then to the Privy Council in England.

As has already been seen, this period of colonial government saw the large-scale adoption of English and Cape legislation. Section 3 of Ordinance 3 of 1902, however, specifically provided that the Orange Free State Statute Book and all republican legislation adopted between 1892 and 1899 were to be retained in so far as they had not been repealed. The English translation of the republican legislation was to be binding, in preference to the original Dutch. Particularly during the sixties, the South African legislature started with the systematic repeal of pre-Union legislation. After the coming into force of the Pre-Union Statute Laws Revision Act 24 of 1979, only two chapters and part of a third chapter of the Statute Book, an 1894 Act and sections of a 1902 Ordinance, remained in force in the Orange Free State. The continued existence of Roman-Dutch law as the common law of the Free State was ensured during the British occupation by section 1 of Ordinance 3 of 1902.

In 1902 the new Raadsaal in President Brand Street was made available to the High Court. In 1907 the legislature again moved to the new Raadsaal. The court was again without a home. It was at this stage decided to erect a building for the court.

Marthinus Theunis Steyn (1857–1916). Steyn was admitted to the Inner Temple, London in 1880. After a successful career as advocate in Bloemfontein, he was appointed attorney-general in 1889 and in the same year as judge. In 1896 he took the oath as president of the Orange Free State. He strove for closer co-operation with the South African Republic while at the same time attempting to elicit a more conciliatory attitude from the Transvaal. Although he prepared his republic for war on all fronts, he also left no stone unturned in his efforts to avoid confrontation. His attempts failed and after the outbreak of war, he threw himself heart and soul into the war effort. Poor health prevented his presence at the signing of the Peace of Vereeniging in 1902. As a Free State representative to the National Convention in 1908 he stated his case for the recognition of Dutch as an official language in the following terms: "We ask this, gentlemen, not as a privilege but as our right." Had his health not been failing, he would in all probability have been the first prime minister of the Union of South Africa.

Reinhold Gregorowski (1856–1922). With an outstanding academic record and after a highly successful period at the Cape Bar Gregorowski was appointed a judge in the Orange Free State in 1881 at the age of twenty-five. His colleagues were (later) Chief Justice Melius de Villiers and Justice F W Reitz. He was appointed a judge of the South African Republic in 1896 and in 1898 became the Republic's state attorney. In 1899 he assumed office as chief justice of the South African Republic. He resumed his practice as an advocate after the South African War (1899–1902) and in 1912 was appointed judge of the Transvaal Provincial Division of the South African Supreme Court.

The new court building was first occupied on 6 December 1909 and is today still the seat of the Orange Free State Provincial Division of the Supreme Court of South Africa. This building too stands in President Brand Street, directly opposite the Bloemfontein municipal fire station.

On Union in 1910 the High Court became, in terms of section 98 of the South Africa Act, the Orange Free State Provincial Division of the Supreme Court of South Africa. Today the court's existence is derived from section 2 of and the first schedule to the Supreme Court Act 59 of 1959. In terms of the first schedule the court has its seat in Bloemfontein and exercises jurisdiction over the entire province of the Orange Free State. As the court's workload expanded, the number of judges increased accordingly. The Free State Provincial Division at present consists of a judge-president and eight judges.

A few highlights in the development of the attorney's profession in the Orange Free State[4]

The first step towards the organization of legal practitioners in the Free State was taken in

4 This summary is based almost exclusively on exhaustive research undertaken by the present secretary of the Law Society of the Orange Free State, Mr G P Greyvenstein. The results of his research were published in 1978 *De Rebus* 74.

The old "Raadsaal" in Bloemfontein.

1884–1885 when a number of advocates, attorneys and notaries founded the first "Association of Legal Practitioners". Among the signatories of the founding document were Abraham Fischer and M T Steyn, both of whom played a prominent role in public life. J G Fraser, the second president of the Law Society of the Orange River Colony, was also a signatory of the document. The first mentioned was the chairman and the last-mentioned the secretary and treasurer of the society after it had received statutory recognition in Ordinance 4 of 1885. This ordinance remained in force (as chapter XX of the Orange Free State Statute Book) until repealed by Ordinance 8 of 1903 of the Orange River Colony. The Law Society of the Orange River Colony was established by Ordinance 9 of 1903.

The law society differed from the republican society in two important respects. In the first place membership was compulsory. In the second, only attorneys and notaries were entitled to membership. In 1929 the society changed its name to "The Incorporated Law Society of the Orange Free State". An Afrikaans equivalent of the name made its first appearance, viz "Die Ingelyfde Wetsgenootskap van die Oranje-Vrystaat". Conveyancers were now also required to join the society. In 1942 the council of the society was given the power to lay down rules and regulations subject to approval by the members. Ordinance 9 of 1903 and its amendments were repealed as from 14 May 1975 when the Law Societies Act 41 of 1975 came into force. The clumsy term "Wetsgenootskap" was removed from the society's name. The

Abraham Fischer (1850–1913) first practised as an attorney and later as an advocate in Bloemfontein. He entered public life as member of the Volksraad for Philippolis in 1879. He acted as intermediary between the South African Republic and the British government before the South African War (1899–1902). After the outbreak of the war he acted in close co-operation with president M T Steyn. After Union he was appointed Minister of Lands and Irrigation, and in 1912 Minister of Internal Affairs.

Sir Andries Ferdinand Stockenström Maasdorp (1847–1931). He was chief justice of the Orange Free State from 1902 to 1910 and later held the same rank in the Orange Free State Provincial Division of the Supreme Court of South Africa (1910–1919). Maasdorp is particularly well known for his translation of Grotius's Inleidinge tot de Hollandsche Regtsgeleerdheid *and as the author of the* Institutes of Cape Law.

society is now known as "The Law Society of the Orange Free State" (in Afrikaans "Die Prokureursorde van die Oranje-Vrystaat"). Act 41 of 1975 was in turn repealed by the Attorneys Act 53 of 1979. This is in essence a consolidating Act and Chapter III (sections 56–77) is virtually a word-for-word re-enactment of Act 41 of 1975. Every attorney, notary or conveyancer practising in the Orange Free State is a member of the Law Society of the Orange Free State (section 57(1) of the Attorneys Act). In broad terms the society aims at maintaining and enhancing the dignity and standards of the profession, protecting the interests of the profession, and effectively controlling the professional conduct of practitioners (section 58 of the Attorneys Act). To realize these aims a variety of powers and capacities are conferred upon the society (see, e.g, sections 59, 69, 70, 71 and, in particular, 72 and 74 of the Attorneys Act).

Apart from Abraham Fischer, M T Steyn and J G Fraser, Charles John Hobern Reitz also played an important part in the history of the Free State law society. He served as secretary and treasurer of the Law Society of the Orange River Colony from 1908 to 1929, and from 1929 to 1944 held the same position in the Incorporated Law Scociety of the Orange Free State. In 1895 Mr Reitz became an articled clerk under Abraham Fischer and in 1899 was Fischer's private secretary in the latter's attempts to avert war with Britain. Reitz was admitted as an attorney in 1904. He was, *inter alia,* director of The Friend Newspapers Ltd for some fifty-one years, and served for fifty years as director of the Old Mutual's regional board.

Francois Petrus (Toon) van den Heever (1894–1956). He was appointed judge of the Orange Free State Supreme Court in 1938 and in 1948 became judge-president of that court. Later that year he was appointed judge of appeal. His original approach and his fearless departure from established legal tenets where he considered it necessary, have ensured him a place as one of South Africa's most renowned judges. His daughter, Miss Leonora van den Heever, is at present a judge of the Cape Provincial Division of the Supreme Court of South Africa. She is the only female judge in South Africa.

The Law Society of the Orange River Colony also played a decisive role in the establishment of what is today known as the Association of Law Societies, an umbrella body which combines and co-ordinates the powers of the law societies in the various provinces. In 1907 the society addressed a proposal to the societies in the other three provinces. The purport of this proposal was that a conference of delegates be held to discuss matters of mutual interest. The conference was held in Bloemfontein in July 1908 after it had been agreed in October 1907 that such conferences should be held regularly. The end result was the formation of the Association of Law Societies of the Republic of South Africa. Statutory justification for the existence of an umbrella body of this sort is currently to be found in sections 58(1) and 59(k) of the Attorneys Act.

The post of secretary was originally part-time. However, as activities were extended, the services of a full-time secretary became essential. The first person to undertake the secretarial duties on a full-time basis was J F Grimbeek. On 1 September 1973 he was succeeded by Mr G P Greyvenstein who still holds the office.

The council of the Orange Free State Law Society at present consists of nine members. The current president of the council is Mr J F A S van der Watt.

S N Roberts BA (Cantab) LLB (Natal) Attorney Pietermaritzburg

6

NATAL 1830–1909

For much more than two-thirds of the time that Natal has been known to Western Europe, Natal has had no recorded legal heritage at all. The Portuguese, the Dutch, the French and the English, however hot in the pursuit of the fabled riches of the East, kept clear of the inhospitable coastline until the first quarter of the nineteenth century.

There was no European settlement before then, and the indigenous tribes had no written language, so perhaps it was a time when the laws of nature were abroad in the land and the romantics of Europe were content.

In 1838 the Voortrekkers arrived in Natal, and established the "Republic of Natalia" commemorated now in the name of the building which houses the Natal Provincial Administration in Pietermaritzburg. The Voortrekkers for the most part were rough frontiersmen who paid little attention to the niceties of constitutional law when they began their Great Trek. The constitution, such as it was, was based upon the laws passed at Thaba 'Nchu and Vet River in 1836 and 1837, as amplified by Jacobus Boshof.[1] The law which the Voortrekkers brought with them was a mixture of the Roman-Dutch law and Cape legislation. As the Volksraad (House of Assembly) never got round to electing a president before the long arm of Queen Victoria, acting through her governor at the Cape, caught up with them, this supreme body paid but lip service to the distinction between executive, legislature and judiciary. The Volksraad itself was the ultimate court of appeal. The court of the first instance was the *landdrost* (magistrate's) court. The *landdrost* had jurisdiction to try petty criminal and civil matters. More serious cases required the assistance of six local *heemraden;* but their decision was subject to an appeal to a full court of *landdrost*, *heemraden* and twelve jurymen, whose decision was by a two-thirds majority. Where sentence was death or banishment, the decision had to be unanimous and it was subject to review by the Volksraad.

So it was that a cutting of the sturdy Roman-Dutch law came to be planted in Natal. For a time it seemed uncertain whether or not the cutting would strike:

> "A certain vagueness – a blurring of the edges – is associated with the Republic of Natalia. Its beginning may well be dated before 1840. Its end may be fixed as early as the 10th May 1843."[2]

Between 1843 and the end of 1845 there was an interregnum with the Volksraad coasting on. In 1843 the governor of the Cape who had been fulminating in Cape Town about annexing Natal sent Commissioner Cloete to sort out land claims in particular and the position in general. And, eventually on 31 May 1844 Queen Victoria in London annexed Natal. Some fifteen months passed before, on 21 August 1845, the governor of the Cape formally proclaimed that she had done so. His support for the Roman-Dutch system of law was somewhat faster. By Ordinance 12 of 1845 dated 27 August 1845 it was provided:

> "The system, code, or body of laws commonly called the Roman-Dutch Law as the name has been and is accepted and administered by the legal tribunals of the Colony of the Cape of Good Hope, shall be and it is hereby established as the law of the district of Natal."[3]

The Natal of that time was defined as the land lying between the Indian Ocean, the Tugela River to the north east, the "Draaksberg" or "Kahlamba Mountains" to the west and the Umzimkulu River to the south. It was only in 1884 that the area around St Lucia Bay was annexed in order to frustrate the Germans. Zululand followed in 1887; and the erstwhile Republics of Utrecht (1854–1860) and the New Republic based on Vryheid (1886–1888) in 1903. The last of Natal's territorial ambitions was realized in 1878 when East Griqualand was excised from the Cape and incorporated in Natal.

The first judge appointed formally to administer the Roman-Dutch law in Natal was Mr Henry Cloete, the former commissioner of Natal and

1 Walker *The Great Trek* 208.

2 Brookes and Webb *A History of Natal* 35–36.

3 Bird *Annals of Natal* vol 2 470.

During the Zulu war, a British regiment under the command of Lord Chelmsford pitched camp at Isandhlwana. On 22 January 1879 they were attacked by a force of 24 000 Zulu warriors and within an hour 800 British soldiers had fallen together with 471 Blacks who had been fighting with them. There were no wounded and only a few soldiers managed to escape. This is an artist's impression of what the battlefield looked like the next day.

(according to Sir Peregrine Maitland, the governor of the Cape) "the only advocate of the colonial bar to whom I could offer the appointment". The post carried with it a salary of £600 per annum with £100 for a house.[4]

With pomp and ceremony the lieutenant governor-designate Martin West Esquire, on his arrival in Natal, immediately swore in Mr Cloete as recorder, and the latter returned the compliment by swearing in West as lieutenant governor. The Whites, however, were but a few of the pebbles on the beach. One of the principal reasons for the annexation of Natal had been to try to preserve some sort of stability in the midst of the indigenous population recovering from the ravages of Chaka. As Lugg points out in the introduction to Stafford *Native Law* (1935) Chaka had not only been a ruthless military commander, but like Napoleon, had been something of a law giver himself and had gone a long way towards unifying tribal custom. Accordingly, within as little as three years from the date of the application of the Roman-Dutch system of law in Natal, regardless of civilization, creed or colour, it had become painfully obvious that that system was hardly appropriate for the 100 000 or so Zulus already then in Natal, and increasing rapidly. Theophilus Shepstone, later to become famous (or infamous) in various fields, had had experience of the Nguni people in the Eastern Cape. He had been anxious to secure the post as British agent "to deal with the large native population" and it was he whom the governor sent to accompany the new lieutenant governor.

Cloete as the expositor of the Roman-Dutch law and Shepstone as protector of native custom were soon at loggerheads. Shepstone succeeded in having an ordinance passed in 1849 whereby the Roman-Dutch law was no longer applicable to the African population and tribal custom was recognized in so far as it was "not repugnant to the general principles of humanity observed throughout the civilized world".[5]

The absence of a colour bar turned out to be illusory. Laws 11 of 1864 and 11 of 1865 made the attainment of the franchise by an appreciable number of Africans impossible. Exempted Africans were entitled to the vote. However, they had to apply for the vote by supporting their applications with proof of twelve years' residence in Natal and the holding of letters of exemption for seven years. In the result the inter-colonial commission of 1903/5 investigating the franchise found that after 39 years only three applicants in Natal and Zululand had ever had the vote.[6] The figure rose to five and then fell back, so at the time Act 18 of 1936 came to be enacted, only one African held the vote. Whilst political rights died of exposure in a

4 Op cit 471.

5 Brookes and Webb 55.

6 Op cit 77.

Lord Chelmsford used a Swedish mission station at Rorke's Drift as a hospital and left a small garrison of 110 men there for protection. After their success at Isandhlwana the Zulus marched to the mission station, but the garrison had been warned by two survivors from Isandhlwana. The small group of men fought very bravely and withstood the attack until daybreak. Eleven Victoria Crosses were later awarded for bravery in this battle. Here is a photograph of what the mission station looked like after the battle.

desert of technicality, tribal custom was preserved and as the result of the efforts of experts was codified first in 1878[7] and then again in 1891.[8] As recently as 1967 the code was re-enacted.[9] In *Mcunu v Mcunu* 1918 AD at 328 Innes, CJ held that:

> "The provisions of the code are not all definite and peremptory . . . But where they embody the rules of law in distinct terms, then those rules must be operative in all cases not expressly or impliedly excluded."

With the increased westernization of the Blacks and their involvement in commercial transactions and land holding it seems unlikely that this source of law will prevail indefinitely.

For the sake of completeness, it is necessary to refer to the arrival in Natal on 17 November 1860 of the first progenitors of the present Indian community. Within a short time 6 000 Indians had been imported into Natal. It is not generally recognized that as early as 1885, the Indian population of Natal nearly equalled the Whites and in the census figures of 1904, 1911, 1921 and 1951 Indians exceeded Europeans.[10] Despite this numerical factor and the special legislative recognition accorded Indians from time to time, their customs have had virtually no influence on the Roman-Dutch law.

7 Natal Native Code GN 194/1878.
8 Law 19/1891 (Natal).
9 Proc R195/1967 GG 1840 dated 1967–09–08.
10 Brookes and Webb 85.

Natal from 1840 to 1902

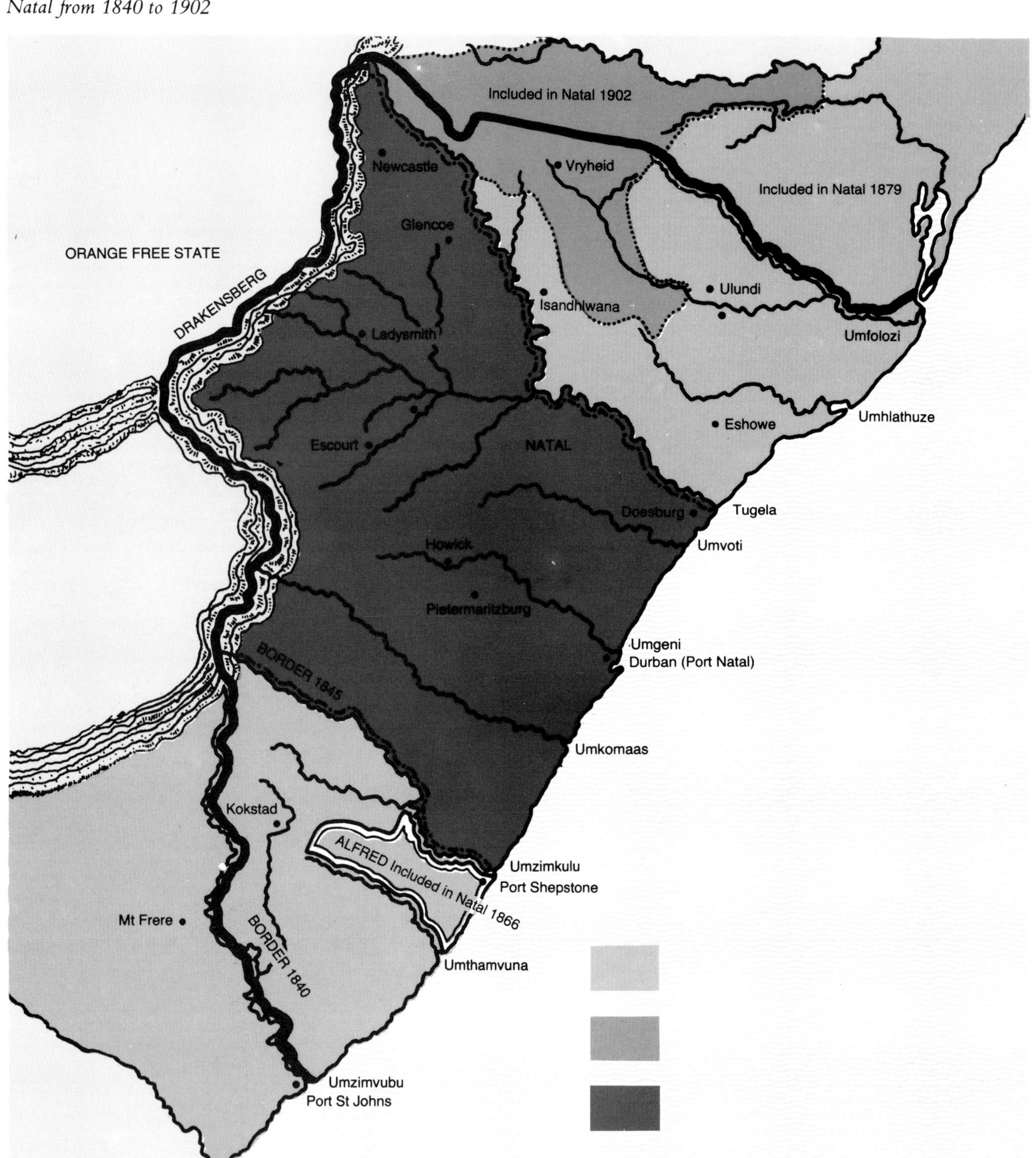

The paramountcy of the Roman-Dutch law was restated in the Supreme Court Act of 1896.[11] But it was not free of outside (some have thought corrupting) influences.

> "Natal, in sentiment and composition the most English of the provinces up to this day, imported many English rules of law, both indirectly through the Cape and directly from England. And in the main, with the notable exception of Connor, Natal judges were more prone than their brethren elsewhere in South Africa to look to the English law for guidance in deciding questions of Natal common law."[12]

Historically, the principal courts in which the Roman-Dutch law has been administered over the years have been the Supreme Court and the magistrate's court. The forerunner to the present provincial division of the Supreme Court of South Africa was the District Court of Natal established by the Cape Ordinance 14 of 1845. The recorder, Henry Cloete, presided over it as a single judge until the Supreme Court of Natal was established by Law 10 of 1857. The new court consisted of a chief justice and two puisne judges who were to be barristers or advocates of the United Kingdom or the Cape. There was a provision for circuit courts and appeals from a non-jury civil judgment were to the Supreme Court with an ultimate right of appeal to the Privy Council. During the next forty years the influence of the English jury system was greatly restricted because of the particular circumstances prevailing in Natal. The seat of the court itself was Pietermaritzburg and initially the court sat in an old building which had previously housed the Volksraad, where the city hall now stands. As the *Natal Witness* of 3 March 1871 put it:

> "The old edifice is an illustration of architectural taste and skill, such as would probably not have been allowed to adorn the metropolis of any other civilised state in the universe. The old barn was built by the Boers who founded the settlement. It is an oblong space with six small windows, with ten small panes of glass each, with a thatched roof and a gable end facing the street. In primitive times the said Volksraad met and made its white washed walls echo to the thunders of Boer eloquence."

11 Act 39/1896 s 21.

12 Hahlo and Kahn *The Union of South Africa: The Development of its Laws and Constitution* 24.

Chaka 1788–1828. His nickname was Nodumenhlezi, which means: the one who makes the earth tremble when he sits down. He built up a mighty army and waged war on a large scale against the other native tribes. The watchword of his warriors was "Victory or death" and they inspired fear as far north as central Africa. In spite of his warlike tendencies, he lived in relative peace with the Whites.

The present Supreme Court building was designed in 1865 by the colonial engineer Mr Peter Patterson. The foundation stone was laid with Gilbertian pomp on 2 November 1865 but then a depression struck Natal. A full bench comprising Chief Justice Harding, Judge Connor and Judge Phillips ("who was indisposed") sat there for the first time on 1 March 1871; but the building was completed finally only in 1875. In 1980, a new Supreme Court building was being completed some 300 metres away in Church Street and there is considerable speculation as to what is to become of the

Queen Victoria

old Supreme Court building. It is very much a part of the Victorian red-brick core of Pietermaritzburg.

The larger city Durban was less well served. A circuit court sitting in Durban from time to time was regarded as sufficient. By 1908, however, there was considerable discontent in Durban and deputations from the Natal Law Society called urgently on the judge president in Pietermaritzburg and his colleague Judge William Broome in Durban.

Shortly after 1910 an imposing building in the Edwardian style was erected on the Esplanade to house the Durban and Coast Local Division, which it still does. It occupies the site of the old Natal Hospital which later became the Durban High School and then the Boys' Model School.

The reputations of many of the early Natal judges have withered under the glare of latter-day sophisticated scholarship. Professors Hahlo and Kahn write that with the exception of Chief Justice Connor,

> "greatest of early Natal judges, as a body they could hardly cope with problems of Roman-Dutch law. Later appointments were almost exclusively from the generally ill or untrained local dual practitioners or civil servants. For example Beaumont J was an ex-soldier turned magistrate, with no legal qualifications whatsoever".[13]

Judge Cloete was memorable for his belligerence. The *Natal Witness* spoke of him sitting "supreme, to deal out his uncontrolled conceptions of justice: with all the danger that attaches to human fallibility".

Sir Henry Connor (1817–1890) qualified at Trinity College, Dublin. Whilst a judge in the Gold Coast he met Sir Benjamin Pine, the former governor of Natal and this probably led to his appointment as a puisne judge of Natal in 1854. About ten years later he was seconded for eighteen months to the new Eastern Districts Court in Grahamstown. In 1867 he sat on the Cape bench for a short time but most of his long South African judicial career of thirty-six years was spent in Natal. In 1874 his old friend Sir Benjamin Pine appointed him chief justice and in 1880 he was knighted. Sir Henry Connor remained a bachelor and lived quietly in the centre of Pietermaritzburg cared for by his Zulu servant. The *South African Law Journal* said of him that:

> "His private benevolence . . . was as generous as it was unostentatious. His gifts were nearly always anonymous. When it was found necessary, during a period of deep depression in Natal, in order to equalize expenditure and revenue, to reduce the salaries of the civil service, Sir Henry offered out of his own pocket to make good the reduction to everyone connected with the supreme court. The offer was declined but the fact will go some way towards explaining Sir Henry's great popularity in Natal."[14]

13 Hahlo and Kahn 222.
14 1919 *SALJ* 224.

Theophilus Shepstone 1817–1893. As the diplomatic representative of the Black people in Natal he went to great lengths to improve their living conditions and to protect their interests. They had a great respect for him and called him Somtseu – Mighty Hunter or White Father. When he was appointed as special commissioner for the British government in 1876 he resigned his post as Secretary of Native Affairs. In his first mentioned capacity he was responsible for the annexation of the Republic of the Transvaal. He retired in 1881.

Another Natal judge to achieve fame was Arthur Wier Mason who was born in Pondoland in 1860. He received his schooling in England, returned to South Africa at the age of twenty and was admitted as an advocate at twenty-one. It was he who appeared before Sir Henry Connor and applied for judgment for rent "to the day of judgment". Sir Henry responded that he was not sure that the court's jurisdiction extended to that period.[15] In 1900 he was a member, with Sir William Smith and Judge Broome, of the special court for the trial of rebels. A year later he was president of that court, and in 1902 was appointed to the Transvaal bench. The *South African Law Journal* said of him:

> "With the exception of the Natal bench, Mr Mason was the only instance that we can remember of a judge being appointed to any of the other colonies or provinces of South Africa whose professional training has been at a bar where the fusion of the two branches was in force."

Thomas Fortesque Carter, erstwhile editor of *The Times of Natal* qualified for admission by sitting throughout the year in court two-thirds of the days of every term, and for two-thirds of the hours of every day's sitting.[16] Carter had other claims to fame. He had been captured at Majuba. He owned one of the first cars in Pietermaritzburg, a Buick, NP1. As attorney-general immediately prior to Union he elevated himself to the bench and took with him the surprised Kenneth Hathorn as another puisne judge. He even had himself locked in solitary confinement for a day or two to find out what it was like. Indeed, he was strong on fact.

But the appointment in 1904 of "Mr J C Dove-Wilson an eminent Scotch (sic) KC"[17] was to be the turning point in the quality of the Natal bench which had gone steadily from strength to strength. He was judge president from 1910 to 1930 and for him "the pastimes of shooting, fishing, golf and the other healthy amenities of an open air life were the antidote to the rigours of the bench".

The lower courts were principally those of the resident magistrate, first created in 1846. An appeal from those courts lay to the recorder. During the second half of the century borough courts were created and the magistrates' civil jurisdiction was expanded so that by the end of the century, the magistrates' courts in Natal were the equivalent of those courts in the Transvaal, and well in advance of their counterparts in the Cape and the Orange Free State.[18] It was not surprising to find the appointment of eminent silks to occupy the office of chief magistrate of Durban or Pietermaritzburg.

15 1916 *SALJ* 1.
16 1925 *SALJ* 247.
17 1905 *Natal Law Quarterly Review* 4.

18 Hahlo and Kahn 223.

Indians selling vegetables in Durban towards the end of the last century.

The 1905 *Natal Law Quarterly Magazine* for example expressed the pleasure of the legal profession in Durban upon the appointment of Mr P Binns KC as chief magistrate of the town. In 1899 William Broome, the founder of a judicial dynasty, had been resident magistrate in Durban.

A consequence of Shepstone's native policy of the control of (as distinguished from the civilization of) the African population was that ultimate judicial as well as administrative power rested with the Crown. This judicial aspect of Shepstone's policy lasted some 25 years before the Native Administration Act of 1875 established the Native High Court with civil and criminal jurisdiction. In civil matters that court was a court of the first instance, or of appeal, depending on the matter. In 1896 it lost its criminal jurisdiction. But in 1898 this was restored on a wider basis; and a bench consisting of a judge president and two puisne judges was given increased jurisdiction. An appeal lay to the Privy Council.

This court came to be housed in a handsome building – now known as "The Old Bailey" – in College Road, Pietermaritzburg, in spite of the protest of the Natal Law Society that the site was inconvenient and that a portion of the show grounds would be more appropriate. The Native Administration Act of 1927 removed this civil

Judge Henry Cloete (1792–1870). He was educated at the first English school to be opened in Cape Town. He then studied in Holland at, among others, the University of Leyden where he obtained a doctorate under Dionysius van der Keessel. Thereafter he entered Lincoln's Inn where he completed the usual studies and was admitted to the Bar. After he had practised at the Cape Bar for a number of years and also acted as a special commissioner in Natal in a matter between the Boers and the British government, he was appointed as a judge in Natal in 1845. In 1855 he was appointed as a judge in the Cape. He remained in this post until his retirement in 1866.

jurisdiction; and Act 13 of 1954 finally abolished the court, two of the judges, Judge President Brokensha and Judge Kennedy being appointed to the Supreme Court bench.

As to the practitioners who practised before these courts, it is difficult now to reconstruct the early days of the Natal Law Society. The society appears to have been founded on 16 February 1871 when eleven worthy lawyers met in the offices of the attorney-general where they were bent upon forming a law association for attorneys and advocates in the colony.[19]

On 3 March 1871 the *Natal Witness* reported:

> "After the opening of the new court on Wednesday last, 13 members of the Society responded to the invitation of the Vice-President Mr Advocate Cope to repair to his chambers where they partook of a champagne luncheon."

And on 21 March 1871 the *Natal Witness* could say that on 17 March the Natal Law Society had finally approved and adopted the constitution of the society. It was a purely voluntary association which was later registered under the Literary and Other Societies Act of Natal 35 of 1874. The attorney-general M H Gallway (later chief justice of Natal) was the first president.

In 1907, after a lengthy debate in the legislative assembly, which makes splendid reading, the Natal Law Society was incorporated in terms of Law 10 of 1907 (Natal). The member for Ixopo, a farming area, was violently opposed to the bill:

> "This is trades unionism with a vengeance. You should not compel a man to join a union. I shall not agree to a man being compelled to become a member of the Law Society or any other society . . . I don't think it is in the interests of the public that these people should be compelled to join the Society. I suppose next year we shall have the charges about treble what they have been before . . . And on the issue of considering, originating and promoting reforms and im provements in the law and 'to consider proposed alterations and oppose or support the same' . . . What is meant by opposing the same? Are they going to put dynamite under this house or not."

The Minister of Justice and Public Works replied (somewhat quaintly): "I understand this has reference to agricultural reform."

Despite this equivocal start, the Incorporated Law Society of Natal regulated the affairs first of both the advocates and the attorneys, until the Society of Advocates came into being and Judge President Feetham's separation of the Bar and the attorneys' profession became effective in the 1930's. It became the Natal Law Society in terms of Act 41 of 1975 and remains so in terms of Act 53 of 1979 and now (1981) has 855 members.

It seems that the records of the Natal Law Society prior to 1907 no longer exist; and there is

19 *The Natal Witness* 21 February 1871.

Arthur Wier Mason. He was admitted to the Bar in Durban at the age of twenty-one. He later went to Pietermaritzburg where he joined the firm Hathorn and Mason. The later Judge Hathorn was the head of the firm and guided Mason in many respects. At that time no differentiation was made between the two branches of the legal profession and Judge Mason was the only person to be appointed as judge in a province other than Natal despite the fact that he had received his legal training under the abovementioned system. In 1896 he was appointed as a judge in Natal, where he acted as chief justice for short periods and in 1902 he was appointed judge in the Transvaal.

Sir Michael Henry Gallway. He was appointed as attorney-general in Natal in 1857 and in this capacity he was also the administrative head of the Department of Justice. After the death of Sir Henry Connor in 1890 Sir Henry Gallway became chief justice of Natal and remained such until his retirement in 1901.

very little in the Natal archives which assists in trying to reconstruct what happened in the early days. In 1875 the society was worrying about disabilities which prevented the admission of colonial attorneys to English courts and from 1880 onwards there were anxious appeals to the government for financial assistance in publishing the *Natal Law Reports*. In 1887 the secretary was soliciting a robing room next to the judges' library in the Supreme Court. In 1902 the secretary, Mr W S Bigby, wrote indignantly to the Colonial Secretary expressing the society's pain at the remarks of the lieutenant-governor upon the occasion of a State visit to Howick. The *Natal Witness* of 13 February 1902 reported the governor as saying that:

> "He had had much experience in dealing with the natives of other races in other lands, and he had no doubt that this teaching would be equally applicable to the natives of these colonies. He wished them to bring all their distress and troubles through their chiefs to the Secretary of Native Affairs and the Governor, because he noted a tendency for the natives of this colony to mix themselves up too much with the lawyers. His advice to the natives is the same he would give to Europeans and Colonists, and was to keep as clear of the law as is possible. They would then be far happier and certainly their pockets would be far heavier . . . He hoped that any member of the legal profession present would forgive his remarks, and he felt sure that in their heart of hearts they knew he was right."

But they did not; and on the minute there is his comment in red ink:

> "For the time there is no necessity for me to assist the Society in the manner indicated and that I do not agree that my remarks at Howick cast any reflection on the whole legal profession."

Frederick Spence Tatham (1865–1934). He was educated at Bishop's College in Pietermaritzburg and showed an interest in military matters at the early age of fifteen by serving in the Basuto War of 1880–1881. He retained this interest throughout his life and held several military posts. In 1886 he was admitted to the Bar and was appointed as KC in 1903. He was president of the Natal Law Society for nine years and performed many public offices until his appointment as judge.

Mohandas Karamchand Ghandhi (Mahatma) 1869–1948). Ghandhi arrived in Natal in 1892 and during the 21 years of his stay in South Africa he continually campaigned for the rights of the Indian community. It was here that he laid the foundations for his philosophy of passive resistance for which he later became world famous and which also played an important role in India's struggle for freedom against Britain. He was a successful attorney in Johannesburg and used most of his money for the protection and promotion of the rights of the Indian community. In 1914 he felt that he had completed his task here and returned to India where, after attaining great fame, he was murdered by a fanatical Hindu in 1948.

One of the things which must strike an interested observer immediately is a pattern of legal dynasties that spread over the province: "Like father, like son." A perusal, for example, of the rolls of advocates and attorneys of the Supreme Court as they were at the last day of the nineteenth century, will reveal many names that are still familiar today. Three generations of Hathorns and Broome's have sat on the Natal bench. The famous F S Tatham KC was the first of three generations of Tathams to be president of the Incorporated Law Society of Natal. He later became a judge and his wife founded the Tatham Art Gallery in Pietermaritzburg. Shepstone, Titren, Dumat, Chadwick, Burne, Millar, Fannin, Bigby, Cameron, Greene, Randles, Tomlinson, Lister, Fraser, Brokensha, Smith and McGillewie are all names to be found in the *Hortors' Diary of 1981* just as they were to be found on the rolls of the Supreme Court eighty years ago.

It is generally acknowledged that in the early days of this century F S Tatham had no equal as a pleader of cases in court, not only for clients of his firm, but in cases conducted on behalf of other firms who were anxious to avail themselves of his enormous forensic skill.

Many years later a retired judge president was to write of him:

> "Tatham's departure left the field open for Graham MacKeurtan a very different type of man – a profound lawyer intellectually far and away Tatham's superior but as a forensic tactician MacKeurtan could teach Tatham nothing."[20]

20 Broome *Not the Whole Truth* 117.

Sir Henry Bale (1854–1910). He was admitted as an advocate in 1878 and was a member of the Natal colonial government from 1897 to 1901, first as attorney-general and later as Minister of Education. In 1901 he became Natal's first Natal-born chief justice, an office held until his death in 1910.

Can it be said that by reason of Natal's legal heritage, the administration of justice in Natal at the time of Union stood on a different footing from that elsewhere in the Republic? Whatever the position may be now, and it seems clear enough that the English taint introduced into the substantive law has been laundered out by powerful Roman-Dutch detergents, the Natal bench then did not enjoy the reputation which the Natal bench enjoys now. The then manner of selecting judges from amongst the civil service in the early days, or flowing from the divided Bar, resulted (with a few exceptions) in a comparative lack of erudition. However, those early members of the Natal bench brought into Natal's legal heritage a homely common sense and a courtesy which together provided the substantial foundations for the solid edifice of the Roman-Dutch law that has been erected since 1910.

Johan Scott BA (Hons) LLB (Pret) LLD (Leyden) Professor in Roman-Dutch Law and Private International Law University of Pretoria

7

THE ADMINISTRATION OF JUSTICE IN THE TRANSVAAL 1836–1910

Roman-Dutch law was carried into the interior of southern Africa by the Voortrekkers who began leaving the Cape Colony in large numbers from the end of 1835 to set up republics of their own outside the reaches of the British Empire. Through the Act for the Prevention and Punishment of Offences commited by his Majesty's Subjects within certain Territories adjacent to the Colony of the Cape of Good Hope (6 & 7 William IV c 57) of 13 August 1836 (usually abbreviated as the Cape of Good Hope Punishment Act) the British government attempted to enforce the criminal law of the Cape Colony in the interior as far as the 25th degree of latitude, hoping thereby to hinder the establishment of independent Voortrekker states and state institutions. However, as early as 2 December 1836 the Trekkers had, under Andries Hendrik Potgieter and Gerrit Maritz, already attempted to establish a representative government at Thaba 'Nchu. Seven *rechters* (judges) were elected to serve on the Burgerraad (citizen's council), the aim of which was to serve not only as legislative and executive body of a Voortrekker state, but also to administer justice as a *landdrost* (magistrate) and *heemraden* court.

This first attempt at the organization of state functions was extremely unsophisticated and it is hardly surprising that the principle of the separation of powers found no application. The so-called Vet River Constitution (Negen Resoluties) of 6 June 1837 wrought no appreciable changes.

Maritz, who was elected as first President-Rechter (judge president), was the only councillor with some legal training in that he had as "agent" been involved in litigation in the Cape Colony. As regards legal sources, the Council was forced to rely on its chairman's scanty law library consisting of: a work by Hugo de Groot – probably his *Inleidinge tot de Hollandsche Rechts-Geleerdheid*; the *Hollandsche Consultatien*; Benedictus Carpzovius's *Practica nova imperialis Saxonica rerum criminalium* translated into Dutch by D van Hogendorp under the title *Verhandeling der Lyfstraffelijke Misdaaden en haare Berechtinge*; Arent Lybreghts's *Redenerende Vertoog over 't Notaris Ampt*; a work by Gerard van Wassenaar which could have been either *Practijk Judicieel* or *Practijk Notarieel*, or alternately a combination of both under the title *Praxis Iudiciaria*; a collection of instructions dating from the Batavian period, and the renowned *Regsgeleerd, Practicaal en Koopmans-Handboek* by Johannes van der Linden. However meagre this collection may appear, it formed the foundation for the development of a legal system based on Roman-Dutch law. Under Maritz's guidance the Council heard cases. Marriage officers were appointed at an early stage and provision was made for the administration of deceased estates.

From October 1837, most of the Voortrekkers headed for Natal. During October 1838 the "Second Voortrekker Constitution" was issued and for the first time a distinction was drawn between legislative and judicial power. From this date litigation would be before *landdrosts* (magistrates), with or without the assistance of *heemraden*. English influence may be discerned from the provision allowing for a jury. Where no relevant legislation existed, justice would be dispensed in accordance with "de Hollandsche regtspleging, zoo civiel als crimineel" (Dutch jurisprudence both civil and criminal). The evolution of a legal administration is furthermore evidenced by the appointment of "gecommitteerdes" as the persons responsible for conveyancing, and the later provision that all transfers of immovable property were to be performed before the magistrate at Pietermaritzburg. The office of Master was also established and the method of administration of estates was adapted to meet the requirements as set in the Cape Colony.

In 1841, after in-fighting, Potgieter crossed the Vaal River and with his party established a council of his own at Potchefstroom. This Adjunkraad (Deputy Council), as it was known, was subject to the Natal council. The British annexation of Natal caused a rift with the community further inland and on 9 April 1844, Potchefstroom-Winburg formally declared its independence and the Burgerraad (Citizens' Council) issued the well-known Thirty-three Articles at Potchefstroom. Although it is doubtful whether this code can be regarded as a constitution in the true sense of the word, it played an important part in Transvaal legal administration in that it was both a manifestation of the Voortrekker vision of law and justice and a tangible expression of the law. It was a conglomeration of criminal provisions, penalties for contempt of court, administrative provisions relating to elections, provisions with regard to relations between the Trekkers and the indigenous peoples, procedural provisions, etc. Of particular importance is article 31 which provides that in all cases where the articles are silent, the "Hollandsche wet" (Dutch law) must be applied "doch op een gematigde stijlvorm en ooreenkomstig van het costuum van Zuid Afrika en tot nut en welvaart van de maatschappij" (but in a modified form and in accordance with the law of South Africa and to the benefit and well-being of the community). This proviso was clearly inserted to limit the excessive and at times savage penalties prescribed in certain of the Roman-Dutch sources.

No specific mention of the establishment of courts of law is to be found in the Thirty-three Articles. The existence of a Burgerraad (Citizens' Council) and of the office of *landdrost* is, however, taken for granted. From this one may conclude that by this stage a reasonably organized legal administration existed. In 1849 the Volksraad adopted instructions and regulations for *landdrosts* embodying a clear definition of their duties.

On account of the absence of organized State authority, it was difficult to determine the area of application of this legislation with any degree of certainty. This problem was complicated when Potgieter broke away in 1845 and established Andries Ohrigstad in the north east as the intended new Voortrekker seat of government. The Potchefstroom council was indeed dissolved on 30 July 1845. This confusion was resolved at an important meeting of all the Trekkers, held at Derdepoort near Pretoria on 23 May 1849 to form a "Verenigde Bond van het gehele maatschappij aan dese zijde van Vaalrivier" (a united association of the entire community on this side of the Vaal River). A Volksraad was sworn in and the Thirty-three Articles re-enacted.

Although Britain recognized the independence of the Boers north of the Vaal by the Sand River Convention of 16 January 1852, the constitution of the South African Republic was adopted only in 1858. An important provision which placed the administration of justice on a sound footing, was section 15 of the constitution which read:

> "Het volk stelt de regterlijke magt in handen van Landdrosten en gezworenen, en laat dit aan hun oordeel en geweten over, om volgens landswetten te handelen."

(The people place the judicial power in the hands of magistrates and justices of the peace, and leave it to their discretion and conscience to act in accordance with the laws of the land.)

The composition and jurisdiction of the various courts were also provided for in detail: the *landdrost's* court was the lowest court, having civil jurisdiction to the amount of 500 *riksdaalders* (£37–10 sterling); where the claim involved a liquid document, jurisdiction was increased to 5 000 *riksdaalders*. In civil cases in which the above amounts were exceeded, the court of the *landdrost* and *heemraden* had jurisdiction. As regards criminal jurisdiction, the *landdrost* court was, as a court of first instance, empowered to hear cases involving a sentence not exceeding three months' imprisonment with or without the option of hard labour and with or without a fine not exceeding £7–10. In the court of the *landdrost* and *heemraden* the period and amount were three years and £37–10 respectively. In cases requiring more severe penalties the highest court, the Hooge Gerechtshof, served as court of first instance. This was also the highest court of appeal following on the court of the *landdrost* and *heemraden*. The jurisdiction of the lower courts was considerably extended in later years.

Although the 1858 constitution is silent on the legal system to be applied, the first schedule, appended in the following year, introduced a *lex citationis* in the true sense. The Volksraad provided that as the term "Hollandsche wetten" (Dutch laws) occurring in article 31 of the Thirty-three Articles and in other laws and council resolutions was a continual source of confusion, the following ruling would apply: the *Wetboek* by Van der Lin-

The Boer Republics

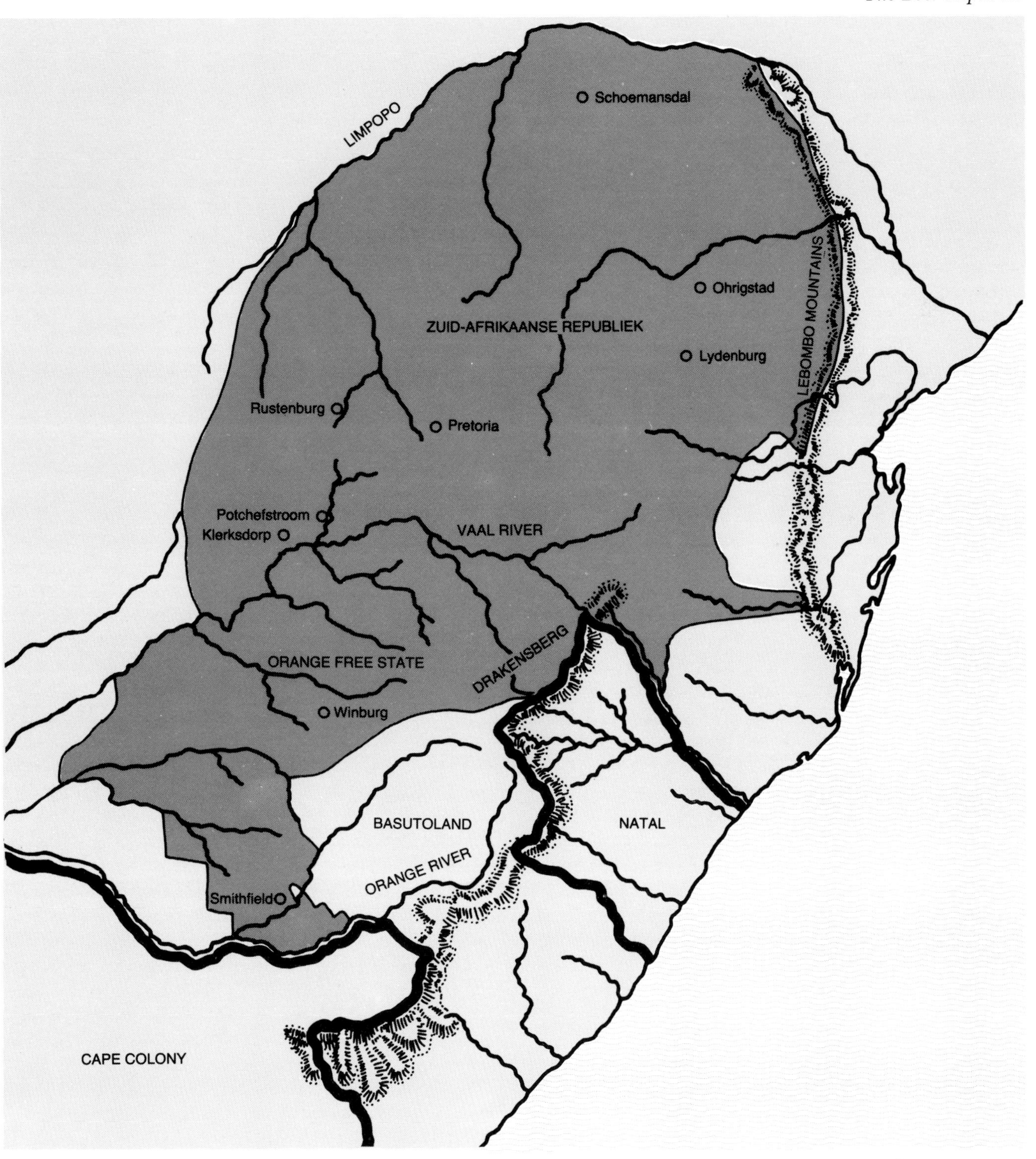

Street scene in Pietermaritzburg circa *1890. Even before the establishment of the Republic of Natalia, the Voortrekkers founded the settlement of Pietermaritzburg in 1838 – named after Piet Retief and Gerrit Maritz.*

den (i e his *Koopmans-Handboek* mentioned above) was to be regarded as the statute book of the State in so far as it did not conflict with any other laws or Volksraad resolutions. In cases not dealt with in this work, or where the work was unclear, the *Wetboek* by Simon van Leeuwen (his *Het Rooms-Hollandsche Reg)* and Hugo Grotius's *Inleidinge tot de Hollandsche Rechts-Geleerdheid* were to be consulted. It was further emphasized that article 31 of the Thirty-three Articles had here to be considered, in other words, that the sources mentioned should be applied "op een gematigde stijlvorm en ooreenkomstig van het costuum van Zuid Afrika" (in moderate form and in accordance with the law of South Africa).

One can hardly imagine a more direct "formal" incorporation of Roman-Dutch law. Practice, however, soon showed that considerable reliance was placed on both the substantive and adjective law of the Cape Colony where English law had already exerted a considerable influence. For example, the third schedule to the constitution – also dating from 1859 – embodied as instructions procedural rules for the Hooge Gerechtshof corresponding largely to those applicable in the Cape. In particular, the attempts by judges to give effect

An early photograph of one of Potchefstroom's most historic buildings which earlier housed the post office and court house. Potchefstroom was established in 1838 by the Voortrekker leader Andries Hendrik Potgieter. In this town the Thirty-three Articles and the first constitution of the Transvaal Republic were accepted. Potchefstroom was also the first Transvaal town to be accorded municipal status (1858).

to article 31 as they were required to do under the first schedule, resulted in the Roman-Dutch law which was applied not being the "pure" law of our old authorities but rather the law of the old authorities as received and developed by the Cape courts. A further consideration which cannot be disregarded, is the fact that certain practitioners, officials and judicial officers received their legal training in England or had formerly practised in the Cape Colony.

Apart from the regular courts, a resident *vrederechter* (resident justice of the peace) also acted as judicial officer in disputes of a less serious nature. The introduction of these inferior courts was undoubtedly inspired by their Cape counterparts. A measure of specialization can be discerned at an early stage in that a special court – the Land Commission – was established for each district to hear disputes regarding farmland. In the proclaimed goldfields, too, special courts were established to hear disputes between diggers.

Although one can thus say that the South African Republic was organized, as far as the judiciary is concerned, at a relatively early stage, an inherent weakness in the system was the poor judicial quality of the officials. Even the *landdrosts* were insuf-

Top: *The first magistrate's court in Lydenburg was in all probability the double-storey building to the left of Archer and McKenzie's shop in the photograph. This building was in any event used as such until the magistrate's offices – now still in use – were built.*

Below: *The Lydenburg magistrate's court during the South African War with British soldiers in the foreground. The building was completed during 1889.*

ficiently qualified. President Burgers, realizing that the low judicial standard could be used as a pretext on which to justify British moves to annex the Republic, thus attempted the introduction of a new dispensation in 1877. In terms of his proposed measures there would be a Supreme Court manned by trained jurists enjoying life tenure, a circuit court presided over by a single judge, and *landdrosts'* courts.

The most important officials concerned with the administration of justice outside the courts were the following:

The "staatsprocureur" (state attorney)

This office combined the present-day duties of an attorney-general, state attorney, secretary for justice, statute drafter (law draftsman), and state legal adviser. The official holding this office was thus in a position to exert a considerable influence on the administration of justice as a whole.

The "veldkornet" (field cornet)

This important official who, in broad constitutional terms, acted in conjunction with the *landdrost* as intermediary between government and populace, had varied duties. He was, inter alia, arbitrator, policeman, prison warder, clerk of the court, and even executioner. He was originally also entrusted with the conducting of preparatory examinations.

"Vrederechters" (justices of the peace)

In addition to his judicial duties mentioned above, the justice of the peace later also took over the conducting of preparatory examinations and the effecting of arrests. He also acted as commissioner of oaths.

As regards legal practitioners, the position in the South African Republic was initially deplorable, as even the most senior of the judicial officers had no relevant training. The lowest category of practitioner was the so-called "law agent" who could appear in the lower courts without any legal training whatsoever. Attorneys, who were entitled to appear before the Supreme Court as well, were required to have undergone some measure of legal

Title page of an 1864 edition, adapted by C P Moll, of the 1858 Transvaal Constitution and the Thirty-three Articles of 1844.

DE

GRONDWET

DER

ZUID-AFRIKAANSCHE REPUBLIEK

BENEVENS DE

33 ARTIKELEN,

MET DE VEREISCHTE VERBETERINGEN
HERDRUKT OP LAST VAN DEN HED
UITVOERENDEN RAAD.

PRETORIA:
BY
C. P. MOLL, Junior.

1864.

The Bar of the South African Republic in 1897: Back (fltr): *S H Barber, J G Dickson, J K Hummel, T L Thome and Jan de Waal (later judge president of the Transvaal),* Middle (fltr): *N J de Wet (later chief justice of the Union), Dr M Farelly, Louis J Jacobsz (later acting state attorney of the South African Republic, 1901–1902), A F S Maasdorp (later judge), A T Rooth, H B Sauer, A F Kock (judge of the South African Republic), W H de Savornin Lohman, S S de Villiers and W Stoney;* Front (fltr): *J G Auret, J W (later Sir Johannes) Wessels (later chief justice of the Union), E Esselen (judge), B de Korte (judge), Dr H J Coster (state attorney until 1897; died in October 1899), J S Curlewis (later chief justice of the Union).*

training and could be required to sit for an examination before being admitted. The offices of notary and conveyancer, too, date from early times. A deeds office was established in 1866.

The British annexation of the South African Republic by Sir Theophilus Shepstone on 12 April 1877 had an important effect on the legal administration. On 18 May of that year, a supreme court as envisaged by President Burgers was created by proclamation. J G Kotzé, a young advocate from Grahamstown who had received his legal training in London, was appointed as the first judge. When, in 1881, after the First Anglo-Boer War, the republican form of government was re-established, Kotzé became chief justice. A further two judges were appointed in 1882, while provision was made for five judges from 1888, and for six from 1896.

J G Kotzé strove actively to improve the standard of the administration of justice. Despite the fact that the old practitioners retained their existing right to practise, the legal profession was divided into a Bar and attorney's profession – as is the case today. More stringent requirements were set for admission to the professions. The practitioners themselves attempted a better distribution of their duties in the interests of the standard of law. An association of advocates was soon created, while a law society was established in 1892. Membership of the latter was compulsory for all attorneys.

Thomas Francois Burgers (1834–1881). This former minister of religion was sworn in as president of the South African Republic on 1 July 1872. During his office Sir Theophilus Shepstone annexed Transvaal (12 April 1877), whereupon Burgers laid down the reins of office and returned to the Cape Colony where he subsequently died in poverty. Although a man of considerable intellectual ability, he was unfortunately very idealistic and impractical. He tried to achieve too rapid a development of his republic and as a result incurred the wrath of the conservative population.

Hermanus Jacob Coster was a Hollander who obtained his doctorate from Leyden University in 1890. He practised as an advocate in Pretoria and in 1895 succeeded Ewald Esselen as state attorney. In 1897, after a clash with President Paul Kruger over the Aliens Act, he resigned his office and returned to practise at the Pretoria Bar. He supported the Boers during the South African War (1899–1902) and fought with them against the British. He was killed at the Battle of Elandslaagte in October 1899. A plaque in memory of Dr Coster was unveiled at Leyden University in 1901.

A further step forward was taken in 1885 when the commissioners' courts were established to decide civil cases between members of the indigenous Black population groups in terms of their own customs and usages. In this way the separate indigenous legal systems were accorded recognition alongside Roman-Dutch law within the borders of the Republic.

The role of the judges as interpreters of common law and thus as founders of the future legal dispensation cannot easily be overrated. Here praise falls particularly to Justice Kotzé who for some twenty years strove to apply Roman-Dutch principles to circumstances sometimes differing radically from those for which the principles were originally created. The conviction and energy which Kotzé brought to bear on his task were unfortunately later to contribute to his dismissal, as they brought him into direct conflict with the executive, in the person of President Paul Kruger.

The constitutional crisis which culminated in the dismissal of the chief justice may briefly be sketched. In 1897 Justice Kotzé held, in the case of *Brown v Leyds NO* 1897 OR 17, that the constitution of the South African Republic was a fundamental law in the sense that any conflicting legislation adopted by the Volksraad would be invalid, and further that the provisions of the constitution laying down formal requirements for the adoption of legislation were to be strictly complied with. In

Sir John Gilbert Kotzé was born in Cape Town in 1849. He received his legal training in London and then practised as an advocate at the Cape. In 1877 he was appointed the first judge of the Transvaal Supreme Court and in 1881 chief justice. In 1898 there occurred a clash between the bench and the executive of the South African Republic which resulted in his dismissal by President Paul Kruger. After the Peace of Vereeniging he served as a judge in other divisions and was appointed judge of appeal in 1922. He retired in 1927 and died in 1940. Kotzé was an outstanding jurist with a thorough knowledge of Roman-Dutch law. He was an ardent proponent of codification.

Willem Johannes Leyds (1859–1940). As state attorney and secretary of the South African Republic, this Hollander exerted a strong influence on President Kruger and the administration of the Republic. Some regard him as the personification of Dutch influence in the Transvaal, an influence which drew sharp criticism against President Kruger. Both before and during the South African War (1899–1902) Dr Leyds was actively soliciting support for the Boer cause in Europe.

effect this judgment meant that the Supreme Court had arrogated to itself the right to test Acts of the Volksraad. The immediate practical implication of the judgment was that the decisions of the Volksraad which President Kruger and the government regarded as valid legislation, were rendered invalid, together with a number of other Acts which had been adopted without compliance with the letter of the constitution. To resolve this situation which the government, of course, regarded as wholly untenable, the Volksraad introduced Act 1 of 1897. In terms of this Act the Supreme Court's testing power was abolished and the president was empowered to dismiss any judge who refused to consent to the new provision. This represented the writing on the wall for Justice Kotzé. Although the chief justice of the Cape, Sir Henry de Villiers, managed to negotiate a compromise between Kruger and his chief justice, by February Kotzé could no longer see his way clear to agreeing with the controversial law, and issued a public protest. President Kruger dismissed him summarily on 16 February 1898. In this way the Transvaal lost one of its greatest jurists, as shortly afterwards Kotzé left the Republic, never to return.

An event which was to play an important part in legal development within the Transvaal, was the

The Palace of Justice was designed by Sytze Wierda as the seat of the Supreme Court of the South African Republic. It was completed shortly before the outbreak of the South African War (1899–1902) and Lord Roberts used it as a hospital for British soldiers after the occupation of Pretoria in 1900. The building currently houses the Transvaal Provincial Division of the Supreme Court of South Africa.

Second British Annexation of 1900. Proclamation 34 of 1901 repealed a number of laws and Volksraad resolutions, including such basic legislation as the Thirty-three Articles of 1844, the 1849 Act confirming these, the 1858 constitution, and the important 1859 schedule to the constitution. Although the works of Van der Linden, Van Leeuwen and De Groot could subsequently no longer be regarded as formal sources of the law, Roman-Dutch law, and consequently also the works of the old Roman-Dutch authorities, remained in force, as in section 17 of the said Proclamation the new colonial legislature provided:

> "The Roman-Dutch Law except in so far as it is modified by legislative enactments shall be the law of this Colony."

Together with the three other British colonies at the southernmost tip of Africa where similar provisions applied, the Transvaal also had explicit statutory authority for the application of Roman-Dutch law until 31 May 1910. The South Africa Act of 1909 which formed the basis for the establishment of the Union of South Africa, brought no changes to the existing position. Section 135 provided that the laws of each territory were to remain in force until altered or repealed.

Sir Arthur Lawley, lieutenant-governor of the Transvaal, opens the Legislative Council of the Transvaal on 26 May 1903.

The British annexation also had a far-reaching effect on the practical legal administration: a new Supreme Court was established. It was made up of the High Court of the Transvaal which sat in Pretoria and consisted of a judge president and at least three judges. The members of the bench were appointed by the governor and were required to be qualified advocates or judges from a British colony. The Witwatersrand District Court sat in Johannesburg as a superior court with a single judge. A few months after the establishment of these courts the Johannesburg division came to be known as the Witwatersrand High Court and the title of judge-president was changed to chief justice. The later renowned chief justice of the Union of South Africa, Justice Innes, became the first chief justice of the Transvaal Colony in 1902. None of the judges from the republican period was reappointed. The other judges who took up office in 1902 were Solomon, Smith and Wessels – the latter the author of the well-known *History of Roman-Dutch Law*.

Right: *Jan Christiaan Smuts (1870–1950) was appointed state attorney of the South African Republic in 1898 at the age of 28 years. He was very active in controlling illegal gold and alcohol traffic and in the reform of the criminal investigation service. As legal adviser to the Executive Council Smuts played a prominent role in the negotiations with the British government directly prior to the South African War (1899–1902).*

Far right: *Stephanus Johannes Paulus Kruger (1825–1904), last president of the South African Republic. He was elected president for four consecutive terms, viz 1883, 1888, 1893 and 1898.*

Sir Johannes Wilhelmus Wessels (1862–1936). He received his legal training in Cambridge and London and practised as an advocate in Cape Town and Pretoria. He was appointed a judge in the Transvaal in 1902 and in 1920 became judge president of this division. He was appointed judge of appeal in 1923 and chief justice in 1932. He was an exceptionally able jurist with a thorough knowledge of Roman-Dutch law. Two of his works are today still highly thought of, viz History of the Roman-Dutch Law *and* The Law of Contract in South Africa.

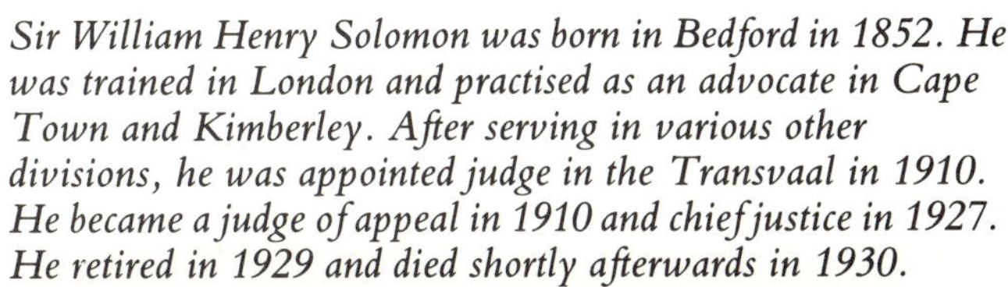

Sir William Henry Solomon was born in Bedford in 1852. He was trained in London and practised as an advocate in Cape Town and Kimberley. After serving in various other divisions, he was appointed judge in the Transvaal in 1910. He became a judge of appeal in 1910 and chief justice in 1927. He retired in 1929 and died shortly afterwards in 1930.

Landdrosts' courts as they existed in the republican period were replaced by magistrates' courts with jurisdiction comparable to those of Natal. The lowest court was that of the resident justice of the peace.

It was particularly during this period that the Cape influence made itself felt more directly than before: for example, the Law of Evidence Proclamation 16 of 1902 was based on the Cape Ordinance 72 (1830). As the Cape Ordinance was based on English law, the latter found its way to the Transvaal. The Transvaal criminal procedure, too, was essentially a simplified version of English criminal procedure.

In conclusion one may consequently state that by 1910 the basic principles of substantive law applying in the Transvaal were based on Roman-Dutch law, despite English traces, but that in both spirit and letter the adjective law reflected English legal norms.

J Dugard BA LLB (Stell) LLB LLD (Cantab) Professor of Law and Director of the Centre for Applied Legal Studies University of the Witwatersrand

8

THE SOUTH AFRICAN CONSTITUTION 1910–1980

The South Africa Act of 1909

At the time that the idea of a union of the four British colonies in South Africa came to be mooted there were two principal constitutional models upon which to draw in the drafting of a constitution. First, there was the rigid American-type constitution with guaranteed rights and judicial review which had proved to be a success in the Orange Free State.[1] Secondly, there was the flexible constitution premised on the principle of parliamentary supremacy – the Westminster model. It is not surprising, considering the politico-legal climate of the time, that the National Convention chose the latter. Judicial review, an inherent feature of the American model, had been discredited as a result of the bitter dispute between President Kruger and Chief Justice Kotzé over the exercise of the testing right in *Brown v Leyds* (1897) 4 Off Rep 17. Federalism, a popular cause until 1908, was now viewed largely as a Natal demand and there was no one of stature to press this cause in the absence of W P Schreiner who had felt obliged to withdraw from the National Convention in order to defend Dinizulu on charges of treason brought by the Natal colonial government. A unitary state with a flexible constitution was therefore almost a foregone conclusion, particularly if one bears in mind the personalities of the two men most responsible for the drafting of the constitution, J C Smuts, then General Botha's second-in-command in the Transvaal, and John X Merriman, prime minister of the Cape Colony. Both were men steeped in English constitutionalism: Smuts was a graduate of Cambridge University and Merriman, according to the historian L M Thompson, "had an almost romantic veneration for the British constitution".[2] More important still, there was a widespread belief that full independence could be achieved only under a British-type flexible constitution and that any constitutional check on the legislature, such as exists in the American constitution, would be a sign of political subordination.

The constitution of the Union of South Africa, which took the form of a British statute (9 Edw 7, c 9) – the South Africa Act of 1909 – created a political order modelled substantially on that of Westminster. There were two legislative chambers, the House of Assembly and the Senate. The House of Assembly consisted initially of 121 members, elected from single-member constituencies which were allocated so as to favour the Orange Free State and Natal. The Senate was composed of forty members, eight of them nominated by the Governor-General-in-Council, and eight elected by electoral colleges in each of the four provinces. Political power was vested in the House of Assembly as a bill rejected by the Senate might later be approved at a joint sitting of both houses by a simple majority vote. Judicial power was organized on a provincial basis with an Appellate Division entrusted with Union-wide appellate jurisdiction. The Privy Council, however, remained the ultimate court of appeal.

The executive was modelled on that of Britain: there was a Cabinet presided over by a Prime Minister which was responsible to the lower house. Cabinet members were obliged to be either members of the House of Assembly or Senators. The operation of the Cabinet was governed largely by conventions inherited from Britain.

Although the South Africa Act created a unitary state, account was taken of the existing colonial identities by means of the system of provincial government which conferred certain limited legislative powers, notably in the field of education, on provincial councils. Executive government in the provinces was vested in an administrator, appointed by the Cabinet, assisted by four members of an executive committe, elected by the provincial council by proportional representation. Certain apparent checks were placed on the power of the Union Parliament to legislate on matters falling within the jurisdiction of the provinces, but in reality there was no such legislative competition.

Although the constitution which emerged from the deliberations of the National Convention was

1 For detailed discussion of this constitution of 1854, see Thompson 1954 *Butterworths South African Law Review* 49.

2 *The Unification of South Africa 1902–1910* 95.

William Philip Schreiner (1857–1919) studied at the South African College and at Cambridge University. After practising as an advocate at the Cape for a period, he entered politics. In 1893 he was appointed attorney-general under Rhodes and in 1898 became prime minister of the Cape Colony – a position he held until his resignation in 1900. He was again elected to the Senate in 1908 and in 1914 took office as High Commissioner for South Africa in London. He remained in this post until his death. A man of integrity with a deep love for his fatherland, Schreiner was sympathetic towards the Afrikaner and at the same time concerned with the fate of the Black peoples.

modelled on the Westminster pattern it was not entirely free of rigid features. One of the most difficult questions to resolve was the franchise. While the Cape delegates favoured a colour-blind franchise, most delegates from the Transvaal, Orange Free State and Natal favoured a Whites-only franchise.

The compromise finally reached allowed the Cape to retain its franchise qualifications, while the northern provinces were permitted to exclude all Blacks from participation in the electoral process. This agreement was entrenched in section 35 of the constitution which provided that no person registered as a voter in the Cape, or capable of becoming a voter in the Cape in terms of the pre-Union requirements, could be deprived of his right to vote by reason of his race or colour only "unless the bill be passed by both houses of parliament sitting together, and at the third reading be agreed to by not less than two-thirds of the total number of members of both houses". Section 137 guaranteed the equal status of English and Afrikaans in the same way and section 152 provided that neither section 35 nor section 137 might be amended save by a two-thirds majority vote of members of both houses of Parliament at a joint meeting. These three sections came to be known as the entrenched clauses and were later to be the subject of a bitter constitutional dispute.

The Statute of Westminster

In 1910 there were several restraints on the legislative power of the Union Parliament which resulted from South Africa's subordinate position. In terms of the Colonial Laws Validity Act of 1865 a South African statute repugnant to British legislation extending to the Union was void to the extent of the repugnancy. In addition it was doubtful whether a dominion parliament could legislate extra-territorially. These two limitations on Parliament were removed by the Statute of Westminster, enacted by the Imperial Parliament in 1931, which provided that no Act of the Union Parliament would be void for repugnancy to any "existing or future" British legislation, empowered the Union Parliament to repeal British legislation so far as it was part of South African law, and declared that the Union Parliament "has full power to make laws having extra-territorial operation". The Statute of Westminster was adopted by the Union Parliament in the Status of Union Act 69 of 1934 which declared:

- that the Union Parliament was "the sovereign legislative power in and over the Union" and that no Act of the British Parliament was to extend to the Union unless so extended by an Act of the Union Parliament;
- that the executive government of the Union in regard to any aspect of its domestic or external affairs was vested in the king, acting on the advice of his ministers of state of the Union.

Henceforth South Africa's independence was assured and the Union Parliament's legislative supremacy placed beyond doubt. As if to confirm

From left to right: L Botha (1862–1919), J X Merriman (1841–1926) and J C Smuts (1870–1950). Three important political figures in the process of unification. Merriman was prime minister of the Cape Colony, Botha of the Transvaal. Smuts was Botha's lieutenant. Despite Merriman's experience and seniority, Botha was elected first premier of the Union of South Africa. Smuts was only later to emerge as a leader destined to make a considerable impact on South Africa's political development.

this latter fact the Appellate Division announced in 1934:

> "Parliament may make any encroachment it chooses upon the life, liberty or property of any individual subject to its sway, and . . . it is the function of courts of law to enforce its will" (1934 AD 11 at 37).

The struggle over the entrenched clauses

The early 1950s saw a bitter constitutional battle over the legal effect of the entrenched clauses which was to emphasize the basic principle of parliamentary supremacy.

In 1931 doubts were expressed as to whether the entrenched clauses of the South African constitution would survive the passing of the Statute of Westminster as in some quarters they were seen to be entirely dependent upon an Act of the British Parliament. In order to assuage these fears, non-binding resolutions were passed in both the Senate and the House of Assembly to the effect that the Statute of Westminster was approved "on the understanding that the proposed legislation will in no way derogate from the entrenched provisions of the South Africa Act". Political assurance was translated into political action in 1936 when the Representation of Natives Act 12 of 1936 which removed African voters from the electoral roll in the Cape Province and gave them separate representation, was passed by the unicameral procedure laid down in the entrenched provisions. When the Act was challenged by an African voter on the ground that this unicameral procedure was, since the passing of the Statute of Westminster, no longer lawful, the Appellate Division held that:

> "Parliament . . . can adopt any procedure it thinks fit; the procedure express or implied in the South Africa Act is so far as Courts of Law are concerned at the mercy of Parliament like everything else . . . Parliament's will . . . as expressed in an Act of Parliament cannot now in this country, as it cannot in England, be questioned by a Court of Law whose function it is to enforce that will not to question it" (*Ndlwana v Hofmeyr NO* 1937 AD 229 at 238 237).

In the light of this decision it was generally accepted that the entrenched clauses had lost their legal efficacy and were at the mercy of the majority party in Parliament.

In 1948, soon after the National Party government came to power, the prime minister, Dr Malan, announced that the Coloured voters in the Cape would be removed from the common electoral roll and would be given separate representation in Parliament, as had happened to the Cape Africans in 1936. Only now this legislative alteration would be effected by a simple majority vote in both houses of Parliament sitting separately. At this stage legal authority appeared to support the government's position.

The National Party government found itself in a difficult position. On the one hand, it lacked the necessary political support for the unicameral procedure, but on the other hand, it was determined to remove the Coloured voters from the mainstream of South African political life. Thus in 1951 it introduced the Separate Representation of Vot-

Conference of ministers of South Africa's self-governing colonies held in Pretoria during May 1908. Back from left to right: R H Brand (Secretary), H C Hull (Tvl), J C Smuts (Tvl), J B M Hertzog (Orange River Colony), Dr Ramsbottom (Orange River Colony), F S Malan (Cape), P H K Lothian (assistant-secretary Inter-Colonial council). Seated from left to right: Dr C O'Grady Gubbins (Natal), A Fischer (premier Orange River Colony), Gen L Botha (premier Transvaal), F R Moor (premier Natal), John X Merriman (premier Cape Colony), J W Sauer (Cape Colony), Chas Hitchins (Natal).

ers Act, which, despite vigorous protests by the United Party opposition, was piloted through both houses of Parliament, sitting separately, and signed by the Governor-General. This enactment was challenged by a group of Coloured voters in *Harris v Minister of the Interior* 1952 (2) SA 428 (A) (the *Vote* case) in which the Appellate Division in a unanimous judgment delivered by Chief Justice Centlivres found that the Act was of no legal force. It held that *Ndlwana v Hofmeyr* had been wrongly decided; that the Statute of Westminster had been passed to remove the legislative supremacy of the British Parliament and not to modify the South Africa Act; that the unicameral procedure laid down in the entrenched sections was an essential feature of Parliament itself when matters affecting the Coloured vote or the equal language rights came before Parliament; and that, by passing legislation dealing with matters falling within the purview of the entrenched sections by the ordinary bicameral procedure, "parliament" had not functioned as Parliament within the meaning of the South Africa Act.

The government's response was to pass, again by the ordinary bicameral method, the High Court of Parliament Act, which provided that any judgment of the Appellate Division invalidating an Act of Parliament was to be reviewed by Parliament itself, sitting as a high court of Parliament. After this high court had set aside the decision in the *Vote* case, the High Court of Parliament was itself struck down by the Appellate Division in *Minister of the Interior v Harris* 1952 (4) SA 769 (A) (*the High Court of Parliament* case). This time the five judges (Chief Justice Centlivres and Judges of Appeal Greenberg, Schreiner, Van den Heever and Hoexter) gave separate judgments in which they all found that the High Court of Parliament was not a court, but simply Parliament in disguise, and that the entrenched sections envisaged judicial pro-

James Barry Munnik Hertzog (1866–1942). After obtaining the degree Dr Iur at the University of Amsterdam, he started his professional career as an advocate at the Bar at Pretoria and later became a politician of outstanding quality, as the following extract from the Bloemfontein Post *clearly indicates: "He is that* rara avis *among politicians, an honest man, and whether he be right or wrong, his purity of motive and perfect singleness of aim are beyond cavil or dispute."*

THE HON. J. B. M. HERTZOG.

tection by a proper court of law. Legislation such as this, which deprived the entrenched sections of their judicial protection, could not be passed by the ordinary bicameral procedure.

Still unable to muster the necessary support for a two-thirds majority at a joint meeting of both houses, despite increased support for its cause in the 1953 general election, the government resorted to more ingenious means of removing the Coloured voters from the Cape roll. First, it increased the size of the Appellate Division from five judges to eleven where the validity of an Act of Parliament was in issue, by the Appellate Division Quorum Act 27 of 1955, passed bicamerally. Secondly, again by the bicameral method, it passed the Senate Act 53 of 1955, which increased the size of the Senate from 48 to 89. The number of nominated senators was increased from eight to sixteen and the method of election of other senators was altered. Whereas before senators had been elected in each province by electoral colleges consisting of members of Parliament and members of the provincial council by a system of proportional representation, they were now elected by a simple majority vote in the electoral colleges. As the National Party had a majority in the Cape, Transvaal and Orange Free State the result was that the government was assured of the support of the overwhelming majority of the new Senate. It now introduced the South Africa Act Amendment Act 9 of 1956 which was passed by a two-thirds majority of both houses sitting together. This Act revalidated the 1951 Separate Representation of Voters Act, removed section 35 from the scope of the entrenching procedure, and provided that

> "no court of law shall be competent to enquire into or pronounce upon the validity of any law passed by parliament other than a law which alters or repeals or purports to alter or repeal the provisions of section 137 of the South Africa Act of 1909".

In *Collins v Minister of the Interior* 1957 (1) SA 552 (A) this legislative plan was challenged before the newly constituted Appellate Division. By ten to one (Appeal Justice Schreiner) the court upheld the validity of the South Africa Act Amendment Act on the ground that neither the Senate Act, nor the South Africa Act Amendment Act, viewed separately, could be described as invalid. The Senate Act was valid because it did not repeal the entrenched sections and therefore had been properly passed by the bicameral procedure. The South Africa Act Amendment Act was valid because it had been passed by a two-thirds majority at a joint sitting. Whereas the High Court of Parliament could not be described as a court for the purpose of the entrenched sections, the same objection did not hold in respect of the new Senate – it was still a senate within the meaning of the South Africa Act.

The dispute over the entrenched clauses convincingly established the principle of parliamentary supremacy. The entrenched provisions were retained to protect the equality of English and Afrikaans, but this was an artificial safeguard as the majority party in the House of Assembly could legally shape the size of the Senate to by-pass the

Albert van de Sandt Centlivres (1887–1966), studied at the South African College School, completing his training as a Rhodes Scholar at Oxford University. He was appointed judge of the Cape Provincial Division of the Supreme Court in 1935 and in 1939 judge of appeal. In 1950 he was appointed chief justice. A number of honorary degrees were conferred upon him by various South African universities in addition to a DCL by Oxford University.

Daniël Francois Malan (1874–1959) prime minister of South Africa from 1948–1954.

obstacle of the entrenched provisions. The vulnerability of the Senate to changes of this kind was further emphasized when, in 1960, the composition of this body was again altered to reduce the number of nominated senators and to restore the system of election by proportional representation in the provinces.

The Republic constitution of 1961

In 1960, when White voters elected by a narrow margin to become a Republic, there were suggestions that South Africa should adopt a new constitutional order. Some suggested a return to the model of the South African Republic with an executive president; while the Progressive Party favoured a rigid constitution, federation and an entrenched bill of rights. These proposals were of no avail, however, as in the course of the struggle over the entrenched clauses the ruling National Party government had identified itself completely with the Westminster model and the principle of parliamentary sovereignty.

The new constitution was brought into life by the Union Parliament, without the co-operation of any other legislative body, by the passing of the Republic of South Africa Constitution Act 32 of 1961. It effected little change to the constitutional life of South Africa, apart from establishing a Republic and replacing the Queen and Governor-General by a State President elected by the Senators and members of the House of Assembly. The powers of the new State President were as limited as had been those of the Queen. Legislative power remained with the House of Assembly, and political power with the Cabinet. The courts' power

Despite serious objections the United Party ("UP") was forced to accept the Senate Act in 1955. Here is a well-known cartoonist's view of the blow suffered by the vanquished in the process.

had been broken in the 1950s, but to emphasize this point section 59 of the new constitution provides:

"(1) Parliament shall be the sovereign legislative authority in and over the Republic, and shall have power to make laws for the peace, order and good government of the Republic.
(2) No court of law shall be competent to enquire into or to pronounce upon the validity of any Act passed by parliament, other than an Act which repeals or amends or purports to appeal or amend the provision of section one hundred and eight and one hundred and eighteen."[3]

The constitution in 1980

Debate over the future constitutional order of the Republic culminated in radical amendments to the constitution in June 1980.[4] The Senate was abolished, the House of Assembly extended to include non-elected members and a President's Council established. The central organs of State may now be described as follows:

(a) The Legislature[5]

Legislative power is vested in Parliament which consists of the State President and the House of Assembly. The State President's role is limited to assenting to Bills passed by the House of Assembly, with the result that political power is concentrated in the House of Assembly. This House is composed of three categories of members namely –

3 Sections 108 and 118 of Act 32 of 1961 replace ss 137 and 152 of the South Africa Act of 1909 which entrenches the equal status of English and Afrikaans.

4 Republic of South Africa Constitution Fifth Amendment Act 101 of 1980.

5 Part V of Act 32 of 1961 as amended.

Johannes Gerhardus Strijdom (1893–1958), known as "The Lion of the North". He was the fifth prime minister of the Union of South Africa.

Hendrik French Verwoerd (1901–1966) took office as prime minister in 1958. In 1960 he called a referendum to determine whether South Africa should become a republic within the British Commonwealth. The result of the referendum showed the majority of White South Africans to be in favour of a republic, but South Africa was compelled to relinquish her membership of the British Commonwealth. Verwoerd was assassinated in Parliament on 6 September 1966.

(i) 165 persons directly elected in single-member constituencies by White voters;
(ii) 4 members nominated by the State President, one from each province;
(iii) 8 members elected by the elected members referred to in (i) according to the principle of proportional representation.

Membership of the House of Assembly is confined to White South African citizens. Elections to the House of Assembly are normally held every five years but may take place at an earlier date.

Parliamentary supremacy is still basic to the constitutional structure of South Africa. Parliament may make laws on any subject it pleases and no court of law may enquire into the validity of any Act of Parliament, except one that affects the equality of the English and Afrikaans languages;[6] but even in such a case the court may only enquire whether Parliament has followed the correct procedure. Normally a Bill is passed if it obtains a majority vote in the House of Assembly, but, where the equal language rights are at issue the Bill must obtain a two-thirds majority vote in the House of Assembly, before it is forwarded to the State President for his approval.[7]

6 Section 59 of Act 32 of 1961.
7 Republic of South Africa Constitution Fourth Amendment Act 74 of 1980.

A cartoonist's impression of the referendum held on 5 October 1960 to decide whether South Africa should become a republic. The majority of voters favoured such a move.

(b) The State President and the Vice State President[8]

The State President is the titular head of the Republic of South Africa. He is elected by an electoral college composed of members of the House of Assembly and holds office for seven years. The Vice President is elected in the same manner for the same period. He acts as chairman of the President's Council. The State President and the Vice State President must be White South African citizens.

(c) The Executive[9]

The executive government of the Republic is vested in the State President, acting on the advice of the Executive Council. The subservience of the State President to the Executive Council is emphasized by section 16(2) of the constitution which provides that

> "save where otherwise expressly stated or necessarily implied, any reference in this Act to the State President shall be deemed to be a reference to the State President acting on the advice of the Executive Council".

8 Part III of Act 32 of 1961 (sections 7–15).

9 Part I of Act 32 of 1961.

South Africa's Black independent and national states

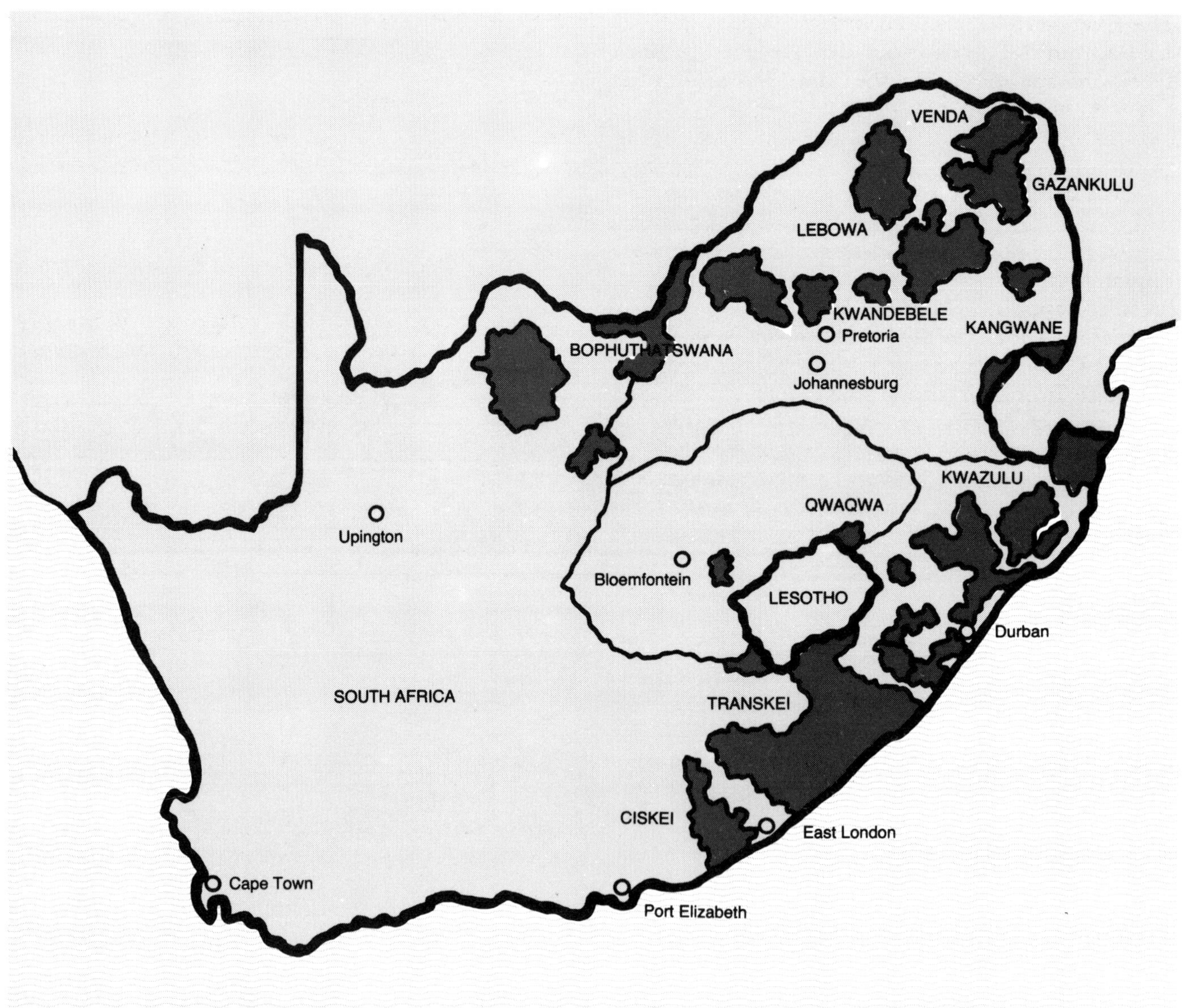

The Executive Council comprises twenty persons who administer the various departments of State. They are appointed by the State President. No minister may hold office for longer than twelve months unless he is or becomes a member of the House of Assembly.

The Constitution Act fails to describe the system of executive government fully as this matter is regulated largely by conventions inherited from England. In terms of these conventions the State President appoints as Prime Minister the leader of the majority party in the House of Assembly, who forms a Cabinet. The Cabinet is then appointed by the State President and constitutes the Executive Council. The Cabinet is responsible to the House of Assembly and if it loses the support of the House it must resign and the State President will then call upon a person able to command the support of the majority of the House of Assembly to form a new government.

(d) The President's Council[10]

In 1980 the Senate was abolished and a President's Council established. This Council consists of the Vice State President and sixty members appointed by the State President (acting on the advice of the Cabinet) who hold office for five years. A member of the President's Council must be a South African citizen above the age of 30 years belonging to the White, Coloured, Indian or Chinese population group.

The President's Council *"shall* at the request of the State President advise him on any matter referred to it by the State President for its advice and *may,* in its discretion advise him on any matter (excluding draft legislation) which, in its opinion, is of public interest".[11] It may also advise on draft legislation before the House of Assembly if so requested by the House.

In essence therefore the President's Council is to be a nominated advisory body composed of Whites, Coloureds, Indian and Chinese on the sidelines of the legislature and executive.

(e) Provincial government[12]

South Africa is divided into four provinces – the Cape of Good Hope, Natal, Orange Free State and Transvaal. In each province there is:

(i) a chief administrative officer appointed by the State President, known as the administrator of the province;
(ii) a provincial council, comprising White persons elected in single-member constituencies by White voters;
(iii) a provincial executive committee consisting of the administrator and four persons elected by the provincial council.

The powers of the Provincial Councils are prescribed by the Constitution. These councils are limited to making ordinances on matters such as provincial taxation, White primary and secondary education, hospitals, municipal institutions, roads and matters of a local nature.

Separate development and the Constitution

Far-reaching constitutional changes have been effected since the late 1950s as a result of the policy of separate development.

The meagre number of White representatives of the African and Coloured people in Parliament were abolished in 1959[13] and 1968[14] respectively; and multi-racial political parties were outlawed in 1968.[15] A Coloured Persons' Representative Council with limited legislative powers was established in 1968[16] but in 1980 this representation was discontinued.

10 Part VIIIA of Act 32 of 1961 as inserted by the Constitution Fifth Amendment Act 101 of 1980.

11 Section 106 of Act 32 of 1961 as inserted by the Constitution Fifth Amendment Act 101 of 1980.

12 Part VI of Act 32 of 1961.

13 By the Promotion of Bantu Self-government Act 46 of 1959.

14 By the Separate Representation of Voters Amendment Act 50 of 1968.

15 By the Prohibition of Political Interference Act 51 of 1968.

16 Coloured Persons' Representative Council Amendment Act 52 of 1968.

A South African Indian Council with limited administrative powers was established for the Indian community in 1968.[17] Sixteen million Africans (excluding the populations of Bophuthatswana, Transkei and Venda) have no voice in the central Parliament or in any other national body. Instead the policy of separate development envisages self-government, and ultimately independence for the different ethnic groups. To date Transkei (1976), Bophuthatswana (1977), Venda (1979) and Ciskei (1981) have achieved independence while Gazankulu, KwaZulu, KwaNdebele, Lebowa and Qwaqwa are self-governing territories, termed "National States", within the Republic of South Africa. Africans living in the urban areas outside the Homelands may participate in the political process in the Homelands ("National States") and in addition they may elect members of local councils – termed community councils – with limited powers of local government.

There is now widespread acceptance of the fact that the Westminster model, as applied in South Africa since 1910, cannot accommodate the political aspirations of the different population groups of South Africa. What will replace this constitutional plan in the future South Africa remains to be seen.

17 South African Indian Council Act 31 of 1968.

Ellison Kahn BCom LLB (Witwatersrand) LLM LLD (Natal) LLD hc (Cape Town) Deputy Vice-Chancellor of and Honorary Professor of Law in the University of the Witwatersrand, Johannesburg

9

THE DEVELOPMENT OF SOUTH AFRICAN SUBSTANTIVE LAW

Legal unification

Before the Union of South Africa came into being on 31 May 1910, in each of the four colonies that were to become the provinces of the Union the Roman-Dutch legal system of the eighteenth-century Netherlands applied as the basic common law; but in all of them that legal system had been influenced, to a greater or lesser degree in the various branches of the law, by the persuasive influence of the law of England. Splendid as it was, classical Roman-Dutch law was expressive of an age gone by. It had to be developed and, occasionally, modified, to meet changing times. Moreover, the Roman-Dutch authorities were in some matters silent, difficult to understand, vague, unsystematic or wanting in detail. In these circumstances the legislatures, judges and lawyers were wont to fall back on the law of England. Many of the judges and practitioners, particularly in the early days, had received their legal education in that country; English was the official language of the Cape and Natal; the textbooks and legal decisions of England were accessible and easy to read, while most of the 'musty manuals of the Middle Ages' (to use the pejorative words of some critics), written in Latin or Dutch, and rarely translated into English, were not; and precedents of contracts, wills and other legal documents of England were available.

In mercantile law recourse to English sources had been a common occurrence. A Cape ordinance of 1843 had set the tone of the insolvency law of the future, a nice mixture of Roman-Dutch and English legal principles. The Cape Companies Act of 1861 had begun the process, never to end, of modelling South African companies legislation on that of the United Kingdom. The enactments on negotiable instruments (that is, cheques and other bills of exchange, and promissory notes), merchant shipping, patents, trade marks and copyright were put, and have remained, on a basis of English law. That legal system also had a considerable influence on the common law – the legal rules not derived from legislation – enunciated by the courts. The expansion of economic activity in the late nineteenth and early twentieth centuries could not be met by the Roman-Dutch legal system that had died long before in the land of its birth. Even scholars most dedicated to the cause of preserving our Roman-Dutch heritage have conceded that recourse to English law in this area has, on the whole, been beneficial.

In the sphere of succession, while the lawmaker did accept certain of the concepts, rules and philosophy of English law, the legal decisions seldom invoked them. In the Cape in 1833 the English system of executorship supplanted the Roman-Dutch principle of universal succession of heirs; in 1845 the very informal and simple English 'underhand' form of will was introduced; in 1873 and 1874 the rights of succession of children and other close blood relations were ended (a surviving spouse, being a stranger in blood, had never had such a right in Roman-Dutch law).

There were some branches of the law in the states and colonies of southern Africa in which English law had comparatively little influence, either through legislation or legal decisions. In particular with the law of persons and family relations, property, the specific contracts (especially sale and lease) and unjust enrichment was this so.

The inheritance of the systematic Roman law made for viability in several of these branches. There were other branches where English law had made some impact through decided cases; for instance, in aspects of the general principles of contract (such as formation, discharge through acceptance of anticipatory repudiation and remedies for breach), in criminal law (especially with certain of the specific offences), in agency, in the rules relating to domicile (but English law was built up on the civil-law foundations basic to the Roman-Dutch law), in aspects of choice of law in the conflict of laws (private international law) and the law of nuisance. And then there were spheres where English law had a strong effect, at some times mainly through absorption in the case law and partially through legislative enactments, and at other times through the reverse process: such as aspects of the law of delict (civil wrongs), notably liability for negligence and the defences in defama-

Reproduction of the preamble and a portion of the Charter of Justice.

George the Fourth by the Grace of God of the United Kingdom of Great Britain and Ireland King Defender of the Faith To all to whom these Presents shall come Greeting Whereas

tion; and all but a small part of constitutional and administrative law.

Unlike most civil-law countries, southern Africa had no code of private law that could form a dyke to hold back the battering waves and penetrating wash of an alien legal system. But there were great judges in the late nineteenth and early twentieth centuries who, aided by scholarly advocates who argued cases before them, preserved the land of the Roman-Dutch law from inundation. On this roll of judicial honour appear such great names as those of William Menzies, E B Watermeyer, Sir Henry de Villiers, Sir William Solomon, J G (later Sir John) Kotzé, Sir Henry Connor, Sir James Rose Innes and J W (later Sir Johannes) Wessels: judges of very high calibre.

All in all, the legislatures, judiciaries and legal professions of the constituent parts of the Union of South Africa had proved pretty canny in what they had imported, consciously or unconsciously, from England into the law of southern Africa. Admittedly, there were instances where the alien corn was a potential danger to the future of the native crop – or at least unsightly. There it would have to be eliminated. That was one task for the future. Another was the harmonization of the rules of substantive law in the country as a whole. To deal with the latter task first.

Title page of the "Code Napoleon enacted for the Kingdom of Holland" which was accorded force of law on 1 May 1809. In broad outline this work is a revision of the French Code Civil, *with the addition of various elements from old sources of the Netherlands, the latter coming largely from the* Ontwerp Burgerlijk Wetboek *(1807–8) by the renowned jurist Johannes van der Linden.*

WETBOEK NAPOLEON

INGERIGT VOOR HET

KONINGRIJK HOLLAND.

TER KONINKLIJKE STAATSDRUKKERIJ,

1809.

Lord Mansfield (William Murray 1705–1793), Chief Justice of the King's Bench from 1756–1788. Mansfield is regarded as one of the greatest and most creative of English judges; up to the nineteenth century only two judges had attained his stature, Sir Edward Coke (1552–1634) and Sir Matthew Hale (1609–1676). Mansfield's finest contribution lay in the development of mercantile law, where his genius for systematization found full expression in the abstraction of principles from a chaotic mass of inconsistent decisions.

Section 135 of the South Africa Act, which created the Union, stated that the legislation obtaining in the four uniting colonies was to remain in force until it was changed by Parliament or, so far as it lay within its competency, by the provincial council concerned. (The South Africa Act did not say this of the common law.) As provincial councils were never given power to legislate on private law or on major topics of public law, it was left to Parliament to iron out inherited differences in legislative provisions. Many of these concerned 'lawyer's law', that is, basically uncontentious matter, largely of a private-law and non-political character.

The lawmakers proceeded at the pace of the ox. The legislative machine does not find lawyer's law a very delectable dish, for it is of little interest to the voter. Political union did not mean legal unification. For decades differences in statute law between the provinces, in areas outside the legislative competency of provincial councils, not only caused additional administrative work for public officials and private legal practitioners, but also created problems of the conflict of laws (private international law) of, as it were, a home-made brew.

In 1912 the first important South Africa-wide enactment appeared on the Statute Book ending

Friedrich Carl von Savigny (1779–1861) may be regarded as the founder of the school of the Pandectists. As such he is held in high esteem in the South African courts and by legal writers. He was interested in Roman law, not as it was interpreted by Justinian and his predecessors, but as a system which could be adapted to serve the needs of the Germany of his day. Savigny's most important works are Das Recht des Besitzes *(a treatise on the law relating to possession),* System des heutigen römischen Rechts, Geschichte des

römischen Rechts im Mittelalter *(a history of Roman law during the Middle Ages) and* Vom Beruf unserer Zeit für Gesetzgebung und Rechtswissenschaft *(which in many ways explains Savigny's philosophical approach to law).*

differences in legislation between the provinces on an aspect of lawyer's law, using that term in the wider sense: the Irrigation and Conservation of Waters Act (the present statute is the Water Act 1956). Four years later came the Patents, Trade Marks and Copyright Act (long since replaced by other enactments). There followed the Criminal Procedure and Evidence Act 1917 and the Magistrates' Courts Act 1917, both of blessed memory to lawyers near the end of their allotted span of life, who today must have recourse to the Criminal Procedure Act 1977 and the Magistrates' Courts Act 1944.

Three years later emerged the first of a series of Acts that gradually brought the prohibited degrees of relationship for marriage into line in the four provinces, in which the common law had been changed in various respects by legislation. The Natal and Transvaal Marriage Law Amendment Act 1920 permitted a marriage in the Transvaal of a man and the sister of his deceased wife or a more remote collateral relation of the latter, and clarified the law of Natal in regard to such a relation (Act 45 of 1898 of Natal had simply permitted marriage by a man to his deceased wife's sister). There followed the Marriage Law Amendment Act 1921, making it lawful throughout the country for a woman to marry the brother, or a more remote collateral relation, of her deceased husband. The Marriage Act 1961 put an end to the long-existent statutory prohibition in the Transvaal and Free State of marriages between double first cousins, and made the rule in those provinces on intermarriage between relations by blood in the collateral line the same as in the Cape and Natal: forbidden if either party was related to the common ancestor in the first degree of descent.

It was not until 1926, however, that another important consolidating measure appeared. It was the Companies Act of 1926 (today the Companies Act 1973 obtains). Only after a further decade was the next significant consolidating enactment passed, the Insolvency Act 1936, still alive and – in theory – a healthy veteran. Thereafter came the Deeds Registries Act 1937, the Merchant Shipping Act 1951, the Wills Act 1953 (creating uniform rules for formalities for wills, an ill-considered measure that has had frequently to be amended), the Marriage Act 1951, the Maintenance Act 1963, the Bills of Exchange Act 1964 and the Arbitration Act 1965, all of which are still in operation.

The cleansing of the Statute Book also required legislation of a more indirect type, for some of the colonies had passed laws that had changed rules of the common law and others had not. In 1879 the Cape and 1902 the Orange River Colony[1] had rid themselves of the elusive doctrine of *laesio enormis.* Born in the late Roman Empire, initially it had

1 General Law Amendment Act 8 of 1879 (C) s 8; General Law Amendment Ord 5 of 1902 (O) s 6.

allowed the seller of land below half its true value to rescind the contract unless the buyer made up the price to its full value. In Roman-Dutch law it grew to a gross manhood, its shadow falling over almost the whole field of contract. In late 1948 the Appellate Division urged its entire abolition.[2] (Our courts do every now and then indicate to Parliament what they consider to be a desirable change of a legal rule; there are limits to the capacity of judges to adapt common-law rules to modern times.) The legislature gave expression to the wishes of the highest court in 1952.[3]

The next step was to bring the divorce law of Natal into line with that of the rest of the country. This was accomplished by the Natal Divorce Laws Amendment Act of 1964, which repealed a certain ancient statute[4] that, *inter alia,* had permitted post-nuptial contracts and had required a minimum period of malicious desertion that would lead to a divorce order. The *hereditas damnosa* of divergent statutes on substantive law dating from before 1910 virtually received its quietus, according to the Government, with the passing of the Pre-Union Statute Law Revision Acts of 1977 and 1979. What remains to be removed is really of no practical significance. The 1977 Act put an end to two ancient laws of the Cape and Orange Free State[5] which had ordained that 'questions of fire, life and marine assurance, stoppage *in transitu* and bills of lading' were to be governed by English common and statute law except where this would be inconsistent with legislation of the particular colony. The 1977 Act also repealed old statutes that had provided for limited liability of certain partners in registered special partnerships in the Cape and Natal.[6] A most important effect of the 1979 Act was the removal from the Statute Book of a bundle of hoary Cape, Natal and Transvaal enactments involving aspects of agency; the main effect was to render sales by auction subject to the common law, unless a South African legislative measure provided otherwise.

2 *Tjollo Ateljees (Eins) Bpk v Small* 1949 (1) SA 856 (A) at 860, 882.
3 General Law Amendment Act 32 of 1952 s 25.
4 Law 13 of 1883 (N).
5 General Law Amendment Act 8 of 1879 (C); General Law Amendment Ordinance 5 of 1902 (O).
6 Special Partnerships Limited Liability Act 24 of 1861 (C); Law 1 of 1865 (N).

Sir William Blackstone (1723–1780), one of the most famous of English jurists, was judge, parliamentarian and academic. His lectures at Oxford University were largely instrumental in the recognition of English law as a subject in its own right alongside Roman and Canon law. His principal work, the classic Commentaries on the Laws of England, *written in a lucid style, represented the first complete, systematic exposition of English law, and for a century was the leading textbook for law students and practitioners.*

The Statute Book is not entirely clear of interprovincial divergences in legal rules, however. On at least one occasion Parliament has legislated to give its imprimatur to a cherished provincial eccentricity. That was in 1932, when it passed the Notarial Bonds (Natal) Act,[7] under which movables specially hypothecated by a registered notarial bond are deemed to have been pledged, so giving expression to what Natalians had for long fondly believed was the common law.

7 Act 18 of 1932, amended by the Notarial Bonds (Natal) Act, 1932, Amendment Act 57 of 1937. See also s 2 of the Insolvency Act 24 of 1936 sv 'special mortgage' as inserted by s 2(c) of the Insolvency Law Amendment Act 16 of 1943.

The Earl of Halsbury (1823–1921) was born Hardinge Stanley Giffard. He held the office of Lord Chancellor for eighteen years. His most important contribution to legal development was his comprehensive work The Laws of England. *Produced entirely under his supervision, this work is a review of the prevailing English law. As such it is invaluable, not only for the English jurist, but for any jurist wishing to research English law or legal systems influenced by English law.*

The legislature has also participated in the modern movement towards international unification of private law (broadly, the law that does not concern legal relations with the state itself). South Africa was a party to the Berne Convention of 1886 on copyright, and its successor conventions, and this found expression in the Copyright Act of 1965; the new Copyright Act of 1978 was modelled on the Berne Convention as amended in Paris in 1975, though subsequently our legislature had to alter a few of its manifestly defective provisions. The Territorial Waters Act 1963 incorporates rules of the Geneva Convention on the Territorial Sea and the Contiguous Zone of 1958. In the domain of the sky, the Aviation Act 1962 gives effect to the Chicago Convention on International Civil Aviation and the Chicago International Air Services Transit Agreement, both of 1944; while the Carriage by Air Act 1946 ratifies the Warsaw International Convention of 1929. Legislative force was given by the Merchant Shipping Act 1951 to the Hague Rules governing bills of lading.

In 1970 South Africa became a member of the International Institute for the Unification of Private Law, known as the Rome Institute, after the site of its headquarters. Only scant success has attended the efforts of the Institute, and the Republic has not contributed in any way to what success has been achieved. The Convention Providing a Uniform Law on the Form of an International Will concluded in Washington DC on 26 October 1973 allows for a form of will that would be valid wherever it is made. South Africa is not among the few signatories to the convention, despite the fact that the form of the 'international will', save in regard to the authentication of a mark, is identical to that of our will, as it is to the will of England.

The Republic has remained aloof from the Hague Conference of Private International Law, which was established in 1892 with the object of 'the progressive unification of the rules of private international law'. On one memorable occasion, however, South Africa did react favourably to a recommendation of the Conference. That was in 1965, when Parliament passed the Wills Amendment Act, which came into operation on 4 December 1970. This remedial statute provides for so many alternative legal systems[8] to test the formal validity of a will that it will be rare indeed for it to collapse on the ground that it had not been properly executed.

One last statute calls for mention as our contribution to co-operation between states in the pro-

8 See s 3 *bis* of the Wills Act 7 of 1953, as inserted by s 2 of the Wills Act Amendment Act of 1965. It is sufficient for the proper execution of a will disposing of movables that it conform to any one of seven laws: (1) the law of the place of execution; (2) that of the domicile of the testator when it was executed; (3) that of his habitual residence then; (4) that of his nationality then; (5) that of his last domicile; (6) that of his last habitual residence; (7) that of his last nationality. With an immovable, an eighth optional testing law is available, that of the place where it is situated.

Sir Johannes Andreas Truter was born in 1763. He studied at Leyden University for the degree of Doctor of Laws, after which he held various posts at the Cape. He was both the first and the last president (in effect chief justice) of the Court of Justice under the old regime at the Cape. In 1820 he was knighted, the first Cape resident to be so honoured. He retired in 1827 when the Supreme Court was constituted and died in 1845. His reputation as a judge was a high one, but in his time there were no law reports, so his contribution to the knowledge and development of the law went with his departure from the Bench.

Sir William Westbrooke Burton (1794–1888) was appointed as one of the first judges of the Cape Supreme Court in 1827, where he sat until 1833. His Observations on the Insolvent Law of the Colony, *published in 1829, may be regarded as the first legal textbook to have been published in South Africa. Burton was related to Robert Burton, author of the famous* Anatomy of Melancholy, *and was the great-uncle of Henry Burton, a member of the South African Cabinet from 1910 to 1924.*

duction of uniform legislation – the Recognition and Enforcement of Foreign Arbitral Awards Act 1977, which takes account of the prevalence of arbitration in conflict-of-laws disputes, especially in commercial matters, with the aim of achieving certainty on which court has jurisdiction and which legal system will be applicable. The United Nations had encouraged states to adhere to a convention of 1958 bearing the same title as our Act. South Africa acceded to the convention on 1 August 1976, and the Act gives expression to it.

The South African Law Commission had recommended accession to the convention, and here its views had been heeded, whereas they had not with the convention on the international will, to which it had advised accession. The Law Commission had been created by an Act, bearing its name, passed in 1973. Its objects are to investigate and make recommendations, in accordance with programmes approved by the Minister of Justice, for the development or reform of the law, including the repeal of obsolete or unnecessary provisions, the removal of anomalies, bringing about uniformity in the law in the country, the consolidation or codification of any branch of the law, and making common law more readily available. Bearing in mind that its members serve in a part-time capacity, one can only praise the work that the Law Commission has done. The time is surely ripe for the acceptance by the Government of the suggestion made by the Law Commission in its Annual Report of 1975, that the commissioners be appointed on a full-time basis. That dispensation has undoubtedly been an important cause of the outstanding success of the Law Commission of England.

Title page of the first edition of L C Steyn's Uitleg van Wette.

DIE UITLEG VAN WETTE

DEUR

L. C. STEYN, B.A., L.L.D., K.A.

Senior Regsadviseur van die Unie-regering.

Agente:

AFRIKAANSE PERS-BOEKHANDEL,

Johannesburg.

1946.

Unification of rules of substantive law of legislative origin was important; but so was unification of the common law (basically, legal rules not emanating from legislation as expounded by the courts), and also consistency in judicial interpretation of statutes. In a very early decision, *Webster v Ellison,*[9] the Appellate Division made the significant observation that there is only one common law of South Africa, and that it is the duty of that court to secure harmony in the true expression of that law. But it was not a case of 'so gesê so gedaan'. In fact, far from 'no sooner said than done', it is a counsel of perfection, mainly because of the peculiar structure of our system of courts, the nature of our doctrine of judicial precedent, and the possibility that the Appellate Division may not be called upon to pronounce on a particular question for decades.

In the classical Roman-Dutch law of the eighteenth century the principle was that a judge should follow a previous decision arrived at after due deliberation unless, after careful consideration, he concluded that there was a convincing reason that it was incorrect.

Before the South Africa Act 1909 created the Union of South Africa, the general rules of the doctrine of judicial precedent had been established in the four uniting colonies, rules which were far tighter than those of the Netherlands a century or so before. Some time after the First Charter of Justice of 1827, when a professionally qualified Supreme Court and English judicial procedure had come into being, the principle *stare decisis* – to abide by decided cases – was accepted. From 1880 onwards the great Cape Chief Justice, Sir Henry de Villiers, explicitly stated that lower courts had to follow the Supreme Court; and the Supreme Court should follow itself, unless it was satisfied that its previous pronouncement was clearly wrong: expediency and equity in giving expression to justifiable expectations demanded this outlook. The Cape attitude was taken, too, in the independent nineteenth-century Transvaal and Orange Free State. By Union the orthodox view was that a single judge was bound by the *ratio decidendi* of a court of two or more judges. By *ratio decidendi* is meant the rule of law that the court expressly considered necessary to state for the decision of the case. A single judge should follow the decision of another single judge of his court unless satisfied it was wrong. As between the four colonies judgments were only of persuasive force, though they might be of considerable weight.

The South Africa Act produced minimal changes. It created the Supreme Court of South Africa, with the Appellate Division at its apex, clothed with appeal jurisdiction but no original jurisdiction. The superior courts of the colonies became provincial divisions of the Supreme Court, lineal descendants of their colonial predecessors, with their satellite local divisions. Each

9 1911 AD 73 at 82, 92–3, 98–9.

provincial division was virtually an *imperium* of its own. The link between the provincial divisions was a common allegiance to the Appellate Division. Subsequent Acts of Parliament trenched very little on the independence of the provisional divisions, of which three new ones were created – the Eastern Cape Division in 1957, the South-West Africa Division in 1959 and the Northern Cape Division in 1969.[10] Seven provincial divisions in a country with four provinces: *ex Africa semper aliquid novi!*

Even such eminent exponents of Roman-Dutch law as Mr Justice F P van den Heever, judge of appeal, and Mr Justice L C Steyn, Chief Justice from 1959 to 1971, emphasized the need to stand by previous judicial rulings.[11] The courts have alluded to the need of the public for certainty in the law, for the protection of vested rights, for the fulfilment of legitimate expectations and for the upholding of the dignity of the judiciary. To these reasons can be added the advantage of a person's being able to plan his actions with some confidence as to their legal effects, and the reduction of litigation. In summary, the requirement *stare decisis* holds out the promise of certainty, predictability, reliability, equality, uniformity, economy and convenience. But, if too rigorously applied, the injunction could lead to the perpetuation of erroneous legal rules, the lack of adaptation to changing times and mores and the stifling of systematic legal development of the common law. In general, fortunately, our courts in expounding and applying the doctrine of judicial precedent have attained an admirable position between undesirable rigidity and undisciplined looseness. The main rules are twofold: First, a provincial division (with its local division or divisions) is absolutely bound by the principle of the decision of a higher or larger court on its level in the hierarchy, in that order, unless the decision had been given *per incuriam* (literally, negligently, but really meaning overlooking something, as for instance a governing enactment or precedent) or there had been later overriding legislation. Secondly, the Appellate Division (whatever the size of the actual bench sitting) and a provincial (including a satellite local division) bench of the same size will follow its own past decision unless it is satisfied that it was clearly wrong, in which event it will refuse to abide by it and so in effect will overrule it. A provincial (or local) division regards itself as free from an obligation to follow the decisions of its fellows elsewhere in the Republic. It regards them with respect, but feels itself to be independent in its own house. Even a single judge sitting in, say, provincial division A need not – indeed, quite often has refused to – follow the decision of a bench of two or three judges in provincial division B. Perhaps a better approach would be that taken in Canada, which, after all, is not even a unitary country like South Africa: as between provincial divisions (with their linked local divisions), a bench should follow a ruling on a new point of law, or a new question of construction of an enactment, of a bench of the same or larger size, unless satisfied it is wrong. Lower courts (being principally magistrates' courts) abide by superior court precedents in the same way; as between decisions of provincial divisions, those of the division of the area take priority.[12] Lower courts do not create precedents of their own.

In general the Appellate Division has been loath to pronounce one of its previous rulings as having been wrong, particularly where people have relied on it in arranging their affairs; and, to a lesser degree, to overrule decisions of provincial divisions if retrospectivity would result. On the other hand, if an earlier decision incorrectly denied rights, this will encourage a departure from it. If anything, provincial and local divisions have been even more disinclined than the Appellate Division

10 See General Law Amendment Act 68 of 1957 s 2(1)(*a*), now s 1(viii) of the Supreme Court Act 59 of 1959; Supreme Court Act 59 of 1959 s 1(ix); Establishment of the Northern Cape Division of the Supreme Court of South Africa Act 15 of 1969.

11 See *R v Sibiya* 1955 (4) SA 247 (A) at 265; *Fellner v Minister of the Interior* 1954 (4) SA 523 (A) at 529; *R v Sillas* 1959 (4) SA 305 (A) at 311.

12 See, for instance, *Credex Finance (Pty) Ltd v Kuhn* 1977 (3) SA 482 (N).

Sir James Rose Innes
Chief Justice 1914–1927

to depart from their earlier holdings.[13] Judges are acutely aware of the fact that they are making a pronouncement on the law, not as it will be, but as it is and was; and that the pronouncement may have a retrospective application – something a court in South Africa, unlike Parliament, is unable to avoid, for, whatever the position be in some countries, the enunciation of a legal rule by the judiciary cannot be made prospective only. (The position may be different with rulings on abstract questions of law in terms of s 333 of the Criminal Procedure Act 1977 or s 23 of the Supreme Court Act 1959, discussed below.) But it is dangerous to be dogmatic on this debatable subject. A court, particularly the Appellate Division, might prove quite willing to wipe clean an erroneous tablet of the law written by judges in the past, even at the price of retrospectivity. Attitudes appear to vary from time to time and from judge to judge. He who has read the law reports over the past three decades could well get the impression that there has been a tendency by our highest tribunal to go back to Roman-Dutch sources – *petere fontes* is the stock expression – and in so doing overrule decisions that did not follow them correctly or evaluate them properly in their modern setting. But only a tendency, for occasionally – if the change of metaphor be excused – a stray sheep has been accepted as part of the flock. Illustrations will follow; but first a word or two on how the Appellate Division can be asked to pronounce on a contentious point of law outside the process of litigation, thereby accelerating the harmonization of the law in the country.

Section 388 of the Criminal Procedure and Evidence Act 1917 stated that where there were conflicting decisions of superior courts on a criminal matter, the Appellate Division could, on application of the Minister of Justice, order argument on a special case and make a ruling which would be deemed by all courts to be correct. The successor statute, the Criminal Procedure Act 1955, stated that where the minister had any doubt on the correctness of a decision of a superior court on a question of law, he could submit the question for argument before the Appellate Division to enable that court to decide it for the 'future guidance' of all courts. The present enactment, the Criminal Procedure Act 1977, in s 333 enlarges the scope of the 1955 statute by adding the conflicting-decisions provision of 1917. It is a power that has been rarely used.[14] The Magistrates' Courts Act 1944 initially contained a similar section relating to clashes between provincial divisions on an interpretation of that statute, but it was repealed when

13 See, for example, *National Chemsearch (SA) (Pty) Ltd v Borrowman* 1979 (3) SA 1092 (T), especially at 1101. But compare *S v Ndhlovu* 1979 (4) SA 208 (ZR) at 215 – '. . . in borderline cases it is better for the law to be certain and wrong than uncertain and right, but this is only in borderline cases'.

14 For illustrations of its use, see *Ex parte Minister of Justice: In re S v Van Wyk* 1967 (1) SA 488 (A); *Ex parte Minister of Justice: In re S v Grotjohn* 1970 (2) SA 355 (A), both decisions of significance.

H A Fagan
Chief Justice 1957–1959

Sir William Solomon
Chief Justice 1927–1929

s 23 was inserted in the Supreme Court Act 1959 in 1974.[15] Section 23 states that whenever a decision on civil proceedings on a question of law is given by a provincial or local division that is in conflict with a decision of another division, the minister may, after consulting with the S A Law Commission, submit the matter to the Appellate Division for argument and determination for the future guidance of all courts. This piece of legislation flowed from a recommendation of the Law Commission, which thought it to be a valuable device for achieving certainty in law without the need to resort to legislation. The Commission conceded that in some instances legislation would be the more appropriate means of resolving the conflict. There is little doubt that this will be found to be the case as a rule, and that scant use will be made of s 23 of the Supreme Court Act.[16]

He who is not schooled in the law of this country may be forgiven for thinking that a common 'common law' is like the horizon: the nearer one seems to get to it, the farther distant it becomes; or like the future infinitive mood – always about to be, and never is. After all, many a vexed question of law takes an unconscionably long time to come before the Appellate Division, and by then new questions will have emerged. But in reality there are vast tracts of law that are uniform throughout the Republic. True, even Parliament recognizes that a province has its own peculiar legal rules. For instance, the law of the Cape applies in Prince Edward Islands[17] and the law of the Transvaal to a

15 By s 36 of the Second General Law Amendment Act 94 of 1974.

16 For an illustration of its use, see *Ex parte Minister of Justice* 1978 (2) SA 572 (A), on a question of computation of finance charges under the Limitation and Disclosure of Finance Charges Act 73 of 1968.

17 Prince Edward Islands Act 43 of 1948 s 2.

L C Steyn
Chief Justice 1959–1971

James Stratford
Chief Justice 1938–1939

South African citizen in Antarctica,[18] which, for legal purposes, it is pleasing to note, is deemed to be situated within the magisterial district of Pretoria, while s 2(3) of the Divorce Act 1979 speaks of the law of a division of the Supreme Court. But differences in rules of substantive law are in truth not common.

The common law: the opposing pulls of certainty, loyalty and virility

The second obvious task that had to be undertaken at Union in 1910 was the removal by the courts of harmful or unsightly alien corn from the field of the common law. It was, of course, only part of a much larger task, that of adapting the legal rules to changing times. Down the years our judges have dwelt on this duty. In 1903 Sir Henry de Villiers, Chief Justice of the Cape, said: 'However anxious the court may be to maintain the Roman-Dutch law in all its integrity, there must . . . be a progressive development of the law, keeping pace with modern requirements.'[19] In 1909 Sir James Rose Innes, Chief Justice of the Transvaal, gave voice to similar sentiments:[20] 'There come times in the growth of every living system of law when old practice and ancient formulae must be modified in order to keep in touch with the expansion of legal ideas, and to keep pace with the requirements of changing conditions.' Then he referred to the perennial problem of the judges: '. . . it is for the courts to decide when the modifications . . . are of a nature to be effected by judicial decision, and

18 South African Citizens in Antarctica Act 55 of 1962 ss 1(iii), 2.

19 *Henderson v Hanekom* (1903) 20 SC 513 at 519.

20 *Blower v Van Noorden* 1909 TS 890 at 905.

Sir John Wessels
Chief Justice 1932–1936

when they are so important or so radical that they should be left to the legislature.' Lord Tomlin, giving the opinion of the Privy Council on an appeal from South Africa in 1934,[21] in the days when it was the final court of appeal, expressed the sentiment that 'Roman-Dutch law . . . is a virile living system of law, ever seeking to adapt itself consistently with its inherent basic principles to deal effectively with the increasing complexities of modern society'. Recently, in the Appellate Division, Mr Justice Holmes said that 'the Roman-Dutch law is a living system, adaptable to modern conditions'.[22]

There are so many forces pulling in different directions. In the words of the most eminent of American jurists, Roscoe Pound,[23] 'law must be stable and yet it cannot stand still'. The courts have to satisfy the demand for legal certainty and yet avoid stagnation; have to show loyalty to our inheritance of Roman-Dutch law and yet try, within legitimate boundaries that they have to fix by an intuitive sense of right, to make the living law reflect justice and the standards of correct conduct and of convenience of today; must feel free to have recourse to a principle of Roman-Dutch law that has never yet been invoked in South Africa, and nevertheless prevent, in Maitland's immortal metaphor,[24] an exhumed 'dead hand' of the past falling with 'a resounding slap on the living body of the present'.

The major task has naturally fallen to the Appellate Division. Save perhaps for a period in the thirties, this court has always had a nice blend of members endowed with exceptional academic scholarship, members with great practical experience of the working of the law and man's mind, and members with special faculties of imagination, intellect and wisdom that enable them to synthesize the rules of law here, and refine them there. To mention the names of but a few of the great judges of appeal of yesteryear: Lord de Villiers, Sir James Rose Innes, Sir William Solomon, Sir John Kotzé, Sir Johannes Wessels, E F Watermeyer, Oliver D Schreiner, L C Steyn, A v d S Centlivres, Leopold Greenberg, F P ('Toon') van den Heever. Each of them would have graced the highest bench of any country. Take the Appellate Division as it was constituted at the beginning of 1950, its members being the Chief Justice, Mr Justice Watermeyer, and four judges of appeal, Mr Justice Centlivres, Mr Justice Greenberg, Mr Justice Schreiner, Mr Justice Van den Heever and Mr Justice Hoexter. It would be difficult to imagine a more powerful tribunal.

The Appellate Division has eliminated certain English law excrescences. A few illustrations of importance must suffice. In 1919 it exorcized the Cape heresy that the Roman-Dutch requirement of *iusta causa* for contract was more or less the equivalent of valuable consideration in English

21 *Pearl Assurance Co v Union Government* [1934] AC 570 (PC) at 579; 1934 AD 560 (PC) at 563.
22 *S v Graham* 1975 (3) SA 569 (A) at 576.
23 In his *Interpretations of Legal History* (1923).
24 F W Maitland *Selected Essays* (1936) 237.

J S Curlewis
Chief Justice 1936–1938

law.[25] In that year it also pronounced that earlier courts which had been guided by English rules as to discharge of contract by supervening impossibility had erred: the matter was governed entirely by civil-law principles.[26] After eighty years[27] of blissful belief by practitioners that the English law of nuisance had taken root in South Africa, our highest court ruled in 1962 that nothing of the sort had happened: ours is 'burereg' – neighbour law.[28] It was regrettable, the court in effect conceded, that so little was said of the detailed rules of this branch of the law in the Roman and Roman-Dutch texts: our courts would simply have to develop it on sound basic principles. So departed dozens of helpful precedents in the law reports and a fully worked-out system; practitioners were left groping when called upon to advise their clients. The adage which comes so trippingly to the tongue of a South African legal academic who has a purist cast of mind, that Roman-Dutch law is rich and English law poor in principles, does seem to take an about-turn here. Two years later[29] the Appellate Division held that it had been wrong in a series of decisions in holding that our law of estoppel is the same as that of England.

There is the possibility of an interesting midway solution: assert the governance of the Roman-Dutch law but concede the adoption of concepts of English law that are compatible with it. That, it appears, is what is happening to the law of defamation, where the Appellate Division in the last twenty years has turned from treating *animus iniuriandi* (the conscious intention wrongfully to defame) from a virtually fictional to an essential element of the delict,[30] but still seems prepared to speak as a rule in traditional English-law terms of the defences of privilege, fair comment and truth in the public interest; blameworthiness and unlawfulness are separate elements; the defences refer to unlawfulness and not to the rebuttal of the presumption of *animus iniuriandi*. The resultant mist enveloping the law of defamation is lifting.

The Appellate Division has also of recent years been engaged in restraining the concept of duty of care, an expression taken over from the English law, from preventing a proper appreciation of the first two of the three requirements of Aquilian liability in delict: a wrongful act by the defendant; fault *(dolus* or *culpa)* on his part; and patrimonial loss to the plaintiff. If the expression 'duty of care' is to be used at all, it should be used in the sense of wrongful conduct. The highest court has also

25 *Conradie v Rossouw* 1919 AD 279.

26 *Peters, Flamman & Co v Kokstad Municipality* 1919 AD 427.

27 Ever since the decision in *Holland v Scott* (1882) 2 EDC 307.

28 *Regal v African Superslate (Pty) Ltd* 1963 (1) SA 102 (A).

29 *Trust Bank van Afrika Bpk v Eksteen* 1964 (3) SA 402 (A).

30 See, for example, *Jordaan v Van Biljon* 1962 (1) SA 286 (A); *Nydoo v Vengtas* 1965 (1) SA 1 (A); *May v Udwin* 1981 (1) SA 1 (A); *Marais v Richard* 1981 (1) SA 1157 (A).

Lord De Villiers
Chief Justice 1910–1914

Jacob de Villiers
Chief Justice 1929–1932

swung from its previous view that liability for an omission necessarily calls for prior positive conduct; it is now speaking of 'the legal convictions of the community' as the appropriate test to determine when there is a legal duty to act.[31]

In practice it does not always prove possible to eject the stranger, and so apply the dictum of Mr Justice Stratford,[32] 'if the decisions had disregarded fundamental principles of our law, we might have to reassert those principles even at the cost of reversing judgments of long standing'. In the early fifties[33] our highest tribunal decided that it could not call back yesterday and restore the Roman-Dutch law relating to contractual penalties that, to the judges' chagrin, had been supplanted by English law through judgments of the Cape Court and the Privy Council. Legislation – the Conventional Penalties Act 1962 – was subsequently passed. Drafted by the brilliant academic, Professor J C de Wet, it was based on Roman-Dutch principles but displayed the impress of modern civil law, especially the German Civil Code and the Swiss Federal Code of Obligations – one of the rare instances of the influence of modern civil-law systems in this country.

The second example concerns the rule permit-

31 Compare the majority view in *Silva's Fishing Corporation (Pty) Ltd v Maweza* 1957 (2) SA 256 (A) with the view of the whole court in *Minister van Polisie v Ewels* 1975 (3) SA 590 (A), especially at 596–7.

32 Stratford ACJ in *Dukes v Marthinusen* 1937 AD 12 at 23.

33 *Tobacco Manufacturers' Committee v Jacob Green & Sons* 1953 (3) SA 480 (A).

E F Watermeyer
Chief Justice 1943–1950

A v d S Centlivres
Chief Justice 1950–1957

ting an agent to act for an undisclosed principal. The doctrine, stated the Appellate Division in a case decided a decade ago,[34] had apparently not formed part of the Roman-Dutch law but had been imported from England. Still, it had been adopted in South Africa and accepted by our courts in many decisions, going back to 1869. In two cases the Appellate Division had accepted it without argument. Whatever its inconsistency with basic principles of contract, the doctrine had not produced inequitable results. Furthermore, to reject it now would foil legitimate commercial expectations. Thus it had to be accepted as part of our law, but because of its doubtful origin, it should be confined to one undisclosed principal.

It can happen that an English legal figure has become so embedded in the South African social structure that it is unthinkable to say that it simply does not exist in the eyes of the law. Then the courts may succumb to the temptation to fit it with a Roman-Dutch legal garb. This, it seems, is what happened to the trust. Senator Sammy Marks once said to Sir Abe Bailey, 'You think you are putting on the coat of Rhodes, but let me tell you, I know something about secondhand clothes, and the coat doesn't fit'. The same may hold for our courts and the trust. If it is *inter vivos* (between living persons), it is regarded as a *stipulatio alteri* (contract for the benefit of a third person); if it is a testamentary, it is regarded (at least by some judges) as a fideicommissum. Neither view seems sound.

In a legal branch or two the judges have frequently dwelt on the importance of remaining true to 'curial practice'. In particular, with the specific

34 *Cullinan v Noordkaaplandse Aartappelkernmoerkwekers Ko-operasie Bpk* 1972 (1) SA 761 (A).

N J de Wet
Chief Justice 1939–1943

crimes the Bench is inclined to say that their nature and scope have been settled by the practice of the courts, and cannot now be changed so as to conform to Roman-Dutch authority, no matter that the practice was largely a result of the influence of English law.[35]

The attitude of the judiciary is a pragmatic one. The decision whether or not to restore a rule of the classical Roman-Dutch law may, to a degree, turn on what is regarded as its appropriateness in modern times. It is hard to think, for instance, that the Appellate Division would hold that there can be nothing against public policy in an agreement in restraint of trade, as provincial and local divisions, taking a line from the law of England, have for decades held to the contrary; and yet in eighteenth-century Holland there was nothing wrong with such an agreement. Again, it is surely too late to eliminate the impact English law has had in determining the vicarious liability of a master for the wrongful acts of his servant.

At the risk of oversimplification, it may be said that the broad tendency of the highest court, one that has become particularly noticeable in the last thirty years or so, in modifying or developing substantive law has been to reflect contemporary social and moral values. In criminal law, the stricter attitude taken to the meaning of *mens rea* has pulled back the boundaries of the area demarcated by the principle that only blameworthy violations of the law are punishable. In contract, there is perceivable a greater concern for fairness even at the cost of cutting into the maxim *pacta sunt servanda* (meaning, in essence, agreements must be adhered to). In delict, the judiciary has on occassion extended the scope of the Aquilian action, which has meant leaning in favour of the injured party.

Occasionally the Appellate Division, in its attempts to keep Roman-Dutch law pulsating with life, will find it possible to expound a legal rule in suitable form by extending a trend already discernible in the classical Roman-Dutch law. Thus the virtual resurrection by it in 1962[36] of the doctrine of *causae continentia* (continuity or connection of cause) in the law of civil jurisdiction and the slotting of it, with adaptations, into the present jurisdictional rules.

Of far greater significance has been the determination of our highest court to give effect to what it holds to be the fundamental principle of the common law, that *actus non facit reum nisi mens sit rea*, expressed pithily as 'geen straf sonder skuld'. The swing to the subjective test for criminal intention had in fact been accepted in 1955;[37] but it took time for the court to insist on compliance with the basic

35 For instance, *Afrikaanse Pers-publikasie (Edms) Bpk v Mbeki* 1964 (4) SA 618 (A) at 627–8 (scope of contempt of court); *R v Badenhorst* 1960 (3) SA 563 (A) (housebreaking with intent to commit a crime).

36 *Roberts Construction Co Ltd v Willcox Bros (Pty) Ltd* 1962 (4) SA 326 (A).

37 In *R v Nsele* 1955 (2) SA 145 (A).

requirement of criminal liability that the accused had the requisite *mens rea* (unlawful mental state) for the very crime charged, and in particular for it to hold that for murder the *mens rea* is *dolus* (intention) and for culpable homicide *culpa* (negligence). *En route* the Appellate Division decisively rejected a doctrine, born in the Middle Ages, popularly (or unpopularly) known by the first four words of the appropriate Latin expression, *versari in re illicita.* It was to the effect that he who committed an unlawful act was criminally liable for all the consequences. If, say, I unlawfully shot at a guinea-fowl lurking in the bushes, and killed a passer-by, I would be guilty of murder even though I did not have the necessary *mens rea* for that crime. The doctrine had not really formed part of the Roman-Dutch law, but it had been applied by courts in South Africa quite frequently. The Appellate Division delivered it a grievous blow in 1961[38] and the *coup de grâce* four years later.[39]

At one stage it appeared as if the *versari* rule had been resuscitated where the accused had committed the act when in a state of self-induced intoxication or subjection to some other drug, albeit he did not deliberately imbibe the drink or take the drug in order to commit the crime; but now the highest court has ruled that this is no exception to the fundamental principle.[40] The problem is a vexed one throughout the world, as the Chief Justice, Mr Justice Rumpff, pointed out in the latest decision, where he adverted to the possibility that Parliament may wish to penalize voluntary drunkenness or subjection to another drug that gives rise to an unlawful deed. In many countries abroad, the comment may be added, there has been considerable concern over the prospect of a 'drunkard's charter' if self-induced intoxication were to be a defence.

Recently[41] the court, in a striking decision, went back even to the principles of Roman law, and in so doing may have performed reconstructive surgery on an important body of law. It appears to have held that every contract is subject to *bona fides* (good faith), implied by law, not being a matter of fact. The scope of good faith, it stated, is not static; it may vary with the times. Our courts, it was held, have a wide jurisdiction to read a term into a contract where justice so requires. The impression to be gained from the judgment is that our law of contract may have entered a new age, in which, at least initially, there may be a hazy zone in legal relations, a tribute exacted from certainty by equity.

On the other hand, it is open to the Appellate Division to jettison a supposed rule of Roman-Dutch law that had been applied by provincial and local divisions, on the ground that the old authorities were in error and the rule is an anachronism. This happened in 1980 in a remarkable decision.[42] Since 1889[43] it has been assumed by various courts, though probably only in *obiter dicta* (remarks made in passing) and not as *ratio decidendi*, and also by a number of writers on our law, that a lessor of premises, in the absence of a cancellation clause, had no right to rescind the lease unless the lessee was two years in arrears with the payment of his rent. But Mr Justice Joubert, delivering the first judgment of the Appellate Division on the question, after an extensive investigation of Roman law and the writings of the jurists of the Middle Ages, of French jurists of the sixteenth and seventeenth centuries and the works of Roman-Dutch authorities, concluded that those among the latter who supported the rule had based themselves on a mistaken view of the Roman law. The so-called rule had become a superfluous historical legal anachronism that could no longer fulfil any useful function in our law and so should not be applied. When the lessee is in arrear with his rent, it was held, the lessor has the right, after sufficient and reasonable notice to the lessee, to cancel the lease.

38 *S v Van der Mescht* 1962 (1) SA 521 (A).
39 *S v Bernardus* 1965 (3) SA 287 (A).
40 Compare *S v Johnson* 1969 (1) SA 201 (A) with *S v Chretien* 1981 (1) SA 1097 (A).
41 *Tuckers Land and Development Corporation v Hovis* 1980 (1) SA 645 (A).
42 *Goldberg v Buytendag Boerdery Beleggings (Edms) Bpk* 1980 (4) SA 775 (A).
43 Starting with *Birkett v Woodroffe and Marais* (1889) 3 SAR 102 at 105 and *Johns v Colonial Government* (1889) 15 SC 245 at 250.

Title pages of sources of law in the appellate court library, Bloemfontein.

INLEYDINGE
Tot de Hollandſche
RECHTS-GELEERTHEYT,
Beſchreven by
HUGO DE GROOT.
Beveſtigt
Met Placaten, Hand-Veſten, oude Herkomen, Rechten, &c. &c.
midsgaders eenige byvoegſels en aenmerkingen op de zelve,
DOOR
Mr. SIMON van GROENEWEGEN van der MADE.
Als mede R. HOGERBEETS, van het aenleggen en volvoeren der Proceſſen, voor de reſpective Hoven van Holland.
En het VERSTERF-RECHT van Hollandt.
Beyde met GROENEWEGENS Aenmerkingen.
Met een GROOT REGISTER voorzien.
Deeze Druk is merkelyk verbeetert, volgens het berigt aan den Leezer.
t'AMSTELDAM,
By JAN BOOM,
M. D. CC. XXXVIII.

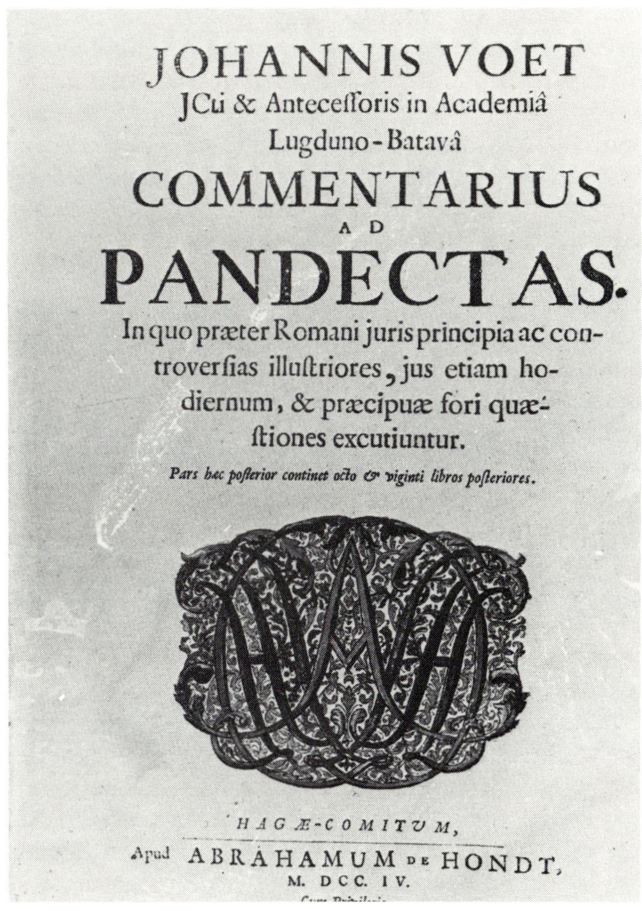

JOHANNIS VOET
JCti & Anteceſſoris in Academiâ
Lugduno-Batavâ
COMMENTARIUS
AD
PANDECTAS.
In quo præter Romani juris principia ac controverſias illuſtriores, jus etiam hodiernum, & præcipuæ fori quæſtiones excutiuntur.
Pars hæc poſterior continet octo & viginti libros poſteriores.
HAGÆ-COMITUM,
Apud ABRAHAMUM DE HONDT,
M. DCC. IV.

The converse can happen: the court can dredge from the old authorities a rule overlooked by our judges and legal writers. A prime illustration is afforded by the decision of the Appellate Division in *LTA Engineering Co Ltd v Seacat Investments (Pty) Ltd*.[44] The effect of the decision is that if a creditor fraudulently cedes his rights in order to defeat the *contra* claim of his debtor, his machination will be of no avail; the *contra* claim may be set up against the cessionary, whose action will be stayed until the *contra* claim against the cedent has been decided. The holding manifestly produces an equitable situation, one that judges in the past had urged be created by legislation.

The court in the *LTA* case held that the rule on which it based its decision, a rule that dated back to the Roman law, had not been abrogated by disuse merely because its existence had been overlooked for a comparatively short part of its long life.

The doctrine of abrogation by disuse, it should be pointed out, permits the abandonment of an ancient legal rule. It applies not only to the common law but also to enactments passed before the British occupation of the particular territory, provided desuetude had taken place before Union in 1910. The particular legal rule must have been out

44 1974 (1) SA 747 (A).

of use for a long time and be discordant with present-day sentiment. It is a doctrine that is seldom invoked. The stock illustration of its employment relates to changing attitudes to adultery. In 1914 it was held that the crime of adultery had become abrogated by disuse; and five years later the subsidiary penalties, such as the inability of the adulterers to marry or inherit from each other, were also found to have come to an end for that reason.[45]

Occasionally the legislator aids the courts in restoring the common law or at least its basic outlook. Two instances stand out. The Prescription Act 1943 (itself founded on earlier South African legislation) was an admixture of the 'weak extinctive prescription' of English law (limitation of actions) and the Roman-Dutch 'strong prescription' that wipes out a debt. The new Prescription Act of 1969, the wording of which flowed from the skilled hand of Professor J C de Wet, plumps for a strong extinctive prescription, going back in essence to Roman-Dutch principles but also invoking aid from certain modern civil-law systems for some of the detailed rules. The other instance is the repeal by the Second General Law Amendment Act 1974 of masters and servants enactments passed in the Cape, Natal, Orange Free State and Transvaal before Union, the earliest going back to 1841; so the common law was restored.

If a question arises before a court in which there does not appear to be any applicable Roman-Dutch authority, the gap will have to be filled by judicial law-making. Legal issues cannot be left in the air. The judiciary acknowledges that, in a secondary sense, it does make law.[46] It does not regard itself as having a blank sheet on which to write its unrestrained will; it fashions a rule within the fabric of the existing law, taking into account, as it considers fit, desiderata such as apt analogies, logic, justice, equity, social utility and trends, public and individual interests, current moral standards, common sense, equality, freedom of the individual, good international relations and persuasive material from other legal systems and legal writers of repute. Courts of law are never beyond the age of legal childbearing, but they wish to produce legitimate offspring.

The law reports are shot through with decided cases that in reality change the law or make new law. For instance, in 1979 the Chief Justice, Mr Justice Rumpff, speaking for the Appellate Division,[47] said that the 'birthpangs' of a right of action in delict to recover compensation for pure economic loss had been endured long enough; the time had come, even by 'Caesarian section' ('keisersnee'), to bring the child into the world. In 1973 the Appellate Division extended the legal remedies for latent defects in the thing sold (aedilitian relief) to incorporeals, such as shares: 'the current climate of opinion is propitious and receptive to such extension by our courts.'[48] Modern South African law, the same tribunal held in 1975, had moved away from the narrow approach of classical Roman-Dutch law to the question whether there could be theft of an incorporeal.[49] At this stage in our legal development, the Appellate Division stated in 1977,[50] in the course of reversing the generally applicable rule, it must be accepted that the cliché that 'every person is presumed to know the law' has no reason for existence in criminal law, and the view that 'ignorance of the law is no excuse' is not legally applicable in the light of the present-day concept of *mens rea*. In short, *mens rea* – *dolus* or *culpa* – must exist in relation to the law as it must in relation to the facts. The decision goes far – perhaps too far. The court endorsed the views of a number of South African legal writers, and in so doing appears in the event to have given

45 *Green v Fitzgerald* 1914 AD 88; *Estate Heinamann v Heinamann* 1919 AD 99.

46 See, for instance, *Sachs v Dönges NO* 1950 (2) SA 265 (A) at 312; *Daniels v Daniels* 1958 (1) SA 513 (A) at 522; *Kroonstad Westelike Boere-Ko-operatiewe Vereniging Bpk v Botha* 1964 (3) SA 561 (A) at 572; *Government of the Republic of South Africa v Ngubane* 1972 (2) SA 601 (A) at 605.

47 In *Administrateur, Natal v Trust Bank van Afrika Bpk* 1979 (3) SA 824 (A) at 831.

48 *Phame (Pty) Ltd v Paizes* 1973 (3) SA 397 (A) at 418, per Holmes JA.

49 *S v Graham* 1975 (3) SA 569 (A) at 576, per Holmes JA.

50 *S v De Blom* 1977 (3) SA 513 (A).

expression to a theory once, but no longer, supported in Germany. In that country, today, ignorance of the law is a defence only if it is unavoidable; otherwise it is simply an extenuating circumstance. Sir Frederick Pollock, one brings to mind, once spoke of the difficulty of striking 'a just middle way between excess of valour and excess of caution'.[51]

The attitude of our courts to foreign precedents is instructive. The most telling statement is that of Mr Justice L C Steyn in 1964, when he was Chief Justice.[52] South African courts are never bound by English decisions, he insisted; nor may even the Appellate Division replace our common law with that of another country – only Parliament can do so. But reference to or consideration of the principles of the law of another country with a related legal system could be a particularly valuable means of obtaining clarity on the best application, adaptation and development of our own principles. This dictum – and there are others in the same vein – makes some play of the benefit to be gained from tapping modern Continental legal systems, with their roots, like those of South African law, in the historical soil of Roman law. Particularly, some jurists believe, is this so with private law and criminal law. English law could more readily be consulted for commercial and procedural law, because of its immense influence in South Africa in these branches. And no one has ever questioned the attitude for so long adopted by our judges,[53] that in the interpretation of a statutory provision modelled on one of England, the decisions of the courts of that country are of considerable persuasive force, except where based on legal principles alien to our system of law.

South African academic writers have traditionally gone for guidance to the law of European countries as well as that of England. But only in the past two decades or so have our judges shown a tendency to do so at times, and then, as a rule, only to Dutch and German legal authorities. There is much to be advanced in favour of taking a wider sweep for comparative material. Nevertheless, a review of recent decisions of our courts has shown the continued predominance of reference to the Anglo-American system of private law.[54]

As will be apparent even from the few decisions that have been cited in this article,[55] there can be no doubt that our courts, in deciding disputed questions of law, have to an ever-increasing extent found assistance in the legal writings of South African scholars of repute. Some legal authors are judges or practitioners, but most are academics. For so small a country, the output and standard of publications on the law have been truly remarkable. In particular has this been so since the last war, after which the number of law schools and teachers swelled and legal education became more scientific and critical in tone.

Parliament and changes in the substantive law

Legal rights and duties, the subject-matter of the substantive law, have been affected by a good deal of legislation. The need to satisfy felt social and economic needs; determination to carry out the policy of the government of the day; the inability of the courts to deal adequately with necessary legal development, because they feel that their hands have been tied by precedent, or because they are unable to fashion detailed rules in one fell

51 'Judicial Caution and Valour' (1929) 45 *Law Quarterly Review* 293 at 296.

52 In *Trust Bank van Afrika Bpk v Eksteen* 1964 (3) SA 402 (A) at 410–11. The judgment was concurred in by three of the four other judges of appeal who sat in the case. See also the judgment of Mr Justice Holmes in *Government of the Republic of South Africa v Ngubane* 1972 (2) SA 601 (A) at 609.

53 For instance, in *Estate Wege v Strauss* 1932 AD 76.

54 In the South African Law Reports for 1979, in ninety-nine of the 684 reported cases source material from Anglo-American legal systems was used, in thirty-five from the Roman and Roman-Dutch legal systems, and in only five from Continental legal systems. See 1979 *Annual Survey of South African Law* 538–9.

55 See, in particular, *Phame (Pty) Ltd v Paizes* 1973 (3) SA 397 (A) at 420–1, where the court recorded its appreciation of the assistance derived from modern textbooks and articles in South African legal journals, in which 'many, divergent and challenging' points of view had been expressed; and *Sperling v Sperling* 1975 (3) SA 707 (A), which raised 'a novel and interesting point of Private International Law' (at 711).

swoop or because the episodic nature of litigation results in an issue not coming before the judiciary for decision: for these and other reasons Acts of Parliament are not infrequently passed, and regulations and other types of delegated legislation are continually being framed, which make or change rules of substantive law.

The faces of the Statute Book and its acolyte, the collectivity of subordinate legislation, have altered almost beyond recognition. To some onlookers it seems to be a change from the innocence and freedom of youth to the cynicism, ailments and neuroses of advanced middle age; to others, a change from the selfishness and lack of concern for one's fellows of adolescence to the wisdom and sense of duty to the community of maturity. As in all relatively advanced societies, there has been an expression of social, economic, moral and racial beliefs and values by Parliament and subordinate legislatures, which has greatly affected the rights and duties of individuals. Labour laws to protect the worker; legislation encroaching on the so-called freedom of contract, so as to restrain leonine agreements; concessions to the claims of consumerism; credit regulation and usury laws; control of misuse of the company, that fictitious entity with neither body to kick nor soul to damn; relief for tenants; the protection of children; the easy untying of the bonds of a broken marriage; the advancement, painfully slow, in the status of wives and recognition of their equity in the property of the family: these are but some of the major changes in the body of enactments.

A number of the statutes have already been alluded to, for they also ironed out inter-provincial differences in legislation. Thus, in the law of persons and family relations, we saw how a surviving spouse was enabled to marry the sibling, or more distant collateral relation, of the deceased spouse. Some of the other major statutory changes in this branch of the law will now be mentioned.

In 1935 the Marriage Law Amendment Act raised the age of marriage of males from 14 to 18 years and of females from 12 to 16 years. The Marriage Amendment Act 1970 reduced the latter to 15 years.

In 1949 the Prohibition of Mixed Marriages Act made a marriage between a White and a Non-White void.

Until 1935 the grounds of divorce remained those of the common law, which were based on fault: adultery and malicious desertion (which may have included a sentence of death or life imprisonment for a crime). Then, by the Divorce Laws Amendment Act 1935, two new grounds were created, the first of which was not based on fault of any sort: seven years' incurable insanity, and imprisonment for five years after a declaration of habitual criminality. A radical change took place in 1979, when our law of divorce crawled out of the woodwork. In essence the Divorce Act of that year substituted the irretrievable breakdown of the marriage for matrimonial offence as the principal ground of divorce. The minor grounds are incurable insanity of the one spouse for two years, or his or her continuous unconsciousness for six months without reasonable prospect of regaining consciousness; both give relief to the unfortunate man or woman whose marriage has really collapsed because the partner is stricken with permanent mental illness or has become, through accident or illness, a human 'vegetable'.

In the past the great majority of proceedings for divorce based on malicious desertion had been a charade, and everyone involved in them knew this. The new law follows the general trend of the West, that divorce is in truth a pronouncement of the death of the union and the defeat of both partners to it. The acceptance by Parliament of the new dispensation was in no small measure due to the unremitting labour of the Law Commission, which had drafted the Bill. The Act has one serious defect, however: if the marriage is by antenuptial contract, that is, the parties are married out of community of property, the court has no general power, as it has in English law, to redistribute property between them. No matter how large the award of periodical maintenance to her be, it cannot make good the true economic value of the wife's contribution to the marriage.

1979 saw another, if minor, piece of legislative divorce law reform. This was the Dissolution of

Marriages on Presumption of Death Act. Up to then an order of court presuming the death of a spouse related only to the administration of his or her estate. Should the other spouse have subsequently remarried and it turned out that the one whose death was presumed was then alive, the second marriage would be void. If, like Enoch Arden, after long years the supposed deceased came home again, he or she could obtain an order of divorce on the ground of adultery. The Act of 1979, following the solution of English law, permits the spouse of the person presumed dead to obtain an order from the court dissolving the marriage.

Reform of the law of matrimonial property has been a perennial and ubiquitous problem. At common law in South Africa a marriage without an antenuptial contract resulted in community of property (to the advantage of the woman if, as is mostly the case, the man made a financial go of things; otherwise very prejudicial to her); but it vested the marital power in the man, which meant that his wife was virtually a minor under his guardianship. If, as became the practice with people of some substance, the parties entered into an antenuptial contract, the invariable result was that both the marital power and community were excluded; and since, as a rule, it is the man who makes the money and the woman who joins what the economists call the most underpaid of all occupations, that of housewife, good fortune shines on the one and not on the other; which to many observers has seemed inequitable, for marriage should really be a partnership and the woman should as of right participate in the acquisitions of the man. Many states of the Western world eventually stumbled on the ridiculously simple answer to the problem in principle: independence of each spouse on marriage, and the sharing of the gains when the marriage ends; community of acquests or, if you like, ultimate profit-sharing. That is what our Law Commission proposes in its tentative Matrimonial Property Bill.[56] A marriage by antenuptial contract excluding community of property and of profit and loss will, unless the antenuptial contract expressly provides otherwise, be subject to the regime of deferred sharing of accruals; where the marriage is in community, the spouses will have equal powers of administration; and the marital power of the husband will vanish from all marriages. The Bill is being closely examined. Up to the present, reform of matrimonial property law in this country has been anything but radical; it has done little more than paste some fancy wallpaper over ever-widening cracks in the structure. The Matrimonial Affairs Act 1953 (revamped slightly in 1962 and 1966) gave a wife married without antenuptial contract a mite of independent legal capacity; enabled her to protect immovable property brought by her into the marriage, or acquired from her out of earnings or by gift or inheritance, against alienation or mortgaging by her husband; allowed her control over her earnings and savings; and increased her rights of guardianship of children. The Act also empowered a court granting a divorce to make a maintenance order against a guilty spouse.

The Suretyship Amendment Act 1971 consigned to oblivion two benefits, dating back respectively to AD 46 and AD 556, called the *Senatusconsultum Velleianum* and the *Authentica si qua mulier,* under which, save in a few exceptional cases, a woman who had not renounced those benefits could avoid liability on a suretyship or other act of intercession. Few tears, if any, were shed at the disappearance of what Mr Justice Van den Heever had splendidly called[57] 'one of the incongruities of this inconsequent age . . . a recognized anomaly, a fossil', enabling women (as he ironically put it) 'in their private affairs to invoke a defence based on their innate fecklessness and incapacity'.

But hark at two attempted reforms that have failed. The first, an endeavour in 1953 to add another *'Hic jacet'* in the churchyard where lie outmoded rules of law, was spurned by the House of Assembly: it was to be a gravestone to mark the burial of the 'prohibition' on donations (other than

56 Published in *Government Gazette* 6740 of 23 November 1979 p 12.

57 *Van Rensburg v Minnie* 1942 OPD 257 at 259.

petty ones) between spouses. The principal reason for the rejection was the belief that the rule acts as a damper on fraud of creditors; but the insolvency law should do this. A subsidiary reason, which had been advanced even in Roman law, was that a spouse could try to buy marital happiness. As the old saying goes, in a marriage there is one who loves and one who is loved. But this ground is not convincing in these enlightened days.

The second effort took place in 1969. In the 1870s[58] the Cape had abolished the legitimate portion of the Roman-Dutch law, under which children, parents and brothers and sisters of a deceased obtained certain fractions of the portions of the estate they would have got on intestacy, albeit there was a will under which they were disherited. The rest of the country followed suit.[59] 'Freedom of testation' was a siren during the springtide of economic individualism. After all, minor children, the courts had held (on a misreading of old authority[60]), would have a claim for maintenance against the estate of the testator; and the surviving spouse had half of the common estate in the ordinary marriage. But rapidly the well-to-do tended to marry with antenuptial contract. Yet when England took a new stance and passed a statute in 1938 empowering the court to make reasonable provision for the surviving or a former spouse and for dependants, our legislature took no notice; nor did it go back to some sort of legitimate portion, favoured by so many Continental legal systems. Illicit passion for a paramour, caprice, or any whim not dictated by insanity continued to permit a person to escape his moral obligations to those close to him, and to society. In 1969 a Family Maintenance Bill, modelled on the then English enactment (today it is the comprehensive Inheritance (Provision for Family and Dependants) Act 1975), was rejected by a select committee of the House of Assembly. It permitted payment of maintenance from a deceased estate to a dependant, the definition covering a surviving spouse as well as close blood relations. The committee was moved principally by the fallacious call of freedom of testation. So the Republic has the dubious distinction of being alone in the civilized world without a legitimate portion or a dependants' relief law.

Strangely enough, in 1965 Parliament had passed a statute that did restrain the tyranny of the dead hand: the Immovable Property (Removal or Modification of Restrictions) Act. Before Union, whatever vestiges of ancient restrictions in tying up property there might have been had been removed; and a person by will or other instrument (such as a trust *inter vivos)* could control all fellow beings for ever. In particular, a fideicommissum (a disposition of a thing to a beneficiary (the fiduciary) subject to the provision that he, either absolutely or on the fulfilment of a condition, pass it, or a part of it, to another beneficiary (the fideicommissary)) was subject to no limitation. (A fideicommissum is normally created by a will, but it may be created by act *inter vivos.)* One will, made by optimists, provided that certain land could not be transferred to anyone other than an heir of the blood of the testators to the ninety-ninth generation.[61] True, by legislation going back to 1916 the courts had been empowered to remove restrictions on land on the ground of the shares of beneficiaries being too small for beneficial use, or the value of the property being affected by unforeseen circumstances; but the proceeds of the sale were still governed by the will or other instrument. The 1965 statute expanded the power of the courts to cover the interests of the public or beneficiaries; and – this being of far greater significance – it limited fideicommissa (and other restrictions on alienation) extending to immovable property to two successive fideicommissary substitutions or beneficiaries. For example, a clause in a will stating 'I bequeath my farm to A for life and on A's death to B for life and on B's death to C' would be quite in order; but if it went on to say 'and on C's death to D', these words would be

58 By the Law of Inheritance Amendment Act 26 of 1873 and the Succession Act 23 of 1874.

59 Law 7 of 1885 (N) s 1; Law Book of 1902 (O) ch 92 s 3; Administration of Estates Proc 28 of 1902 (T) s 128.

60 See *Glazer v Glazer NO* 1963 (4) SA 694 (A) at 706.

61 See *Ex parte Barnard* 1929 TPD 276.

inoperative, and C would take the farm free of any burden. Thus, to a degree, Parliament has accepted the truth of the famous words of Thomas Jefferson: it is 'self-evident that the earth belongs in usufruct to the living, that the dead have neither powers nor rights over it'.

Two other legislative changes to the law of succession call for mention. The first concerns the right of succession of a widow or widower whose spouse died without leaving a will. At common law there was no right at all. Presumably it was felt in the eighteenth century that as the great majority of marriages were in community of property, the half share in the joint estate that came to her or him sufficed. But with the growing popularity of antenuptial contracts, our legislature had to intervene. The Succession Act 1934 dealt with the matter comprehensively. In essence, the survivor never gets less than a child's share.

The second statute was the Wills Act 1953. At common law the age for making a will was 14 years for boys and 12 for girls. In 1868 Natal had fixed the age for both sexes at 21 years;[62] the rest of the country abided by the common law. The Wills Act fixed the age at 16 for both males and females. The minimum age of a witness was made 14 years, the position by statute in all provinces other than Natal. The Act clarified the requirements of the standard 'underhand' will of England, signed by the testator and two witnesses, that had long since been accepted in all provinces; and it abolished the notarial will and all privileged wills other than the soldier's will, which simply has to be in writing.

The exhortation to freedom of action is found in the law of contract too. There was a time when South African judges were wont to speak in such terms as the 'spirit of modern jurisprudence is in favour of the liberty of contract'[63] and 'contracts when entered into freely and voluntarily shall be held sacred'.[64] But of course in every legal system limitations have always been imposed on the nature and content of legal commercial bargains where the general interest has been thought to take priority over freedom of action of the individual. And in the modern state *laissez faire* has to a considerable extent given way as an ideal to social security. Judges have, understandably enough, been loath to use the common law as a mechanism to interfere with the processes of the market-place or to take an excursion into the territory of economic theory in order to reduce inequality of bargaining power or protect the improvident, foolish or ill-informed against their lack of attributes. The legislature has thus been compelled to intervene to protect and aid the citizen. But not only on this score; also in order to safeguard the economy of the country, for instance, by controlling the granting of credit.

The expression 'freedom of contract' as a child of nineteenth-century liberalism had four qualities, each of which has to an ever-increasing extent been diminished by legislation, particularly since the last war. They were the freedom without state interference to negotiate the terms of a contract and the correlative freedom from having them imposed upon one; the freedom to choose the other party to a contract; the freedom not to contract; and the freedom from having one's contract interfered with. Concurrently, fair-trade and consumer-protection legislation, on such matters as monopolistic practices, usury (beginning with the Usury Act 1926, now replaced by the Limitation and Disclosure of Finance Charges Act 1968), weights and measures, pure foods and drugs, trade coupons and trade descriptions of goods, while mainly (though not invariably) resulting in criminal sanctions and not voiding contracts or provisions of contracts, has had an impact on the contractual scene. These enactments have generally had a salutary economic and social effect, facilitating more rational choice, allowing for greater competition, encouraging the entrepreneur and protecting the honest and scrupulous trader and manufacturer from the excesses of that unattractive creature, *homo oeconomicus*.

There are statutes that require certain clauses, prohibit and void others, and give the debtor cer-

62 Law 2 of 1868 (N) s 6.

63 Per Kotzé JP in *Osry v Hirsch, Loubser & Co* 1922 CPD 531 at 546.

64 Per Innes CJ in *Wells v South African Alumenite Co* 1927 AD 69 at 73.

tain rights no matter what the contract states. Prime examples are the Credit Agreements Act 1980 (replacing the Hire-Purchase Act 1942), the Sale of Land on Instalments Act 1971 and the Insurance Act 1943. Section 37(5) of the Insolvency Act 1936 states that a stipulation in a lease that it will terminate or be varied upon the sequestration of the estate of either party is null and void. Many aspects of the contractual relationship of employer and employee are controlled by complex labour legislation.

Numerous enactments require formalities for the conclusion of a contract, the object being the promotion of certainty, the elimination of fraud and, occasionally, the protection of third persons. For instance (to speak in broad terms), a contract of suretyship must be signed by or on behalf of the surety (the General Law Amendment Act 1956 s 6); a sale of land must be in writing and signed by the parties or their agents acting on their written authority (the Formalities in respect of Contracts of Sale of Land Act 1969); and a long lease (roughly, one for ten years or more) is invalid for more than ten years against a creditor or a successor under onerous title of the lessor (i e one who has given value for the property) unless the lease has been registered against the title deeds or the creditor or successor at the critical time knew of it. The Credit Agreements Act and the Sale of Land on Instalments Act also lay down formalities.

The state has interfered with certain private rights arising out of contract, such as the fixing of rents and the protection from ejectment of the so-called statutory tenant, beginning with legislation in 1920 as a consequence of the housing shortage after the First World War, the present statute being the Rent Control Act 1976.

Parliament has compelled the entering into a contract, as with third-party motor vehicle insurance, initially by the Motor Vehicle Insurance Act 1942, today by the Compulsory Motor Vehicle Insurance Act 1972; a forced sale of the holding of minority shareholders on a take-over, in terms of s 321 of the Companies Act 1973; and a compromise or arrangement imposed on a dissenting creditor under s 311 of the last-mentioned statute.

A fascinating piece of legislation in the sphere of control of contracts, of a character known nowhere else except Norway, is the Price Control Act 1964, which is to be read with the regulations under it. The statute creates administrative control largely through the criminal law. The regulations, among other things, control certain prices and charges, prohibit certain contractual terms, require marks of selling prices of certain goods and control multilevel marketing (pyramid selling) and various aspects of advertising.

The question arises whether, as is the position in many countries, there should be a general statutory provision aimed at eliminating onerous stipulations in contracts. These appear frequently in standard-form contracts, sometimes called, after the French expression, contracts of adhesion, where a party, in a position of monopoly or economic power, such as the supplier of water, electricity, gas or transport, a building society, an insurance company or a master builder, is prepared to contract only on certain terms. There is no true freedom for the other side. Either he agrees or he goes without. Standard-form contracts are not all oppressive, and they hold out the promise of certainty and immediacy of legal terms. But they can be cruel.

As has been pointed out, perhaps the Appellate Division in the *Tuckers Land* case[65] has set in motion the vesting in the judiciary of a general equitable jurisdiction over contracts. As far as legislation is concerned, at present there is only the Conventional Penalties Act 1962. It states that a stipulation for a penalty on breach of contract is enforceable, but that the court may reduce it to an equitable amount if it appears to be out of proportion to the prejudice suffered by the creditor.

The legislature has changed the common-law rules of the law on delict in one very important respect. This took place in 1956, when the Apportionment of Damages Act was passed. Up to then a claim for damages based on negligent conduct

65 *Tuckers Land and Development Corporation v Hovis* 1980 (1) SA 645 (A).

could be countered by a defence of contributory negligence by the plaintiff. This 'all or nothing' principle produced such unfair, indeed bizarre, answers that our courts in desperation took over from England the 'last opportunity' rule: he who had the last opportunity of avoiding the harmful result by the exercise of reasonable care was alone responsible for the damage. But this rule also proved to be a wayward horse. The last opportunity may have been available to the party whose negligence was insignificant compared with that of the other. A realistic and equitable answer was to follow the pattern of the remedial legislation adopted by England in 1945. That is what the 1956 Act did: to apportion damages on the basis of the parties' degrees of fault in relation to the damage sustained and to consign the last-opportunity rule to perdition.

One legislative enactment that has effected a radical change of the common law rule remains to be mentioned. It belongs to the law of property, called by some jurists the law of things. Its name is the Sectional Titles Act 1971. At common law the principle is that whatever is built on to land accedes to the land; in other words, the ownership of land comprehends all buildings on it. Ownership of flats or other portions of buildings was not possible according to Roman-Dutch law. In the past, all that could be done was for land to be vested in a company and a shareholder to be given a right to occupy a particular flat or other portion of the building. The Act of 1971 allows for the division of a building into sections, each of which can become the property of a different owner, with common property (which includes the land) being owned jointly in undivided shares. So was introduced into the law the concept of horizontal division of ownership.

Sufficient has surely been said in appreciation of the value of our heritage of substantive law, and our loyalty to it. But loyalty does not connote absence of change. For law is made for man, not man for law. In the words of Ambrose Bierce,

'Yet the Past is the Future of yesterday,
The Future is the Past of tomorrow.
They are one – the knowledge and the dream.'

Crest of the Republic of South Africa

J A van S d'Oliveira BIur (Pret) LLB LLD (SA) Deputy Attorney-General Transvaal

10

THE ADMINISTRATION OF JUSTICE IN SOUTH AFRICA

The legal administration, i e those persons and institutions involved in the application and execution of the law and the judgments of the courts, is no less essential to the administration of justice than is the law and is as much part of our legal heritage as the law itself. For the layman, however, these institutions are associated with the historical, political, and sociological development of the country as a whole, rather than with legal evolution – the field which attracts the jurist.

Space does not permit a background study of all our legal institutions – indeed, the evolution of the administration of justice is, in any event, covered in other chapters of this work. Within the confines of this chapter, which deals with our legal administration, we shall, however, occasionally refer to the roots of our administrative system in the hope that the reader will gain some insight into the colourful history surrounding our institutions and offices.

In his daily life the man in the street constantly comes into contact with facets of the administration of justice – either directly or indirectly. He is aware of the existence of the Minister of Justice; he reads of sensational murder trials in the Supreme Court; he consults an attorney for an antenuptial contract, to draw up a will, or to register his land. Does he, however, understand the connection between the Department of Justice and the courts; is he aware of the hierarchical system within which the courts function; does he understand the functions of the Deeds and Master's Offices? Examples are legion, but we must now proceed to the presentation of the administration of justice in South Africa.

At the vanguard stand the courts and their staff. The other instances follow, with the Department of Justice and, to a lesser extent, the Department of Co-operation and Development, being the agencies which are widely involved. As the constitutional development and the historical background of the South African judicial system are dealt with in chapters 4, 5, 6, 7 and 8 in this book, the emphasis in this chapter will be on the present state of the administration of justice.

1 The courts

Broadly stated, the difference between the various courts is based on jurisdiction and competence. While the jurisdiction of the lower and special courts is statutorily limited to certain causes, to actions of a certain amount or type, to certain crimes and penalties, or as regards area and person, the Supreme Court enjoys wide and original jurisdiction coupled with powers of review and appeal. Although in Europe presiding officers generally bear the appellation of "judges", in South Africa this is a title reserved for the presiding officers of the Supreme Court.

A Lower Courts

I Magistrates' courts

The magistrate's court is the court most intimately involved with the day-to-day life of the man in the street. Traces of the office of magistrate and of the magistrate's court can be seen early in Cape history. In Holland and Batavia, too, one finds traces of the office of "landdrost" – an official whose police duties were emphasized. Between 1682 and 1685 the college of *landdrosts* and *heemraden* came into being. This semi-official body concerned with civil law, was to become the local judicial organ peculiar to the Voortrekkers (see chapters 4, 5, 6 and 7).

A consolidation Act passed in 1917 placed the magistrates' courts of the four provinces on an equal footing and perpetuated the term magistrate. In 1944 a new Act was adopted which (with a few amendments) today still regulates the position. In passing it may be mentioned that in 1957 official recognition was given to the use of the Afrikaans term "landdros" as an equivalent of the term "magistrate".

The current position

The Republic (and South West Africa) is divided into magisterial districts, each under the control of a magistrate to whom certain judicial and administrative duties are entrusted. The primary task of the magistrate and his personnel is to act as presiding officer in the trial of civil and criminal cases in the magistrate's court and to perform the allied administrative duties. In addition, magistrates' offices fulfil a number of agency functions for other government institutions. Further powers and duties are entrusted to the magistrate by legislation. With the exception of Pretoria, the magistrate is the senior government representative in his district. There are today 325 magistrates' offices throughout the country. The Johannesburg magistrate's court is the largest single court, not only in South Africa, but, at least, in the southern hemisphere.

The magistrates' courts fall under the magistrates' section of the Department of Justice and their personnel are officers of that department. In the exercise of his judicial function the magistrate is, however, independent.

The jurisdiction of a magistrate's court is determined by Act 32 of 1944. As regards criminal jurisdiction, the Act provides that persons who commit offences within (or in certain specific instances even outside) a magistrate's district, may be tried by the court of that district. The court exercises jurisdiction over all crimes except treason, murder and rape. Unless otherwise stipulated, its penal jurisdiction is limited to the following: twelve months' imprisonment, a fine not exceeding R1 000, and as regards corporal punishment, corporal punishment with a cane only.

As regards civil jurisdiction the position is more complex. Reduced to basics, it may be stated as follows: in respect of persons, the magistrate's court has jurisdiction not only over persons resident, employed or carrying on business within its district, but also over persons where the entire cause of action arose within its district. As regards cause of action it may be broadly stated that the court does not have jurisdiction if the amount in issue exceeds R1 500, or in certain instances R3 000, except where the parties have expressly consented to jurisdiction in writing. The Act specifically excludes magistrate's court jurisdiction in, *inter alia,* the following cases: marriage, wills, the status of a person, with regard to mental capacity, etc.

2 Regional courts

The court of the regional magistrate with increased penal jurisdiction was established in 1952. Regional districts made up of a number of magisterial districts may be established in terms of the Magistrates' Courts Act. There are at present six regional districts. In 1981 the office of Regional Court President was created, which entailed a magistrate heading a regional district.

A regional court is an exclusively criminal court and has no civil jurisdiction. (A regional magistrate is, however, appointed as additional magistrate for a district for purposes of civil actions.)

A regional court has jurisdiction over all crimes with the exception of treason and murder. Its penal jurisdiction is subject to the following limitations: ten years' imprisonment, a fine not exceeding R10 000, and, as regards corporal punishment, the same provisions as are applicable in the magistrate's court.

3 Courts for Blacks (Tribal law)

The Black population is, of course, also subject to the laws of the land and has full access to the normal courts of the country. During the evolutionary process a conflict was found to exist between the traditional laws and customs of the Blacks on the one hand, and on the other, national law. With the passing of time special courts were set up (or recognized) to deal solely with the adjudication of issues between Blacks in terms of indigenous law and custom.

The present co-existence of national and indigenous law was preceded by a general recognition of traditional law (in so far as it was found not to conflict with civilized legal norms) and the establishment of special courts with a history of their own.

Background

Until 1859 the Cape managed to avoid the problem of national versus indigenous law by administering British Kaffraria in terms of martial law. The subsequent official policy was that only

A sketch of the magistrate's offices at Du Toitspan (now Beaconsfield) by Dr Emil Holub. The sketch was found in the Napistek museum in Prague by Dr Fock of the McGregor museum in Kimberley. A translation of the caption below the sketch reads: "Magistrate's office at Du Toitspan, twelve steps from where my shack, which blew away during a thunderstorm, stood." The magistrate's office is the building in the middle (with flag). The building on the left is a canteen and the one on the right is an attorney's office.

Roman-Dutch law was to be applied although the magistrates continued to apply indigenous law *sub rosa*. The same was true of British Bechuanaland. In Transkei, however, the pattern was different; tribal law was officially recognized from the outset (1879). In 1894 civil appeals in this territory could be heard by the Native Territories Court.

In Natal, particularly under Sir Theophilus Shepstone, tribal law was recognized in so far as it did not conflict with civilized norms. The chiefs were permitted to continue with the exercise of their civil and criminal jurisdiction. In 1875, however, the Native High Court, a court of appeal, and the courts of the (White) Administrators of Native Law were established. The chiefs were stripped of their criminal jurisdiction. In 1894 the appeal court and in 1895 the Native High Court were abolished and their duties were transferred to the Supreme Court. The Native High Court, was, however, reintroduced in 1898.

The initial Transvaal attitude was that Blacks should be subject to national law. Although during the British annexation all courts recognized indigenous law, this was altered in 1881. The state president was appointed supreme chief of the Blacks and was empowered to appoint commissioners. The latter, together with chiefs appointed by the government, were granted jurisdiction over civil causes between Blacks.

In the Orange Free State it was regarded as unnecessary to accord tribal law general recognition.

The magistrate's office in Potchefstroom has been declared a historical monument. The photograph shows President Paul Kruger addressing the burghers in front of the office. The notice "Landdrost-Post-en-Telegraafkantoor" (Magistrate's, Post and Telegraph Office) can still be seen in front of the office today.

This, in broad outline, was the position before the adoption of the Bantu Administration Act in 1927.

The present dispensation

The court system is as follows:

(a) Chiefs' courts

The Minister of Co-operation and Development may empower a captain or chief (recognized or appointed by the State President) or his nominee, to hear and decide civil cases between Blacks which arise from tribal law and custom. The parties may elect to have their case heard before the commissioner's court. There is in any event a right of appeal from the chief's court to the commissioner's court.

(b) Commissioners' courts

These courts are established by the aforesaid minister to try civil cases in which only Blacks are involved. The presiding officer is a commissioner who is a member of the public service (more specifically, of the Department of Co-operation and Development which also administers these courts).

As in the case of the magistrate's court, certain matters are wholly excluded from the jurisdiction of these courts. On the other hand, the same limitations on, e g the amount of an action, do not exist. Generally it may be said that the court exercises jurisdiction in causes where the defendant resides or carries on business within the area of the court, where the cause of action originated in the area, or where the parties consent to jurisdiction in writing.

As regards the problem of the applicable law referred to above, section 11 of the 1927 Act provides that the commissioner may, as he deems fit, decide questions of custom in accordance with traditional law save in so far as such law has been repealed or amended, and subject to the proviso that such law should not conflict with state policy or natural justice. The practice of *lobola,* for example, is not regarded as incompatible with the above.

The commissioner's court is consequently both a court of first instance and a court of appeal (cf 1 above). It also serves as a maintenance court for Blacks. Where a commissioner's court has been established for a certain area, the magistrate in that area has no jurisdiction over civil cases between Blacks.

In addition to its civil jurisdiction the commissioner's court is also endowed with criminal jurisdiction in respect of statutory violations relating to the Black population. The Supreme Court is the appeal and review authority.

(c) Black children's courts

A children's court may be established for the area of a commissioner. Failing the establishment of a separate court, the commissioner's court also serves as the children's court for the territory. A children's court is empowered to hear any application, to make any order or give any decision which a magistrate's or children's court may hear, give or make in terms of the Children's Act. The jurisdiction of the Black children's court is concurrent with that of the latter two courts. Provision is made for appeal to the Black appeal court.

(d) Black appeal courts

In 1928 two appeal courts, and in 1948 an additional court, were established. These courts had jurisdiction extending beyond provincial boundaries. The courts are in Johannesburg, Pietermaritzburg and King William's Town and hear civil appeals from the commissioners' courts. Appointments are made from the ranks of senior commissioners.

Further appeal lies to the Appellate Division of the Supreme Court subject to leave from the Black appeal court and on points of law reserved by that court.

(e) Black divorce courts

These courts, the territorial jurisdiction of which corresponds to that of the appeal courts above, hear cases relating to the nullity of, divorce and judicial separation in marriage between Blacks.

Provision is made for appeal to the Supreme Court.

(f) Homeland courts

The 1971 constitution for the Black Homelands provides that in self-governing territories the existing courts continue to function until altered or dissolved by competent authority. The constitution further provides what maximum powers the Homelands enjoy. Basically these provisions mean that the courts so established may not exceed magistrate's court jurisdiction and that the magistrates' courts as such, are not affected. The Homeland governments have used these powers to establish their magistrates' courts with jurisdiction equal to, and procedures similar to those of the traditional magistrate's court. The judgments of these courts apply only to Blacks.

On independence (as in the case of Transkei, Bophuthatswana and Venda) the administration of justice as a whole is transferred to the state concerned and the magistrates' courts become the lower courts while a Superior Court which takes the place of the Supreme Court is established. The right of appeal to the Appellate Division is, however, retained unless or until the fledgling State creates its own appeal court.

B Superior courts

We may now move on to the next rung in the hierarchy of the courts in our country, and here we shall be concerned principally with the Supreme Court. These courts owe both their existence and present form to the strong English law influence exerted on our legal administration; at the same time, however, internal influences cannot be underestimated.

1 The Supreme Court

From Union to to-day

After Union the existing Supreme Courts became the Provincial Divisions of the Supreme Court of South Africa, while the Eastern Districts, Griqualand West and Witwatersrand courts became local divisions of their respective provincial divisions. The latter retained the original appeal and review jurisdiction which they had previously enjoyed over the lower courts. The judges remained in office, the four colonial chief justices retaining their titles. Their successors, however, would be known as judges president.

At the head of the Supreme Court a central appeal body, the Appellate Division of the Supreme Court (the appeal court) was established. This court will be discussed below.

To date the development in the provincial and local divisions appears as follows: the Transvaal and Natal provincial divisions retained jurisdiction over their respective provinces, while the Witwatersrand and Durban and Coast courts became local divisions of these two provincial divisions respectively; the Eastern Districts court first became a local division of the Cape court, but in 1957 the latter relinquished the area to the Eastern Cape court which became a provincial division. The Eastern Cape division today has a local division of its own (South Eastern Cape division) with its seat in Port Elizabeth. The High Court of South West Africa (established in 1919) became a provincial division, while the Griqualand West local division of the Cape became the Northern Cape provincial division about a decade ago. While the Cape provincial court relinquished territory in two instances the Orange Free State relinquished no jurisdiction. It may further be mentioned that the Transvaal, Natal and Eastern Cape provincial divisions have concurrent jurisdiction in the areas of the Witwatersrand local division, the Durban and Coast local division, and South Eastern Cape division respectively. Judges of the provincial divisions preside over the courts of the local divisions.

Jurisdiction

While the lower courts may correctly be termed "creatures of statute" with limited and clearly defined jurisdiction, the jurisdiction of the Supreme Court is original and unlimited within its respective provincial boundaries. In general terms it may be stated that the Supreme Court exercises jurisdiction over all persons residing or finding them-

Old building of the high court of justice of the South African Republic (ZAR) at the corner of Bureau Lane and Andries Street, Pretoria.

selves within the area of the court, and over all causes of action and crimes originating or committed within its territory. To this may be added all other matters of which it may take cognizance in terms of legislation. The Supreme Court has exclusive jurisdiction over, for example, all matrimonial matters originating from a civil marriage. A provincial division is further empowered to hear appeals from a lower court and to review the proceedings of lower courts and of administrative bodies.

As regards criminal matters, the provincial and local divisions have jurisdiction over all crimes committed within their areas. In practice murder, treason and very serious cases are brought before the Supreme Court. The penal jurisdiction of the Supreme Court is generally unlimited and includes, for example, life imprisonment and the death penalty.

2 Special courts

At this point brief mention should be made of the superior courts other than the Supreme Court. The following specialized courts exist:

(a) In the first place, the *Water Court* established in 1912. In terms of section 34 of the Water Act 1956 there are today six water courts (seven if one

The new magistrate's office in Klerksdorp which was inaugurated in 1972.

includes South West Africa) with areas of jurisdiction corresponding roughly to those of the provincial and local divisions of the Supreme Court. A water court is presided over by a judge of the Supreme Court assisted, if he so wishes, by two or three assessors whom he may appoint.

The court hears and decides any matter arising from or in connection with the use or appropriation of water from a *public* stream or of underground water. Unless the parties otherwise consent, the court has exclusive jurisdiction. Appeal lies to the Appellate Division unless the parties agree that the finding of the court will be final.

(b) In the second place, there is the *Special Income Tax Court* (established in 1914) which has since 1949 been presided over by a judge of the Supreme Court.

This court hears appeals from all persons dissatisfied with a ruling of the Commissioner for Inland Revenue with regard to their taxation (or estate duty, etc). Contrary to practice in the other courts, the tax court hears the complaint from one side only, viz that of the taxpayer. The court is a type of review court which means that neither the court nor the commissioner is bound by earlier decisions. Like the magistrate's court, this court is a "creature of statute" without the inherent powers of the Supreme Court. The procedures and practices applied are those of the magistrate's court. The special court, which is established by the State President, consists of a judge of the Supreme Court, an accountant (of at least ten years' standing) and a representative of commerce. In matters relating to the mining industry the third member may be a mining engineer if the applicant so desires. An applicant need not have legal representation but may act directly or through an agent. Strict confidence is maintained. Provision is made for appeal to the provincial division, or, with the consent of the president of the court, directly to the Appellate Division.

(c) In the third place, the State President may by

The main entrance of the Johannesburg magistrate's office. The building which was completed in the 1930's, covers four street blocks. It comprises 44 court rooms, 384 offices and 6,7 kilometres of passage. The building is decorated with sculptures and murals.

proclamation constitute a *Special Court in terms of the Maintenance and Promotion of Competition Act* (the successor to legislation designed to control monopolistic conditions).

The function of this court is to hear appeals from the decisions of the minister and actions against persons who have applied restrictive commercial practices. The court, which may be constituted for the entire Republic or for a specific area, comprises a judge of the Supreme Court (who acts as president of the court) and two other members, experts in the field of economy and the industrial, commercial or financial fields. The findings of the special court are not subject to appeal or review by a court of law.

(d) In the fourth place is the *Court of the Commissioner of Patents*. In terms of the Patents Act, the judge president of the Transvaal provincial division appoints two or more judges or acting judges as commissioner(s) of patents. They are endowed with the jurisdiction of a provincial or local division as courts of first instance in cases relating to the infringement, repeal, or granting of or opposition to a patent. The court also hears cases which, had they not been defended, could have served before the Registrar of Patents. It also hears appeals from the decisions of the registrar.

The commissioner has the powers and privileges of a single judge of the Supreme Court, and Supreme Court rules are applied. The commissioner may appoint experts to advise him. A decision or order given by the commissioner has the same effect and is regarded as the equivalent of an order or decision of a single judge of a provincial division of the Supreme Court. Where the parties so agree they may appeal directly to the Appellate Division; failing this, appeal lies to the Supreme Court.

(e) In the fifth place we find the *Court of the Registrar of Trade Marks*. Where an application for the registration of a trade-mark is formally opposed, a trial is held before the registrar. As regards the proceedings before him, the registrar generally enjoys all the powers and capacities of a single judge in a civil action before a provincial division of the Supreme Court. The decision of the registrar may be taken on appeal to the Supreme Court of the area concerned as if it were an appeal against the finding of a single judge. Further appeal to the Appellate Division is possible. Direct appeal (i e without intermediate appeal) to the Appellate Division is permitted where all the parties agree thereto in writing.

3 The Appellate Division

At the head of the country's judicial system stands our highest court, the appeal court or Appellate Division of the Supreme Court of South Africa, with its seat in Bloemfontein. This has not always been our highest court and it has also not always sat in Bloemfontein.

Background

Before Union, provision was made in the Cape for appeal to the High Court in Batavia. During the British occupation the Privy Council in England represented the highest court of appeal for both the Cape and Natal. Eventually this was extended to cover the Transvaal and Orange Free State as well.

From Union until the establishment of the Appellate Division as the highest court within the Union, the Privy Council was retained as the ultimate appellate body. Few cases were, however, taken to the Privy Council for final decision. Our Appellate Division attained full independence only in 1950 when, after a number of unsuccessful attempts, the right of appeal to the Privy Council was abolished.

For interest's sake it may be mentioned that for the first two or three years after Union, the Appellate Division was a circuit court sitting in the various provincial capitals. The first chief justice, Lord De Villiers, was particularly eager for the court to sit in Cape Town. The Orange Free State, however, was jealous of its position – Bloemfontein had, after all, been designated as the seat – and in highly exceptional cases only did the court sit at a place other than Bloemfontein.

Today

The Appellate Division today consists of the chief justice of South Africa and as many judges of appeal as the State President may determine. There are at present fourteen judges of appeal, including the chief justice.

The Appellate Division is not a court of first instance but solely a court of appeal. Subject to what was said above, only matters taken on appeal from the other divisions of the Supreme Court serve before the Appellate Division for final decision. Appellate Division processes, judgments and orders apply and are enforceable throughout the Republic; its orders are enforced in a division as if they were original orders of that division. We may here mention that the *stare decisis* doctrine applies in the Republic, and any and every court in the Republic is bound by the authoritative interpretation of the law by the Appellate Division. (Within a provincial division the lower courts are bound by the decisions of the provincial division concerned, while the latter's views give way before those of the Appellate Division.)

To ensure that the Appellate Division is not overburdened with cases without reasonable hope of success on appeal, the provincial division must grant leave to appeal in all criminal cases. This applies to certain civil cases as well.

Until recently, civil appeals were heard by a bench of five judges; today three judges are sufficient. In criminal appeals there are generally three judges; while in the case of constitutional questions eleven judges of appeal are appointed.

Details with regard to the seats and number of judges serving in the various divisions of the Supreme Court may be summarized as follows (June 1981):

Division	*Seat*	*Number of judges*
Appellate Division	Bloemfontein	Chief justice + 13
Cape Provincial Division	Cape Town	Judge president + 15
Eastern Cape Division	Grahamstown	Judge president + 8
South Eastern Cape Local Division	Port Elizabeth	
Northern Cape Division	Kimberley	Judge president + 2
Natal Provincial Division	Pietermaritzburg	Judge president + 13
Durban and Coast Local Division	Durban	
Orange Free State Provincial Division	Bloemfontein	Judge president + 8
Transvaal Provincial Division	Pretoria	Judge president + 31
Witwatersrand Local Division	Johannesburg	
South West Africa Division	Windhoek	Judge president + 1

(Acting judges appointed periodically – generally for a six-month term – are left out of consideration.)

We must now briefly discuss those persons or officials involved in the courts – on both the judicial and administrative sides.

The magistrate's office at Somerset West which was built in 1897. It has recently been declared a national monument.

II Presiding and other officers

A Presiding officers

1 Judges

Judges are appointed by the State President from the ranks of advocates (more specifically, senior advocates – SC's, formerly QC's). There is a strong tradition limiting appointments to private advocates, although, theoretically, the choice is not limited to advocates or even jurists – the Supreme Court Act speaks only of "suitable persons". In a few instances senior advocates in the service of the State have been appointed; the late Chief Justice L C Steyn, for example, was a government legal adviser. Acting judges are appointed by the Minister of Justice for a specific period.

A judge may be removed from office only by the State President acting on address of the House of Assembly made during the session of Parliament at which a request for the removal of the judge on the grounds of misconduct or incompetence is made. A judge's salary may not be reduced while he holds office.

2 Magistrates

Magistrates and regional magistrates are public service officials (Department of Justice) and as

The new magistrate's building in Durban.

such are subject to the rules and conditions of service of the public service. As we have noted magistrates also perform a number of administrative functions. As regards their judicial functions they are as independent and unfettered as judges are.

Magistrates are appointed by the Minister of Justice. The minimum academic qualification required for appointment as a magistrate is the *diploma iuris,* although preference may be given to persons holding higher qualifications. No person is appointed a regional magistrate unless he complies with the requirements for the *baccalaureus legum* (LLB) degree or the *diploma legum* (or an equivalent or higher qualification). Appointment as regional magistrate is further subject to selection by the advisory council for appointments to regional divisions.

The position of commissioners is similar to that of magistrates except that they are appointed by the Minister of Co-operation and Development; so, too, the Homeland magistrates who are appointed by the Minister of Justice of the Homeland government concerned.

Plan of the old supreme court building, Cape Town, after the completion of the architect Thibault's alterations.

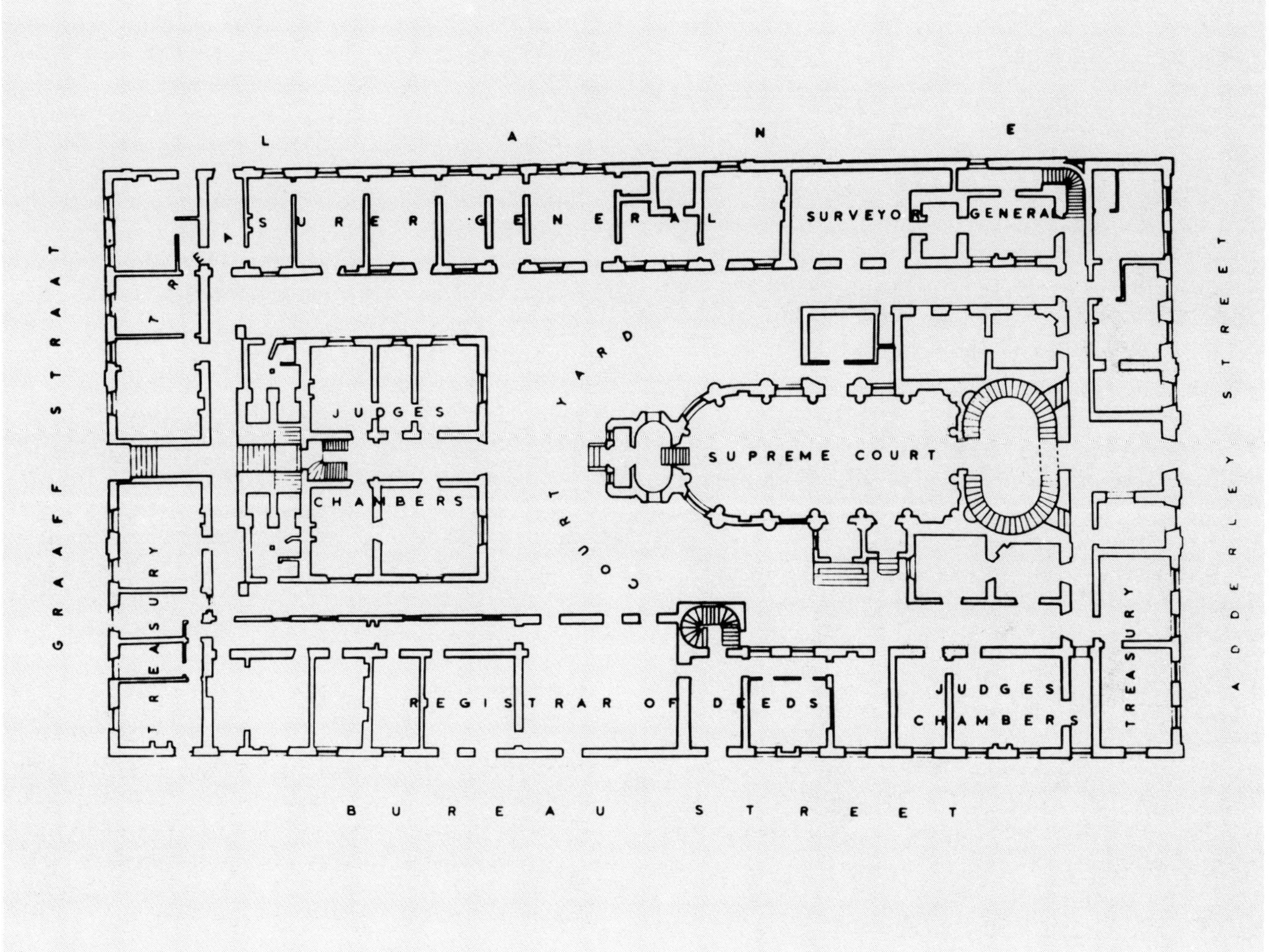

B Court officers

The other officials involved in the administration of justice differ slightly depending on whether the case is criminal or civil. In a criminal case there is always a prosecutor (public prosecutor or state advocate) whose position will be discussed below (*q v* the attorney-general). There is no further difference between the legal practitioners appearing in criminal and civil cases except that attorneys are prohibited from appearing before the Supreme Court if an advocate is available. (The case where a party appears in person is not discussed here.)

1 Legal practitioners

As for the legal profession, the dual-bar system applies: it is divided into advocates and attorneys. There are certain important differences between the two branches. Although both advocates and attorneys are admitted to practice by the Supreme Court, their admission requirements differ (viz LLB for advocates as against LLB or B Proc plus a period of articles for attorneys). While advocates may appear in both the magistrates' and Supreme Courts, attorneys do not, subject to a few exceptions, have access to the Supreme Court. On the other hand, attorneys are consulted directly by the public while an advocate may only act when briefed by an attorney.

An attorney, furthermore, performs a variety of functions: he advises his clients (as opposed to the advocate who gives legal opinions at the request of an attorney); he draws wills, administers estates and acts as representative in various matters. He is generally also a notary who draws notarial deeds (e g antenuptial contracts) and a conveyancer who, *inter alia,* draws deeds for the transfer of fixed property and prepares bonds for registration.

Advocates and attorneys were not always in the position in which they today find themselves; previously in the Cape (and later in the Transvaal as well) attorneys could appear before all the courts. There have, however, also been changes as regards their qualifications; until 1903 only advocates and conveyancers could prepare notarial bonds and deeds of transfer. We shall, however, not trace the subsequent development.

Both professions are today subject to a strict ethical code and members may be struck from the register by the Supreme Court if they are guilty of professional misconduct. Their interests are protected and their codes of conduct upheld by their respective professional bodies, viz the Bar Council and the law societies.

2 Attorneys-general

The attorney-general's section, just like the magistrates' courts, falls under the Department of Justice. There are at present nine attorneys-general in the Republic and South West Africa.

The Criminal Procedure Act provides that the State President appoint an officer, the attorney-general, for every provincial division of the Supreme Court. The attorney-general, who conducts prosecutions for the state, exercises his powers subject to the control and instructions of the Minister of Justice.

The office of the attorney-general (formerly sometimes termed state attorney) features throughout our history (e g in the Cape as the unpopular fiscal). Before Union the attorney-general was *de facto* the Minister of Justice. In the South African Republic he was the "state attorney" who acted as government legal adviser, draftsman and State representative in civil suits.

Since Union the office of attorney-general has been non-political and is held by a public servant concerned solely with prosecutions. The position and duties of an attorney-general are today determined by the Criminal Procedure Act. The attorney-general may appear personally before any court but in practice his power is delegated to his personnel of state advocates (appearing in the superior courts) or suitably qualified officers who act as public prosecutors in the lower courts (including the Homeland and commissioners' courts). The attorney-general has other duties as well: he is, e g, *curator ad litem* to mentally-disturbed persons referred to institutions within his jurisdiction; in terms of the relevant legislation, he is further required to have access to the records and reports on mining and factory accidents – and likewise to the records of inquests.

It may be mentioned that where the attorney-general declines to prosecute on behalf of the state, provision is made for a private individual to institute a prosecution under certain circumstances.

One must clearly distinguish between the attorney-general and the recently established office of *advocate-general.* The latter is appointed by the State President and his position is entrenched in a particular manner. He is not directly involved in the administration of justice. His province is rather the public administration in general and the misapplication of State funds. More particularly, it is his duty to investigate allegations that State funds have been used in a dishonest manner or that persons have been illegally or improperly enriched or have benefited through the act or omission of a public servant. He compiles a report which is submitted to Parliament. If he feels that the commission of an offence is involved, he advises the attorney-general and/or the police accordingly.

A typical court scene. On the left is the state prosecutor and a regional court magistrate is on the bench. On the far right is the interpreter. Interpreters are used in most cases in which Blacks are involved.

3 Administrative officers

(a) Registrar

The Supreme Court Act provides that the Minister of Justice may, with due regard to the provisions governing the public service, appoint registrars or assistant registrars.

The registrar and his staff are entrusted with the administrative duties surrounding the Supreme Court. He oversees, e g, the running of the courts, the receipt of pleadings, the issue of summons, and the recording of judgments. He also acts as taxing officer. There are today eleven offices in the registrar's section of the Department of Justice. Under the same provision, the minister is empowered to appoint persons (who are not public servants) to act as sheriffs or deputy-sheriffs. The sheriff serves all judgments, orders, decisions, summonses, warrants and procedural documents of the division of the supreme court to which he is attached and reports to the court on his duties. He also makes attachments and arrests.

(b) Clerk of the court

This is the magistrate's court equivalent of the registrar. He falls under the magistrate's section and performs his duties under the control of the magistrate for the district concerned.

In addition to his duties as court official, the clerk of the court is also called upon to perform a number of administrative tasks, in particular where agency services are undertaken for other government departments.

Sketches of several court building by the artist Minette van Rooyen. They are (upper left) the Palace of Justice, Pretoria, (upper right) the Appeal Court, Bloemfontein, (lower left) the Supreme Court, Durban, (lower right) the Supreme Court, Cape Town. The sketches were commissioned by the editorial committee of De Rebus – the South African Attorneys' Journal.

In the magistrate's court the equivalent of the Supreme Court sheriff is the messenger of the court, who is appointed by the minister in terms of the Magistrates' Courts Act.

III Other officials in the administration of justice

Although the courts are the most obvious instances of the administration of justice, they are not the only ones. There are other officials and institutions which perform important legal administrative functions.

1 State attorney

The state attorney's section of the Department of Justice was established in 1925 to perform for the state all the work which a private attorney would perform for his client. The state attorney is the public sector's counterpart of the private attorney. State attorneys (and their personnel) qualify and are admitted to practice in the same manner as any other attorney in terms of the Attorneys' Act and enjoy the same rights of appearance. They, however, hold salaried posts in the public service. There are seven state attorney offices in the public service. As far as the definition of their functions is concerned, the State Attorneys Act provides as follows:

> "The functions of the office of the State Attorney shall be the performance in any court or in any part of the Republic of such work on behalf of the Government of the Republic as is by law, practice or custom performed by attorneys, notaries and conveyancers."

2 State law adviser

This section of the department consists of the chief state law adviser and other law advisers, all advocates, who advise the government and public service institutions (including the provincial administrations) on a variety of matters (one immediately here thinks of the legal opinions of advocates), including whether or not clemency should be granted. They also draft statutes. Like state attorneys and state advocates, they are salaried public servants.

3 Master of the Supreme Court

An office which has existed since 1673, the Master was in former times (particularly in the republics) known as the orphan master or master of the chamber of orphans. The title "Master of the Supreme Court" was introduced during the British occupation and has existed ever since.

The Estates Act provides that the Minister of Justice shall appoint a Master for the jurisdictional area of every provincial division of the Supreme Court. His duties are principally the supervision of the administration of deceased and insolvent estates and control over the guardian's fund. The Master also has exclusive rights of supervision over the administration of the property and estates of minors, the mentally disturbed, persons under curatorship, and persons permanently absent from the country (and who have appointed no representative). The Master issues letters of guardianship and curatorship.

Generally speaking, the Master performs his duties under the eventual control of the Supreme Court which often calls for his advice – e g on whether or not a person who has been declared insolvent, should be rehabilitated.

4 Registrar of Deeds

An office for the registration of title deeds was established as early as 1714; by 1732 an "Erf Brief Boek" (deeds register) existed. The British authorities built on these foundations and we today find a body with comprehensive duties which from one point of view are of great legal significance, and from the other, offer the man in the street an important form of protection.

The Deeds Registries Act provides that there will be eight Deeds Registry Offices each in its own area. It also, however, provides for the continued existence of the registration office for Rand towns in Johannesburg. There are thus nine offices at present.

The registrar is required to apply the provisions of the Act which provides for the registration of land, rights to immovable property and antenuptial contracts. A number of ancillary duties are listed in the Act, e g the preservation of documents in the archives of the registration office, the examination of all documents submitted to the registrar for signature or registration, the registration of grants and transfers, of bonds, etc.

The registrar may, generally speaking, not register, attest or sign a deed or certificate that has not been drawn up by a conveyancer. As regards antenuptial contracts and bonds on movable property, however, the practitioner concerned is the notary.

5 Other registrars

Of the statutory registrars, two appointed by the Minister of Commerce, Industry and Tourism warrant brief mention.

(a) Registrar of Companies

The importance and scope of this registrar's duties are clearly discernible from the role played by legal entities in the commercial and legal life of the community. The establishment, existence and termination of a company are subject to statutory control.

Documents of incorporation must be submitted to the Companies Registration Office in Pretoria. A company comes into existence only once the registrar has certified on the memorandum and articles of association that it has been incorporated. Even before this, however, the registrar must have approved the company's name.

The registrar is responsible for the administration of the registration office which, within the framework of the Act, fulfils a key function. In company law the doctrine of disclosure (viz the requirement that certain information on companies always be available to interested parties) is of great importance; it replaces the alternative method of detailed regulation by the State. The information relates to the company's incorporation documents which embody, *inter alia,* the aims, powers and scope of the company; the issue of shares; financial statements (where applicable), etc. This documentation must be submitted to the registrar who in turn makes it available to interested persons.

The extent of the registrar's duties can only be fully understood against the background of the English developments in company law and our own legislation.

(b) Registrar of Patents

In England legislation to protect immaterial property and inventions appeared quite some time ago. As early as 1860 similar legislation was introduced at the Cape. Building on this tradition the Union and Republican legislatures established a Patents Office under the control of the Registrar of Patents.

The registrar is required to examine every appli-

A few of the first Secretaries of Justice of the Union of South Africa. On the left below is Jacob de Villiers Roos BA LLB, who was appointed Secretary of Justice when the Union came into being. On the right is Willem Eduard Bok D Iuris (Leyden) who fought on the side of the Boers during the South African War (1899–1902), was taken prisoner of war and later practised as a lawyer. He was appointed Secretary of Justice in 1916. After his period of service as Secretary of Justice, the person on the far left, Francis Petrus (Toon) van den Heever BA LLB, achieved fame as a judge and Afrikaans poet. He was an expert on the old sources of law and played an important part in establishing Afrikaans as a legal language. His daughter, The Honourable Leonora van den Heever was appointed as a judge of the Northern Cape Division of the Supreme Court on 1 July 1969 and is the first woman in South Africa to have been honoured in this way.

cation for a patent and every complete specification in the prescribed manner to determine whether it is legally valid. If it complies with the requirements set in the Patents Act, he must accept and register it. He is further required to maintain a register of patents in which, *inter alia,* details with regard to applicants for patents and persons to whom patents have been granted, to inventors and to the classification of patents in accordance with their subject matter, must be recorded. The registrar must further arrange for the periodic publication of a patents journal containing detailed particulars of all full specifications accepted.

Nothing further need be said of the importance of this body to the national and international legal and commercial community.

(c) Registrar of Trade Marks

In the sphere of industrial property, mention should also be made of the Registrar of Trade Marks who controls the Trade Mark Office in Pretoria. This registrar's specialized court has already been discussed.

A person claiming to be the owner of a trademark which he uses or proposes using, and who wishes to have the mark registered, must apply to the registrar in the prescribed manner for registration in the trade-mark register. The application may be accepted, or rejected, or accepted subject to such amendments, conditions or limitations as the registrar may deem fit. Any objection to a decision of the registrar is heard by the registrar either formally or informally.

As in the case of patents, the international convention for the protection of immaterial property applies to trade-marks. This is indicative of the importance of the registration office.

6 Police and Prisons

In any discussion of the instances controlling criminal justice one must perforce also mention the police (who investigate cases for submission to the prosecutor) and the prisons (who are responsible for the custody of and the execution of sentence on a convicted person).

(a) Police

The pre-Union colonial police forces (e g the Cape Mounted Police and the Orange River Colony Police) together with various urban police forces (e g those of Durban and Pietermaritzburg) continued to exist after Union, while at the Lonsdale conference of commissioners of police the establishment of a national force was discussed. The South African Police Force came into being on 1 April 1913.

In terms of the Police Act, the duties of the South African Police include the maintenance of national security, the maintenance of law and order, the investigation of offences, and the prevention of crime. The composition of the force reflects these functions.

The activities of the specialized *security branch* of the police are well known. After their initial training, these detectives – like all policemen – first become members of the uniformed branch who perform general duties such as patrol, investigation of motor accidents and less serious offences, charge office duties, etc. While crime prevention is the principal task of the uniformed branch, the detective force is concerned primarily with the investigation of crime. Highly trained detectives are also to be found in the specialized divisions, for example, in the commercial branch and in the South African Criminal Bureau with its fingerprint and handwriting experts, its forensic laboratories, ballistic section, etc. Here modern scientific techniques and equipment are put to the service of the investigation of crime.

Our second police force, too, should not be overlooked. This is the Railway Police Force which operates primarily within the sphere of the railways and harbours and fulfils the same functions and enjoys the same statutory powers as the South African Police.

(b) Prisons

Before 1910 each colony had its own laws governing prisons and rehabilitation centres. The majority of these Acts were repealed in 1911 when the national prison service was established. The 1911 Act was later repealed by the 1959 Prisons Act.

Not only is it the duty of the Directorate of Prisons to ensure that every prisoner is held in safe custody, but it is also required to ensure, as far as is possible, that convicted prisoners receive treatment and training which will lead to their rehabilitation so that a basis for habits of diligence and industry is formed.

The emphasis placed on positive socio-scientific treatment is illustrated by the training and modern penological approaches given to the more than 16 000 members of the prison service. Social care of prisoners is an on-going process, and apart from the employment of trained social workers to support prisoners the department works in close cooperation with the Department of Social Welfare and Pensions to ensure the adaptation, employment and housing of released prisoners.

Space unfortunately does not permit a discussion of the classification, treatment and training of prisoners, or of the types of prisons and their facilities, or of the prison boards and the parole system.

General: the Department of Justice

This contribution could have been approached from a different angle, viz that of the government department entrusted with the administration of justice in our country. Not only is it responsible

The crest of the Department of Justice. It consists of a shield with two scales balancing on the edge of a sword. As a whole it symbolizes justice, reasonableness and honesty. The scales weigh up the different interests against each other and the sword (by means of punishment and compensation inter alia) ensures the balance.

for the day-to-day flow of the legal administration, but also for the maintenance and promotion of a proud part of our legal heritage. In what has been dealt with we touched upon various sections of the department, for example the magistrates, attorney-general, Master's office etc. Much could be said of the other sections, but unfortunately that would be beyond the scope of this chapter. One could easily expand on the duties of those behind the scenes at head office, the personnel section, training, legal planning and law formulation and the internal security sections. There are, of course, also those responsible for the physical facets of administration, for example, the provision of office and court space, furnishings, library services, finance, etc – in short, the auxiliary service section. We shall, however, content ourselves with this mere listing of the organization and manpower underlying the maintenance and execution of administration of justice in South Africa.

SA Law Commission

The legal planning section of the department is responsible for the administrative arrangements pertaining to the appointment and the channelling of the commission's reports to the minister. There is a strong secretariat, of which most officials are research officers.

The law commission (established in 1973) replaced the Law Reform Commission of 1950, and consists of five to seven members appointed by the State President and serving in a part-time capacity. Provision is also made for the appointment of *ad hoc* members. The chairman and deputy-chairman must both be judges; the former generally a judge of appeal.

In terms of the Act, the aim of the commission is to conduct research with regard to all branches of the law, and to study and investigate the law with a view to recommendations for the development, improvement, modernization or revision thereof.

The secretariat examines each proposal received, to determine whether it warrants the attention of the commission. To achieve its goals, the commission draws up programmes listing the various matters for consideration in order of preference. These programmes are laid before the minister for his approval. The secretariat undertakes research and may also call upon experts. Consultation with all interested bodies is an important part of each project. If after the completion of its investigation the commission feels that legislation is called for, it draws up draft legislation. This is submitted to the minister to whom the commission's annual report is also submitted.

The recent divorce legislation is the fruit of the labours of the law commission.

Legal aid

Before 1969 legal aid consisted principally of the voluntary provision of assistance by legal practitioners to needy litigants. In 1969 the Legal Aid Act instituted an independent Legal Aid Board to organize and control a countrywide system of legal aid to needy persons. The duties and powers of the board are, *inter alia,* to secure the services of legal practitioners and to determine conditions on which legal aid can be granted.

The Legal Aid Board comprises ten members under the chairmanship of a judge. The other members include five legal practitioners and the directors-general of Justice, Co-operation and Development, and Health, Welfare and Pensions.

The legal aid scheme which was instituted in March 1971, is administered under the provision of the director of legal aid (in Pretoria).

Legal aid officers are appointed in the major cities; officials attached to the magistrates' and commissioners' courts throughout the country are also appointed legal aid officers.

The concept "needy person" is not defined in the Act, and to determine who is entitled to legal aid a means test (which is revised from time to time) is set by the board. Despite this test, however, aid may still be granted in deserving cases. The fees payable to practitioners are determined in consultation with the professional bodies concerned.

Legal aid is granted for civil, criminal and quasi-judicial suits. Provision is made for appeal to the director against the refusal of aid by a legal aid officer.

Conclusion

Part of our legal heritage is the satisfaction of the demands of the legal community. This is the task facing legal administration today – just as legal administration served a young South Africa in times past – and in its tremendous growth to meet the demands of modern society, our administration of justice is building upon a colourful and proud legal heritage.

D H Sampson BA (Hons) MA (Oxon) Attorney Durban

11

LEGAL EDUCATION

Early developments

Legal education in South Africa has been slow to evolve. It has been said that the law lags behind in providing solutions to the social, economic and political problems of the day. Lawyers are notoriously conservative, and as the development of legal education is bound up with the growth of the law and of the legal system itself, it is not surprising that reforms have usually followed at a sedate pace.

"Our present system of legal education, if it can lay claim to such a name, is very unsatisfactory."[1] These words were written in 1919, more than a century after the British system of administration of justice had been introduced at the Cape.

The story of the evolution of legal education together with the survival and growth of the Roman-Dutch law during the nineteenth century is colourful and interesting.[2]

Of the early pioneers in the field of legal education there were several whose contribution was outstanding. The beginnings of organized tuition appeared to have coincided with the lectures introduced by Mr (later Professor) J H Brand, later to become the president of the Orange Free State Republic. As the first professor of law at the South African College in Cape Town, Professor Brand helped to prepare candidates for admission as advocates for the examinations set by the Board of Public Examiners. A successful candidate obtained the Certificate of Higher Class in Law and Jurisprudence which by virtue of Act 12 of 1858 became an additional qualification for the Bar.

Several worthy successors followed Prof Brand, until one Casper van Zyl arrived on the scene. Initially he conducted large private classes for both the advocates' and attorneys' examinations without, it should be noted, charging any fees. Later he became a lecturer at the South African College in Cape Town which had by 1874 introduced examinations for the degree of LLB.

Van Zyl's contribution to legal education was by no means limited to lecturing. His work entitled *The Theory of the Judicial Practice of the Colony of the Cape of Good Hope and of South Africa generally*, first published in 1893, was a beacon to light up the paths of many students and practitioners of the generation of that time. Indeed, with the exception of Burton's *Law of Insolvency*,[3] published in 1829 and Tennant's *A Notary's Manual*, published in 1844, there was virtually no other textbook of any consequence which had emanated from this country.

In 1873 when the Board of Public Examiners was replaced by the University of the Cape of Good Hope, the conferring of a law degree in South Africa became possible for the first time. It should be noted, however, that although lectures were provided by the South African College, the university itself was merely a degree-granting institution. It had no provision for the tuition of students and it was Van Zyl who in 1889 put forward the following plea for the establishment of a "school of law":

> "I call it by the humble name of 'school', I dare say others would like to fly higher and prefer to call it a college or university. It matters, however, very little to me by what name it is called, so long as we know that we have a place in this colony where law can be systematically and scientifically taught by competent men trained in the knowledge of law."[4]

Although there had been a faculty of law in the making for a number of years, it does not appear to have been a faculty in the modern sense. True, lectures were given, examinations were set and degrees were conferred, but there were no full-time teachers of law. The position was stated as follows in 1918:

> "Before the inauguration of the three universities established by the Acts of 1916, there existed no teaching university in South Africa; the then existing University of the Cape of Good Hope was merely an examining body. Students at that time mostly picked up their knowledge of law as best they could; for years many of them must have studied the authorities of the old law of Holland with very

1 Bodenstein 1919 *SALJ* 358.
2 Cowen 1959 *Acta Juridica* 1.
3 For an interesting biography of Sir W W Burton, see 1935 *SALJ* 257.
4 1889 *Cape Law Journal* 247.

Johannes Henricus (Jan) Brand (1823–1888) obtained a master's degree in law from Leyden University (LLB). He then practised as a barrister at the Inner Temple in London and later as an advocate in Cape Town. He earned a formidable reputation as an advocate and taught as a lecturer and professor at the South African College. In 1856 he entered the political arena and in 1864, at the age of forty years, was sworn in as the fourth president of the Orange Free State. He was re-elected for five terms and held office until his sudden death in 1888.

little knowledge of the interpretation and application of that law in South Africa. In some cases of late years, there have been examiners who took for granted on the part of students a knowledge of leading cases decided by the local courts, but . . . a student could hardly be expected to know without instruction which of the many hundreds of cases which have been decided by the courts are to be regarded as leading ones, and if he did know which were such, he could as little be expected to go to the very great expense of acquiring the books in which such cases are recorded. Something has been done to remedy previously existing deficiencies; it would seem to be invidious to point out in what respects these remedies were lacking in those qualities which might yield fruitful results."[5]

Former Orange Free State judge, Melius de Villiers, then went on to describe the true nature of a law faculty as he had experienced it at the University of Leyden. There were eleven professors in the faculty of law, besides lecturers and "privaat-docenten". They were men thoroughly proficient in their department; the professor of Roman law for instance was a man who had made that system of law his life's study. The professor of history of Roman-Dutch law was the foremost authority in the world on that subject having also made that the study of a lifetime. "Such men," wrote De Villiers, "who devote themselves to one special department of law and have made a scientific study of the same I venture to say we have not had in South Africa, nor shall we ever have until ample funds are available for the purpose of obtaining such men and a sufficient number of them to enable each to confine himself to his own special department."

By the Act of 1916 referred to above, the University of the Cape of Good Hope was abolished and three new universities were established, namely that of Cape Town, that of Stellenbosch and that of South Africa. The last-mentioned at that time consisted of a number of constituent colleges, or what may be called "sub-universities". At that time it was considered by De Villiers

> "hopeless to expect a proper and fully equipped faculty of law at any of the constituent colleges, and even at the other two universities the outlook did not seem hopeful".

He went on to say:

> "The fact is that one university – at the very utmost two – would have been ample for the needs of a population so small as that of South Africa is; and even with one it seems doubtful whether there would have been funds available for a fully staffed professorate. With the three universities thus fully staffed there would probably be more professors of law than the students of that subject."[6]

Some sixty years later academics were to be heard to question whether sixteen law schools were not too many, and to suggest that the "proliferation of law faculties" was a great pity as it was one of the reasons "why legal education in this country is in a state of flux and even confusion"![7]

5 Melius de Villiers 1918 *SALJ* 157 – see biographical sketch in 1978 August *DRP* 417.

6 Op cit 158.

7 Van Wyk in *Legal Aid in South Africa* 172.

Casper Hendrik van Zyl (1842–1914) was a prominent attorney who worked for reform in the profession. He was the driving force behind the establishment of the Cape Law Society in 1883. He also served as professor of law at the South African College for a number of years. As author, the following works speak of his valuable contribution to legal literature: A summary of the Leading Principles of the Law of Costs *(1882),* Judicial Practice *(1893), and* Notarial Practice *(1909). Speaking on behalf of the judiciary, at the time of his death, Chief Justice Kotzé paid the following tribute to his memory:*

"Dr van Zyl was a man of many parts. He was entirely a self-made man, which goes very much to his credit, and we always looked upon him as certainly one of the leading lights of the honourable profession with which he has so long been connected. From my earliest training in the law I have always looked upon the profession of an attorney as a very important branch. Much depends upon the attorney in the early preparation of the case, and Dr van Zyl always set a very excellent example in that direction, and also to the articled clerks in his office who have spread themselves, I may say, all over the Union of South Africa. He has taken in them a most kindly and fatherly interest, and shown others what their duty really is towards their articled clerks. He was also well known for his great industry and research. We are all acquainted with what he has written from time to time, and when the culminating honour came to him, when he was honoured with the Degree of Doctor of Laws by our University (Cape Town), all of us, not merely the members of his own profession but I feel sure all members of the Bar – I may say the brotherhood of the law – rejoiced that at last his services had been recognized. I am sure that far and wide throughout the Union of South Africa the news of his unexpected and sudden death will be received with the greatest regret, and with feelings of great sympathy for those who are near and dear to him."

However, the foundations for the future had been laid and in 1920 Prof George Wille (a name well known to law students up to the present day) was appointed to the chair of Roman-Dutch Law at the University of Cape Town, whilst in the same year Mr Henry Fagan (later chief justice) was appointed to the Stellenbosch University chair. In the words of Prof D Pont:

> "Legal education in the proper sense of the word commences in South Africa in 1920 with the faculties of law of the universities of Cape Town and Stellenbosch."[8]

In the words of Prof D V Cowen:

> "And with the appointment in South Africa of full-time professors of Roman-Dutch law, it could, I think, fairly be said that the future of that system was assured."[9]

The survival of the system of Roman-Dutch law had indeed been in jeopardy for reasons which are dealt with in chapters 4 and 9 of this work.

Whatever the difficulties which hampered the growth of the law, its practice went on regardless throughout the century, and many illustrious names can be listed of those who achieved prominence and contributed much to the building up of our legal system.

The education of practitioners of law had always been as it now is, a twin-stream system. The distinction between advocates and attorneys had existed both in Holland and in England, and so it continued at the Cape. Elsewhere, due to a paucity of advocates, elements of duality existed: in the Orange Free State Republic and originally in the Transvaal attorneys could appear in the superior courts and dual practice continued in Natal until much later.

Advocates

The legal education of advocates in the early days at the Cape was non-existent, as advocates were all trained either in Holland or, after the British occupation, in England. As we have seen, a local LLB following the Certificate of the Higher Class in

8 1969 *Acta Juridica* at 112.
9 Op cit 18.

South African College Schools (SACS) and the University of Cape Town both developed out of the South African College, established in 1829. In 1857 Sir Langham Dale presented the first lectures in law in the college buildings.

Law and Jurisprudence was later introduced as a qualification for admission. The system of reading in chambers in pupillage as it existed in England was unknown, and it would appear that the preparation of an advocate for his practice left much to be desired. Judge Melius de Villiers writing in the *South African Law Journal* in 1918 associated himself with an earlier article by Prof Bodenstein and expressed himself as follows:

> "The reason why in this country more particularly strict attention should be paid to the scientific teaching of our law is the desirability of neutralizing as far as may be possible the effects of the very extraordinary and anomalous rules prevailing here relative to admission to the bar. Generations of lawyers have contentedly put up with the fact that hitherto and still at present a man may be called to the bar in London after 'eating his dinners' and passing certain not very exigent examinations, without the slightest knowledge of our law being required, and, coming out to the Cape, is at once fully qualified to be admitted to practice as an advocate."[10]

These complaints did not go unheeded and it was soon to be provided by the Admission of Advocates Act of 1921 that only certain degrees from specific Dutch or British universities would be recognized as a qualification for the admission of advocates, and then only provided that the candidate had passed an examination in Roman-Dutch law and in South African statutes. A further step forward was taken in 1946 when this Act was amended to provide specifically for the right of admission as an advocate of any person who had obtained the degree of bachelor of laws as a postgraduate degree in any South African university.

10 1918 *SALJ* 155.

Professor R R R B Howes, first dean of the University of Cape Town Law Faculty (1912–1919).

By Act 74 of 1964 it became necessary for the course of study to be of five years' duration, including *inter alia* one-year courses in Latin, Afrikaans and English. This degree has thus become the basic qualification for an advocate, but two further steps were to be taken before the present-day situation was arrived at. The first was the introduction of the system of pupillage by a uniform rule adopted by the provincial societies of advocates which provided that a newly admitted advocate must spend at least four months in chambers as a pupil to three of his more experienced colleagues. This form of training, based on the English model which had been in operation for a number of years was designed to add a modicum of practical experience and knowledge of procedure to the novice before letting him loose, so to speak, in the courts of law.

It had been a criticism of the system that the mere attainment of a university degree, even a post-graduate LLB, was no guarantee that a newly admitted advocate would be competent to assume the responsibilities with which he might be confronted soon after admission.

The second step which has recently been taken with a view to countering this criticism, has been the introduction of a Bar examination on a national basis which all newly admitted advocates are obliged to pass before being admitted to membership of the relevant society of advocates.

Attorneys

According to the observations of one Sir John Barrow, the reputation of attorneys at the Cape in 1801 seems to have reached a low ebb. This is not surprising since, as he put it: "To become a procureur it is by no means necessary to study law. Hence any bankrupt shopkeeper or reduced officer or clerk in any of the departments may set up for an attorney."[11]

However, in 1829 the system of apprenticeship in articles of clerkship was introduced, the period being five years. Unlike the position in England where 100 years earlier an Act of 1729 had made a term of five years articles obligatory, the law of Holland made no provision for articled clerks, and as Van Zyl puts it "gentlemen there were admitted to their profession after examination without indentureship". Until 1829 it was the same at the Cape, and although some form of examination was apparently required, it was of a formal nature to test character and fitness. In 1858 a Cape Act provided that those who passed the second class law examination as it was then known might be admitted after three years' service in articles. This was, however, a discretionary concession. When the university was incorporated in 1873 it was provided that before a clerk could enter for his university law examination (then known as the law certificate examination), he must have passed the university matriculation examination.

In 1877 at the request of the Cape town attor-

11 See Van Blommestein *Professional Practice for Attorneys* 1.

Henry Allan Fagan (1889–1963) started his studies as a student of literature at Stellenbosch University. He later enrolled as a theology student and in 1910 commenced his legal studies at London University. He was admitted to the English and Cape Bars in 1914. He was involved in the founding of Die Burger *and served for three years as assistant-editor on the editorial board of that paper. In 1920 he was appointed the first professor of Roman-Dutch law at Stellenbosch University. He returned to the Bar and produced a number of*

literary publications. After a spell in politics during which he served under General J B M Hertzog as, inter alia, *Minister of Native Affairs, Education and Social Welfare, he was appointed to the Cape Bench in 1943. In 1950 he was appointed judge of appeal and in 1957 chief justice.*

neys a rule of court was passed which made it compulsory for an articled clerk to pass an examination in the practical branch of his profession. This was perhaps the origin of the practice and procedure examinations which candidate attorneys must pass in order to qualify at the present time.

In due course as the university law faculties were established, the university law degree came to be recognized as an important element in the training and qualification of attorneys.

The automatic remission of two years' articles after a university degree had been obtained was the next logical step, and a jump to 1934 brings us to the pattern, founded over the past century or more, which became the basis of future extension and development into the modern era.

The Attorneys, Notaries and Conveyancers Admission Act of 1934 for the first time prescribed uniform rules for admission which applied throughout the country. The requirements in so far as legal education is concerned were basically threefold:

(a) Service in articles: two years after attaining an LLB degree, three years after obtaining any other approved university degree, local or otherwise, or five years in any other case.
(b) The passing of examinations in practice and procedure.
(c) The passing of the Attorneys Admission Examination conducted by the Joint Committee for Professional Examinations, or the attainment of a university law degree recognized by that body as its equivalent. A person admitted or entitled to be admitted as an advocate was exempted from this examination.

This framework has continued to the present day, subject to two basic changes:

(a) In 1959 the place of the Joint Committee for Professional Examinations was taken by the Board for the Recognition of Examinations in Law appointed in terms of s 4 of the University Amendment Act of 1959. Under the new dispensation university examinations recognized by the board, which had previously been only an alternative course open to candidate attorneys, now became the only avenue for admission. Save for those already committed to the previous course, the examinations by the joint committee fell away.
(b) In 1970, at the instance of the Association of Law Societies (which had come into being in 1938) a special degree known as the *Baccalaureus Procurationis*, a new degree of four years' duration, was instituted at the various universities.

After sitting for his admission examination in Utrecht, the Netherlands, William Mortimer Robertson Malherbe (1875–1964) returned to South Africa to fight in the South African War (1899–1902). He was captured and exiled to India until the end of the war. He obtained a doctorate in law from Leyden University in 1906 and thereafter practised as an advocate in the Transvaal. He was editor of Die Brandwag *and in 1921 was appointed professor of Roman-Dutch law at Stellenbosch University – a position he held for thirty years. He was a staunch supporter of Afrikaans as medium in legal matters.*

This degree was placed under the control of the Board for the Recognition of Law Examinations which has laid down the minimum requirements with which the curricula for the new degree in the various law faculties must conform in order to be recognized.

This degree, popularly known as the B Proc, replaced the Attorneys Admission Examination which had been introduced in 1959, and in so doing rendered obsolete a number of approved degrees, diplomas and certificates of the various universities, which had been recognized as equivalent to the admission examination.

Dealing in turn with the above elements, one might at the outset observe that over recent years a much greater awareness of the requirements of legal education and the deficiencies in the present system has developed. This has been largely due to the circulation amongst all attorneys of the journal *De Rebus – the SA Attorneys' Journal,* originally created under the name *De Rebus Procuratoriis* as the organ of the Transvaal Law Society, some twenty-five years ago.

Articles of clerkship

Casper van Zyl wrote of the duty of an attorney to instruct his articled clerks that it was so obvious as scarcely to admit of argument. After citing the words of Warren in his *Moral, Social and Professional Duties of Attorneys* he stated:

> "It follows that if the principal cannot instruct his articled clerks owing to want of work, he should do the next best thing, viz: give them imaginary cases to deal with; and if he is so fully occupied as to have no time to attend to them, he should employ others to do so, himself supervising the work at reasonable intervals as he cannot wholly divest himself of this necessary obligation. For just as he can call upon them to fulfil their part of the contract, so they can require him to fulfil his: each, of course, within reason."[12]

Although the system of articles has certain admirable features, for instance, the right of an articled clerk to appear in the magistrate's court on his principal's behalf, the standard of training is apt to vary from one office to another. In some cases attorneys do not have the time to devote to systematic training of their clerks, whilst in other cases their practice is too specialized or limited to provide complete coverage. To some extent this weakness is remedied by the examinations in practice, procedure and bookkeeping which are designed to ensure a minimum uniform standard of competence in those areas, and this is a positive feature of our system of legal education.[13]

But perhaps the situation has not improved since Dr H D J Bodenstein wrote as follows in 1919:

12 *Judicial Practice* 760.

13 Described as a "safeguard in the interests of the public" by Van Zyl *Judicial Practice* 173.

The President C R Swart Building houses the Law Faculty of the University of the Orange Free State. The building was named after Dr C R Swart, a former State President of the Republic of South Africa and chancellor of this university. Dr Swart also practised as an advocate.

"It is the duty of the attorney to instruct his clerk, but this duty is only too often made light of. The clerk does the work of an ordinary clerk, and must try and get hold of such knowledge of the law as he requires for his examination in his spare time, and by such means as he can lay hands on. Often he has to do the reading without any assistance at all. When he is so fortunate as to serve his articles in a big town he may hope to attend such classes as he himself and his fellow clerks have succeeded in establishing by their contribution. The instructors themselves are as a general rule practising lawyers who cannot devote all their time to this part of their work, and must avail themselves of spare hours suitable to their students. Neither can a clerk devote all his time to instruction. Instructor, as well as instructed, generally meet each other after a day's work, hard work sometimes, rendering them less fit either to impart or take in knowledge."[14]

At that time, of course, the position was different since as Dr Bodenstein points out the university law faculties were barely emerging, and the average articled clerk had no previous background of systematic teaching and training in legal principles and method.

In certain of the larger centres, classes are arranged to assist articled clerks to pass their practice and procedure (and now bookkeeping) examinations. The three-weeks' winter school run by the Cape Law Society is a notable example of a practice training school in embryo.

Awareness that the practical training of attorneys should be improved, has caused the Association of Law Societies to focus attention on the whole system of legal education in the Republic.

An ad hoc committee was accordingly appointed to carry out investigations and to make recommendations. During the course of its investigations it considered in particular the introduction of institutionalized training for articled clerks on the model of the so-called "colleges of law"

14 1919 *SALJ* 361 – see, too, 1971 Sept *DRP* 373, 374.

which exist both in the United Kingdom and Australia. These institutions in particular concentrate on giving an articled clerk the type of practical training for the work which he will encounter in his early years in practice. It is accepted that the system of apprenticeship to a practising attorney does not, taken as a whole, meet and fulfil this need and that some means must be found of ensuring that a uniform level of practical training can be made available for all articled clerks. Information on overseas institutions was gathered[15] and as an experiment a four weeks' course was conducted in Pretoria in July 1979. This was attended by articled clerks from throughout the Republic and tuition was administered by practising attorneys and others who could speak from practical experience. This "pilot project" was regarded as a success and during 1981 practical schools for articled clerks were presented in Cape Town, Bloemfontein, Johannesburg and Durban. Steps are now being taken to create an institute of legal education which it is hoped will serve as a vehicle for introducing this type of training on a permanent basis.

Academic training

The other aspect of legal education which has been the subject of review is the academic training of law students during the process of obtaining the necessary university degree. Here too, awareness and interest have increased in recent times. Presently the only two degrees recognized for admission as an attorney are the B Proc and LLB degrees. In addition a person in possession of an LLB or B Proc degree must serve articles of clerkship for two years. An important landmark was the formation of the Society of University Teachers of Law in South Africa, which held its inaugural meeting at Pretoria on 23 July 1957.

This society has held regular conferences, and today comprises representatives of sixteen university law faculties. No longer could it be said as it was said by Dr Bodenstein that "it is plain that the present system is really a sham. It purports to be a complement to the theoretical training of the future attorney, whereas in fact it can hardly be such, as the theoretical training is lacking".

Melius de Villiers (1849–1938) studied at the South African College and was admitted to the Cape Bar in 1872. He was appointed a judge of the Orange Free State in 1876, and in 1879 became chief justice of the Orange Free State. Despite numerous offers, he chose to remain in the Orange Free State until 1900 when he was sent to the Cape as a prisoner of war and thence allowed to travel to England. In 1899 his well-known work Roman and Roman-Dutch Law of Injuries *appeared. After the war he practised as an advocate at the Cape until his appointment as professor of Roman-Dutch law at Leyden University – a chair which since his retirement in 1909 has never been filled.*

The addresses delivered at the conference of the society held at Cape Town on 28 January 1959[16] indicate that much careful thought was being given to the scientific planning of university curricula, and also to the methods of tuition.

In 1975 at Port Elizabeth a further conference was convened by the university teachers of law, this time the spotlight being focussed specifically on legal education. A wide-ranging assortment of papers was delivered covering the various facets of our system of legal education. These papers have been collected and are valuable as perhaps our first record of any conference devoted solely to this subject.

15 See 1976 Aug *DRP* 380, Sept 473 (Canada) and 1977 October *DRP* 629 (Australia).

16 1959 *SALJ* 310 et seq.

Continuing legal education

For some time it has been recognized that legal education is a continuing process which does not cease upon qualification and, furthermore, that it is essential that the process be continued if proper standards of competence on the part of the attorneys' profession are to be maintained. For some years the Association of Law Societies has given serious attention to the arranging of lectures, seminars and the like with a view to ensuring that attorneys have the opportunity of keeping abreast of new legislation and developments in the law, and ensuring too, that they are kept informed by experts of the latest trends, concepts and procedures in different areas of the law.

In 1974 a Standing Committee of Continuing Legal Education (CLE) was appointed by the Association of Law Societies to develop these programmes, and at first they were arranged on a Republic-wide basis through an agency employed for the purpose, speakers and tutors being recruited from the ranks of the profession, the universities and the public service.

In 1976 it was decided that the standing committee could and should take over the running of the CLE programmes itself and a director of legal eduction, Dr C F Eckard, was appointed to organize programmes and recruit lecturers.

Such was the success of the standing committee and the director that in 1977 seven different programmes were conducted, those being repeated in smaller centres where appropriate and where there was a demand. These have proved very popular and during the years 1977–1980 more than 9 200 attorneys attended one or other of the twenty-four programmes which were conducted at 162 different meetings throughout the country.

The committee is also working on publications to be issued to attorneys providing guidance in the more typical procedures and the opportunity of keeping up to date with new trends and developments in the law.

Public service lawyers

The contribution of the Department of Justice to the development of our legal system and its influence on legal education should not be underrated.

Public service law examinations have catered for the education and training of future magistrates, prosecutors, registrars and other government officials for a century or more.

In 1919 a strong plea was made by Prof H D J Bodenstein for higher standards of education for prospective magistrates.

In his words:

> "[Our future magistrates] enter the service without legal qualifications, and are for their legal training, cast on their own resources. When fortunate they might share in the classes for future attorneys, but more often they are attached to offices in centres where they have to help themselves. Is it possible to expect under such circumstances properly trained lower judges? The fact that they pass a legal examination is no proof whatsoever of a harmonious and proper training.
>
> "It is ridiculous that the judges should be in possession of a lower qualification than the legal practitioners. Therefore the theoretical examination of attorneys as well as civil servants of the legal branch should be the same."[17]

A change in the system came about in 1959 when the Board for the Recognition of Law Examinations took over the control of these examinations from the old Joint Committee for Professional Examinations. Thenceforth, the Public Service Law and Public Service Senior Law Examinations were to be conducted by the universities, subject to minimum requirements as to curricula set by the Recognition Board.

Typically, the Public Service Law Examinations (now known as the *Diploma Iuris*) course comprises elements of private law, mercantile law and criminal law, civil and criminal procedure and interpretation of statutes, and is spread over a period of three years.

The Public Service Senior Law Examination (now known as the *Diploma Legum*) takes a further two years and is open to those who have passed the Public Service Law Examination *(Diploma Iuris)* or an examination deemed to be its equivalent.

Much progress has been made in the intervening

17 1919 *SALJ* 362.

years since 1919 when the question attracted the attention of Prof Bodenstein.

Today the Department of Justice conducts intensive and continuous in-service training programmes for prosecutors and examiners in the Master's and deeds offices. Officers of the department have arranged and participated in numerous seminars for attorneys, and many products of the Department of Justice Training Division find their way into the private sector of the profession as attorneys and advocates.

The department does everything in its power to co-operate with other bodies pursuing the same objectives, and in particular the universities.

Its task as the department sees it is "to give the graduate his professional grounding and the necessary practical experience to round off his academic training".[18]

A particularly useful aspect of the department's activities is to run regular refresher courses for magistrates and future regional magistrates. In the lecture room many exasperating problems that magistrates have to cope with are thrashed out by the students and much interest is generated by these discussions and much benefit derived from them.

Today, it is by no means uncommon for a magistrate to hold an LLB degree, so perhaps the pleas of the past did not fall on deaf ears.

In this context it is interesting today to read the view of Prof Hahlo expressed some twelve years ago:

> "My own views which have not changed over the years, and which are, I am able to say, being increasingly shared by present members of the profession, are that every lawyer, advocate, attorney or magistrate should be required to qualify initially in the same way: by obtaining the BA (or B Com) LLB degree by full-time study at a university."[19]

In 1961 similar views were expressed by Prof Pont:

> "Legal education in South Africa would be placed on a proper footing by having one and the same qualification for advocates, attorneys and law officers in the magistrates' courts, namely the LLB degree of one or other of the teaching universities ... Candidates for service in the law offices of the government, after obtaining the LLB degree, should be required to serve in a magistrate's court and the offices attached thereto for a similar period (one year) and after office hours to attend classes held by competent and qualified teachers in court practice and the conduct of cases."[20]

Latin

The question whether or not Latin should be a requirement for a law degree has been much debated over the years. Despite a recent move to have Latin relegated to the position of an optional subject in the academic qualification of an attorney, the position remains unchanged. Latin is required to matriculation standard as a prerequisite for the B Proc degree, and to first year university standard for the LLB, the latter being the academic, requirement for admission as an advocate.

Control over legal education

The evolution of our present system of legal education has over the years resulted in some diversity in the influences and power which are brought to bear on the law student and the qualified lawyer.

- The full bench of the Supreme Court in each province admits advocates and attorneys to the rolls as officers of the court (and where appropriate removes them).
- The judge president of each division appoints examiners for the attorneys' practice, procedure and bookkeeping examinations as recommended by the law society concerned.
- The chief justice has power to regulate the qualifications for examiners and also the method of conducting examinations.
- The law society of each province, besides recommending examiners, controls admission to articles, and exercises jurisdiction over the training and conduct of articled clerks.
- "The Association of Law Societies now arranges for courses for articled clerks to assist them

18 Report of Department of Justice 1978.
19 1969 *SALJ* 465.
20 1961 *Acta Juridica* 17.

in the preparation for their future careers: sometimes lectures are arranged locally by attorneys' circles."

- The university law faculties educate prospective advocates, attorneys and public service lawyers to the levels required for their respective qualifications.

Liaison between judges, attorneys and advocates on the one hand and the university law faculties on the other often exists through the various law faculty boards or advisory boards on which judges and practitioners are sometimes invited to sit. Judges are usually invited to attend conferences of the Society of University Teachers of Law and frequently deliver papers, as do attorneys and advocates.

The Board for the Recognition of Examinations in Law, which regulates curricula for the B Proc degree comprises representatives of each law faculty and an attorney representing each provincial law society.

The Association of Law Societies, a federal body representing the five law societies (including South West Africa), itself elects annually a Standing Committee on Legal Education and a Standing Committee on Continuing Legal Education. As stated above, it had also appointed an ad hoc committee consisting of three university professors and four attorneys to investigate and report on legal education, which brought out its report in 1977.

The Association has close links with the Attorneys, Notaries and Conveyancers Fidelity Guarantee Fund, created under Act 19 of 1941 and re-enacted in the Attorneys Act 53 of 1979, and the delegates of the law societies who comprise the board of control of the fund are often the same delegates comprising the council of the Association. The significance of this in the sphere of legal education is that the fund's board of control is empowered, so long as the fund amounts to not less than two million rand, to –

(a) make grants, with the approval of the Minister of Justice, to any individual or university for the purpose of education or research in law; and

(b) pay honoraria to any person for services rendered with the object of enhancing the professional standards of practitioners.

These functions are fulfilled by two committees appointed by the fund, one of which is chaired by a judge nominated by the minister, and has as a member a representative of the Department of National Education.

Funds which for the most part emanate from interest earned by attorneys' trust accounts, can in this way be channelled to the universities and the profession for the promotion of legal education and the consequent raising of professional standards.

The future of legal education

The inter-action of the various elements – the universities, government departments, the profession and the judiciary – has led to our present system by an evolutionary rather than a planned process.

The question which must sooner or later be faced, is whether this is a sufficient answer to the demands of modern society in the field of legal education.

Is the end-product, the qualified attorney or advocate, well enough equipped for the challenges of a changing world?

There is today a strong reformist movement in legal education, more vociferous abroad perhaps than in the Republic. It is contended that the law as taught today is no longer relevant to the times and that the way in which it is applied is no longer suited to the needs or the pocket of the man in the street.

Subjects ought to be regrouped, it is said, and greater emphasis should be placed on the social evils which the law should seek to remedy. Instead of concentrating on the acquisition and retention of wealth, more attention should be given to such aspects of the law as consumer protection, social security and justice, environmentalism, criminology and the like.

In some quarters the emphasis sought to be placed on this type of course is regarded as "unreal". "Too often," it is said, "these subjects are taught not by persons well qualified in sociology or economic philosophy, but by enthusiastic young lawyers filled with reforming zeal who find it easier to ride the hobby horse of social reform than walk behind the plough of disciplined legal reasoning."[21] This may be so elsewhere, but the reformist views of some leading South African academics should not lightly be disregarded.[22]

However, if lawyers are to serve the needs of society, should their education not be planned more systematically? The case for the establishment of a council of legal education or similar advisory or controlling body to co-ordinate and plan legal education, was considered by the ad hoc committee appointed by the Association of Law Societies.[23]

The function of such a body would be to provide a permanent liaison between the various elements concerned with legal education, and the framework within which to enable legal education to be planned throughout its various stages. With a more concerted effort we might then bridge the gulf between the conservatism of the past and the predictable demands of the future.

Is the time not ripe for such a venture?

A final thought for the future: the high cost of litigation has recently caused to be resurrected the old question of fusion or amalgamation of the advocates and attorneys, wholly or partially, into a unified profession. This perennial question was the subject of debate at the South African law conference in April 1978.[24]

It is perhaps coincidental that both branches of the profession are feeling their way towards some form of institutionalized practical training to supplement or supplant pupillage and articles. One of the problems in running these schools will be the shortage of manpower – of experienced and able practitioners willing to devote their time to giving tuition. This difficulty would largely fall away, it is submitted (as seems to be the case elsewhere) in circumstances where a single profes-

Helgard Dewald Johannes Bodenstein (1881–1973). In 1907, after having travelled widely and studied in South Africa and the Netherlands, Bodenstein obtained a doctorate in law with distinction from Leyden University. He studied under professors Fockema Andreae and Melius de Villiers. He was simultaneously admitted as a member of the Middle Temple and as a Barrister-at-Law in London. Subsequent to his return in 1908 he served consecutively as attorney, public prosecutor, secretary to the judge president, and professional assistant to the attorney-general of the Orange Free State. He was appointed professor of South African law at the Gemeentelike Universiteit of Amsterdam; a post he held from

1912–1919. He then returned to South Africa to become assistant-editor of Die Burger. *Academic life, however, remained his first love, and in 1912 he was appointed professor at Stellenbosch University. In 1927 he was appointed as South Africa's first Secretary of Foreign Affairs.*

21 Nash loc cit.

22 Dugard *Legal Aid in South Africa* 161.

23 Par 29.17 et seq of Ad Hoc Committee Report. See also, Van Wyk de Vries Commission Report, par 12.13 and recommendations 1 and 2 for a "standing conjoint committee".

24 For powerful arguments for fusion, see Hoppenstein 1959 *SALJ* 296, and address by late Mr Justice A B Beyers to Law Society of the Cape of Good Hope in 1964 in Van Blommestein op cit 142 seq; also address by Mr Justice (as he then was) Anton Mostert to 1978 SA Law Conference published in 1978 *DRP* 531.

sion is able to deploy its forces to the task of planning and running such establishments. To this extent, legal education could stand to gain from fusion – a consideration which, however, is purely academic at the time of writing.

The need for a closer liaison with others concerned with legal education was canvassed on the initiative of the attorneys present at the 1981 conference of the Society of University Teachers of Law held in Pietermaritzburg, and it was then agreed to form a liaison committee comprising academic and practising lawyers as a channel of communication and a forum for discussion of matters of mutual concern. This, it is hoped, may serve as a useful platform for future planning in the field of legal education.

G W Cook BA LLB (Witwatersrand) Attorney Johannesburg

12 THE LEGAL PROFESSION IN SOUTH AFRICA

In considering the organization of the legal profession, it should first be noted that South Africa, like England, divides practising lawyers into two groups – advocates and attorneys. The organization of the advocates' branch of the profession differs materially from that of the attorneys' branch.

There is a law society in each of the four provinces. It is interesting to note that the provincial law societies have, in one form or another, been in existence for a considerable time. According to Randell and Bax *The South African Attorneys' Handbook*, the dates from which it can be said that there was an organized law society in each province of what is now the Republic, are the following:

Cape of Good Hope	1883
Orange Free State	1885
Transvaal	1905
Natal	1907

The four societies presently operate in terms of the provisions of the Attorneys Act 53 of 1979. This is a comprehensive measure dealing with all aspects of the control of the practise of law by attorneys. It also controls the operation of the legal practitioners' fidelity fund which was first created by Act 19 of 1941.

The Attorneys Act perpetuates the existence of the four provincial law societies, the names of which are stated to be:

The Law Society of the Cape of Good Hope
The Law Society of the Orange Free State
The Law Society of the Transvaal
The Natal Law Society

The Act also applies to South West Africa and the law society of that territory is designated:

The Law Society of South West Africa

Section 57 of this Act provides that every practitioner (attorney) who practises in any province, whether for his own account or otherwise, shall be a member of the law society of that province. It also provides for the admission and enrolment of attorneys who have served articles of clerkship and who have the necessary academic qualifications.

Application for admission is made to the court. Court is defined as any court of a provincial division. On admission the attorney becomes an attorney of that court. Having been so admitted, an attorney may apply to the registrar of any court other than the court by which he was admitted, to have his name placed on the roll of attorneys of the court for which such registrar has been appointed. It should be noted that if, having had his name placed on the roll of attorneys of a court other than the court which admitted him, he practises in the area of that court, he has to become a member of the law society of the province in which that court is situated. It may, therefore, be necessary for an attorney to be a member of two or more law societies.

Notaries and conveyancers are only permitted to practise as such if they are admitted as attorneys, have obtained the necessary academic qualifications entitling them to practise as a notary or conveyancer as the case may be, and have been enrolled by the court in the same way as attorneys are enrolled.

The Act prescribes the objects of the provincial law societies. These include the following:

To regulate the exercise of the profession; to encourage and promote efficiency in and responsibility in relation to the profession; to uphold the integrity of practitioners; to provide for the effective control of the professional conduct of practitioners.

An onerous duty carried out by the law societies is that of exercising control of the professional conduct of practitioners. This involves the exercise of extremely important disciplinary powers.

In order to enable the councils of the law societies to discharge their duties, they employ full-time permanent staff. The officers of each law society in fact perform a vast number of duties and are engaged in extensive activities in the interests of the practice of law and of legal practitioners.

The Association of Law Societies has presented ten national law conferences since 1960. Papers dealing with topical subjects such as "The jurist in a changing world" and "Consumer protection" were delivered at these conferences. Overseas guest speakers are often also invited.

Suid-Afrikaanse
Regskonferensie
Mount Nelson Hotel
Kaapstad
1 tot 4 April 1975

Foto deur: "Charles Field Studio", Kerkstraat, Wynberg, Kaapstad.

South African
Law Conference
Mount Nelson Hotel
Cape Town
April 1 to 4, 1975

Photograph by: "Charles Field Studio", Church Street, Wynberg, Cape Town.

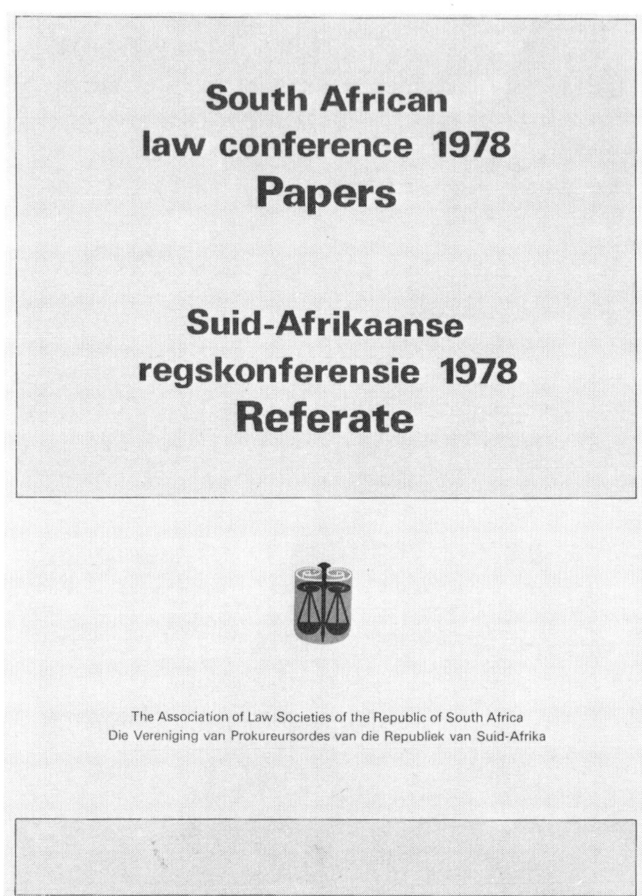

The Act provides that the affairs of each society shall be managed and controlled by a council which is given wide powers to manage and control the affairs of the society. The council of each law society is elected by the members of the law society concerned.

The income of each society is obtained, in the main, from subscriptions from members. The councils of the law societies are vested by the Act with considerable disciplinary powers and may enquire into cases of alleged unprofessional or dishonourable or unworthy conduct and are given the power to apply to court for the removal or suspension of an attorney from practice, to impose a fine not exceeding R500 or to reprimand a member and to recover from him the costs incurred by the council in connection with the enquiry into his conduct. They are also given disciplinary powers over articled clerks, having the power to cancel or suspend articles of clerkship, impose a fine not exceeding R100, or reprimand a clerk.

The rules of each of the provincial law societies make provision for the establishment of what are termed "circles". Each province is divided up into circle areas, and the attorneys in each area constitute a circle of the law society. In terms of constitutions approved by the law societies, the circles, speaking generally, elect office bearers and meet from time to time to consider local matters affecting members in the particular areas. The circles are

also called upon by the councils of the law societies of which they are circles, to assist in supplying information and expressing opinions for the guidance of the council in question. In addition to circles, attorneys in several areas have, with the authority of the responsible law society, constituted local attorneys' associations. The constitutions of such associations have to be approved by the responsible law society.

Although it has been suggested from time to time over the years that there should be constituted a South African Law Society, the provincial law societies have always expressed the view that they should retain autonomy over the control of the attorneys practising in the provinces over which they have jurisdiction. There is no doubt that the councils of the provincial law societies have exercised a very firm and satisfactory control over the practice of law and that it is probably unwise to tamper with a system that works extremely well. Furthermore, local traditions have evolved and these are often somewhat jealously guarded. However, the provincial law societies do not work in a vacuum. At a conference of law societies held in December, 1938, the idea of creating a South African Law Society was discarded and it was unanimously decided to establish the Association of Law Societies. The Association of Law Societies (now known as the Association of Law Societies of the Republic of South Africa) has operated successfully ever since and today performs a very useful function. It co-ordinates the activities of the provincial law societies; it constitutes a forum for debating all matters affecting the legal profession on a nation-wide scale and affords the profession a mouthpiece particularly in its dealings with government departments and ministers of state. The constitution of the Association of Law Societies has been amended from time to time over the years. The following is a very brief summary of the main provisions of this constitution:

The objects of the Association are set out at length, but in the main they provide that the Association shall promote the interests of the profession and encourage legal education. The foundation members of the Association are the four provincial law societies of the Republic of South Africa. The Law Society of South West Africa has been accorded the status of associate membership having no voting rights. It is specifically provided that the autonomy of the constituent societies shall in no way be altered or abridged by the existence of the Association. The decisions of the council of the Association or of the executive committee of the Association are, however, binding on constituent societies unless, at the time a decision is taken, all the representatives of any constituent society, present and having a vote, vote against it. In this event the decision shall not be binding on that society until it is ratified by the council of that society. The Association and every

other society shall, however, act on such a decision but the dissenting society shall not be bound until its council does so ratify. In other words a decision of the council or executive committee will bind the members of the Association save a dissenting member, which is then absolved from the duty of complying with the decision, but which may subsequently ratify and thereby become bound by the decision.

The constitution further provides that the business of the Association shall be managed by a council which consists of the president of the Association, three members of each of the constituent societies being the president and vice-president and one additional person who is a member of the council of the constituent society which he represents and who is nominated by such council.

Provision is also made for the appointment of an executive committee consisting of the president of the Association and the four presidents of the constituent societies. The immediate past president of the Association continues to attend meetings of the executive committee for one year in order to give continuity, but he exercises no vote.

The Association employs a secretary-general and staff and its headquarters are situated in Pretoria. Its funds are mainly obtained by contributions paid by the constituent societies. These contributions are paid on a per capita basis, the amount of which is determined by the Association

The attorneys' profession provides a special service to the public by publishing brochures on different aspects of the law. Thousands of brochures on subjects such as "Getting married?" and "Consult your attorney" were distributed in the last few years.

from time to time. The president of the Association is elected annually by members of the councils of the constituent societies in accordance with a somewhat detailed procedure.

The Attorneys Act of 1979, in addition to regulating the four law societies, reconstitutes the Attorneys, Notaries and Conveyancers Fidelity Guarantee Fund which was originally established by section 8 of the Attorneys Admission Amendment and Legal Practitioners Fidelity Fund Act 19 of 1941. This fund is customarily referred to as the Fidelity Fund. It is controlled by a board of control consisting of the serving presidents of all the law societies including the Law Society of South West Africa and two members of each law society elected annually by the council of that society. The sources of revenue of the Fund are mainly contributions by practitioners, income from investments and interest on trust money invested by attorneys which is referred to more fully below.

Every attorney pays a first contribution of R50 to the Fund on his admission and is required to pay an annual contribution unless the free assets of the Fund exceed R1 million in which event, as is presently the case, annual contributions are not required.

The purpose of the Fund is to reimburse persons who may suffer pecuniary loss as a result of theft committed by a practising attorney, his clerk or employee of any money or other property en-

Advocate Gladys Steyn was the first woman to act as public prosecutor in the circuit court at Senekal in 1926. Today the legal profession is popular with women and there are many women who are attorneys, advocates, prosecutors and law lecturers.

A page from the minutes of the Transvaal law society. The date on the minutes is 11 November 1892.

Notulen van Vergadering van Raad va[n] Bestuur gehouden ten Kantore van den Voo[r]zitter op Vrydag 11 November 1892.

Tegenwoordig. Voorzitter (E. Rooth) en de Heeren H. C. Scholtz en A. W. Baker.

Secretaris — (1) De Heer Maudby was aangesteld als Secretaris pro tem.

Rule nisi tegen J. T. M. Thwaits Procureur enz. — (2) Voorzitter maakt Vergadering attent op procedu[re] in de zaak van "Mills v. Breytenbach" gehoord te Heidelberg by den laatsten zitting van het Rondgaande Hof. Uit de getuigenis gebleken, dat Eischers Procureur J. T. M. Thwaits een gedeelte van de vonnis in de zaak zou kregen indien het door hem gewonnen was. Dat daarop eene Rule Nisi door het Hof uitgereikt was den Heer Thwaits oproepende om redenen aan te toonen waarom hy niet van de Rol geschrapt zou worden wegens (Champerty) zyne mishandeling

Rule Nisi en extract van getuigenis gelezen en na discussie besluit de Raad

Dat Korte Brief gegeven wordt aan Adv. Wessels om namens de Orde te verschijnen en te melden dat aangezien het Hof reeds Kennis genomen heeft van de zaak vóór d[e] in werking treding van het Reglement, de Orde alleen de attentie van het Hof roept [op] het feit dat zy nu ingelyfd zyn.

Goedgekeurd 2[?]. 12 92. — Edw Rooth Voorzitter.

trusted by or on behalf of such persons to him or his clerk or employee in the course of his practice or while acting as executor or administrator in the estate of a deceased person or as a trustee in an insolvent estate or in any other similar capacity.

In addition to meeting claims by persons from whom monies have been stolen, as above set out, and paying certain incidental expenses incurred by claimants, the Fund is empowered to apply its assets for a number of purposes, the most important of which are the following:

It may reimburse a practitioner's bank charges incurred in connection with the keeping of his trust account as required by the Act.

It may pay the premium (or portion thereof) in respect of professional indemnity group insurance taken out in favour of practitioners and it may meet the costs (or portion thereof) incurred by a practitioner in connection with his obtaining what is termed his fidelity fund certificate.

Provided the free assets of the Fund exceed R2 million which is presently the case, the Fund is empowered, with the approval of the Minister of Justice, to make grants, subject to such conditions as the board of control may determine, to any individual or to any university or university college for the purpose of education or research in law and may pay an honorarium to any person for services rendered at the request of the board of control with the object of en-

The old Market Hall in Pretoria during the trial of the Reformers.

hancing the professional standards of practitioners.

Sections 48 to 50 of the Act should receive particular attention from all practitioners as these sections contain details regarding the procedure for establishing claims against the Fund. It usually falls to the lot of an attorney to act for a person who has, by virtue of the theft of money by an attorney or his clerk or employee, a claim against the Fidelity Fund. The procedure laid down by the Act has to be followed and attorneys should be particularly careful not to expose themselves to claims for professional negligence by failing to follow the prescribed procedure.

Section 78 of the Attorneys Act provides that a practitioner may invest in a separate savings or other interest-bearing account at a banking institution or building society any money deposited in this trust account which is not immediately required for any particular purpose. It is further provided that the interest accruing on such deposits must be paid over to the Fidelity Fund by the practitioner concerned in the prescribed manner. This provision is an extremely interesting and important one. Many years ago, an investigation into the legal position established that interest earned on trust monies did not accrue to the attorney who was the agent of the client whose money it was, with the result that collectively a vast sum of money was lying idle and not earning interest. As a result of representations made by the Association

De Rebus – the SA attorneys' journal is the mouthpiece of the SA attorneys' profession. It is South Africa's largest legal journal with a circulation of more than 9 000, read by practising attorneys and their staff, judges of the Supreme Court, many advocates, legal advisers and other lawyers on the staff of companies, municipalities, banks and universities. The journal publishes articles on

law and practice, finance and office administration, professional news, practical aids, new books and other matters related to legal practice. The cover themes of the journal have proved to be popular with readers and thousands of offprints have been sold since 1975.

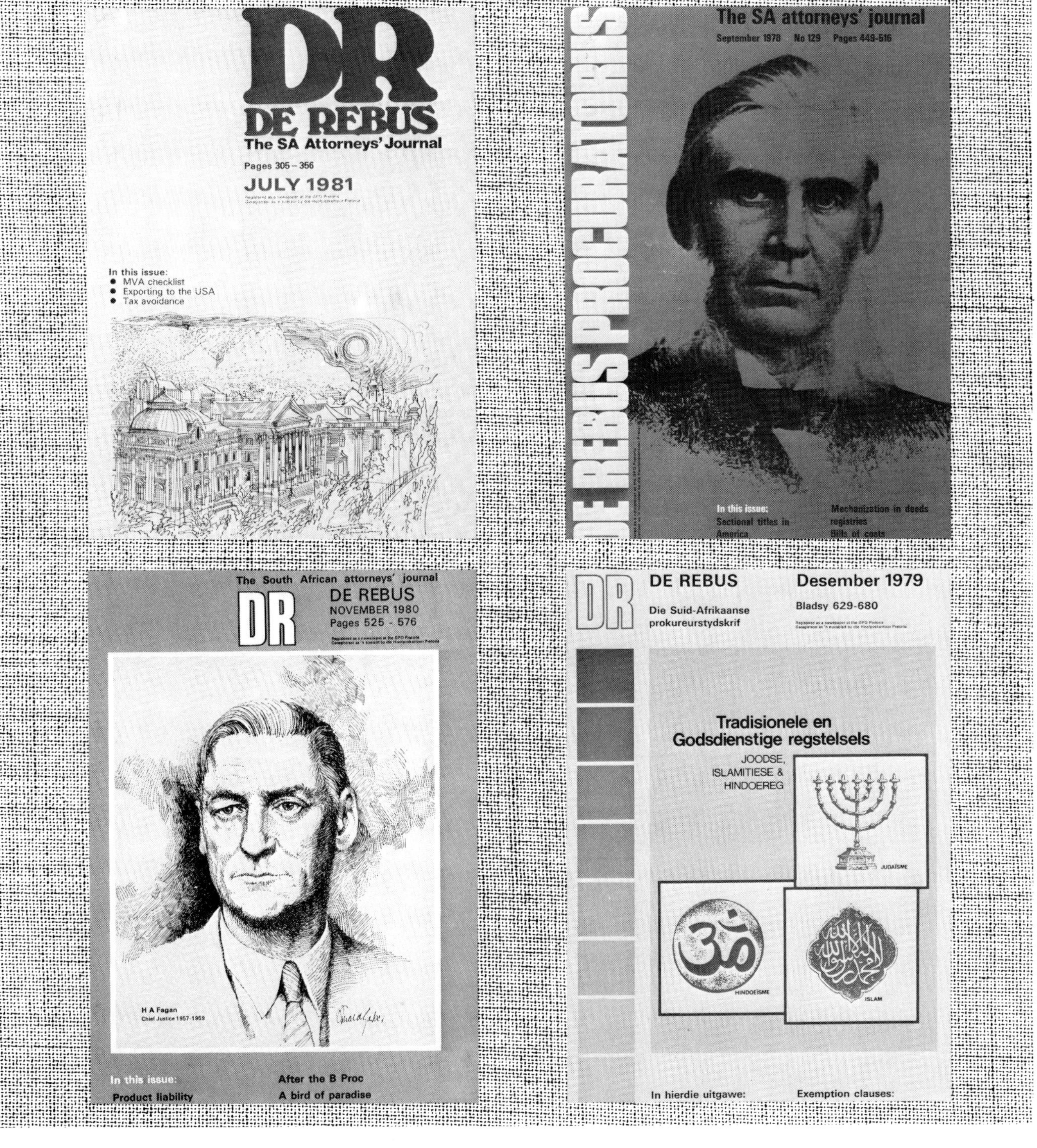

In 1926 Constance Mary Hall was the first woman to be admitted as an attorney in South Africa. This memorable occasion was witnessed by three well-known brothers in the legal profession: on the bench was judge B A Tindall; counsel for the applicant was adv R J L Tindall and Miss Hall's principal was Mr W A Tindall.

of Law Societies, the then legislation was amended so as to permit, what might be termed the fixed residue of attorneys' trust accounts, to earn interest and the payment of this interest to the Fidelity Fund. The uses to which the Fidelity Fund can put its monies are, of course, restricted. These uses fall into the following categories:

(a) The payment of claims.
(b) The advancement of legal education.
(c) The raising of the standard of the legal profession.
(d) Defrayment of attorneys' costs incurred in maintaining trust accounts.

It is apparent that collectively, these objects may be regarded as being in the public interest, thus justifying in full measure the use of the interest accruing on trust accounts for the purposes prescribed. The extent to which money is available for these purposes depends on the goodwill and co-operation of attorneys in investing trust monies in accordance with the provision of the Act.

It is appropriate to make mention of the other branch of the profession, viz the advocates. There is very little legislative provision governing advocates. In terms of the Admission of Advocates Act 74 of 1964 any division of the Supreme Court shall admit to practice and authorize to be enrolled as an advocate, any suitably qualified person who makes application. Having been admitted to practice, and having had his name entered on the roll of advocates, an advocate may practise in any court in the Republic. An advocate can appear in all courts, including the lower courts, but he may not practise as an attorney and as an advocate at the same time.

The practising advocates in the Republic and South West Africa have formed themselves into voluntary societies. Such societies exist in every area in which there is a Supreme Court, for example, Cape Town, Pietermaritzburg, Pretoria, Johannesburg and Bloemfontein. The societies of advocates regulate their own professional conduct and have domestic rules concerning minimum fees, the necessity (at certain Bars and in certain matters) for senior advocates to have juniors briefed with them and, very important, all members of the various societies of advocates are, in terms of their domestic rules, prohibited from taking instructions directly from the public and are obliged to take instructions only from practising attorneys.

An admitted advocate can practise as such without being a member of a Society of Advocates, but if he takes instructions directly from the public he may be doing the work reserved to attorneys and may then fall foul of the Attorneys Act.

The several societies of advocates are associated together in a further voluntary association known as the General Council of the Bar of South Africa,

The crest of the Association of Law Societies of the Republic of South Africa.

The crests of some of the provincial law societies. From left to right: the Law Society of the Orange Free State; the Law Society of Transvaal. The provincial law societies have approximately 5 300 members.

on which all the societies are represented and which meets periodically to discuss matters of general interest to the legal profession and in particular, to practising advocates and further, to consider, promote and deal with all matters concerning the teaching and practice of the law and the administration of justice.

Finally, reference should be made to a large number of persons qualified either as attorneys or advocates or both, who are employed in government, provincial and municipal services; in the various semi-state corporations such as Amcor, Iscor and Escom; in banking institutions and in major public companies. These persons are not regarded as practising attorneys or advocates. They are in receipt of regular salaries and, not being in practice, the attorneys among them are not presently required to be members of a law society. The Societies of Advocates restrict membership to persons in full-time practice.

Section 57 of the Attorneys Act requires every practitioner who practises in any province to be a member of a law society. The powers vested in the councils of the law societies under section 69 of the Attorneys Act contemplate that provision may be made in fixing subscriptions to differentiate among members belonging to different categories determined by the council in question. Attorneys who have been admitted as practising attorneys and who retire, may be permitted to continue as non-practising members and it is competent for law societies to admit to membership duly qualified and enrolled attorneys who are not in practice, but in employment. This, in fact, is the case in the United Kingdom and a non-practising attorney has even held the position of president of the English Law Society. It may well be appropriate for the councils of our law societies to make provision for membership by admitted attorneys engaged in legal capacities, but not in private practice. In fact, the Law Society of the Transvaal has already promulgated certain rules in this regard.

The attorneys' branch of the profession has over the years been extremely active in relation to many matters of public interest and welfare. These activities of the profession are on occasion organized by particular provincial law societies but more generally are the responsibility of the Association of Law Societies of which, as mentioned earlier, the provincial law societies are all members. It is of interest to give some examples of the far-reaching initiatives which have been taken by the Association. It has studied and proffered advice on proposed criminal law revision, on sectional titles legislation, on sale of land by instalments legislation, on legislation to amend the Companies Act and on many other similar issues. The Legal Aid Act which was enacted in 1969 and is now in operation throughout the country was largely the result of research conducted by and recommendations made by the Association. Members of the legal profession now render aid to poor persons in terms of this Act. They are remunerated at reduced rates by the Legal Aid Board on which they are represented. The necessary funds are voted by Parliament. The Association also took the initiative with regard to the creation of the South African Law Commission. As a result of representations made to the Department of Justice in 1969 the South African Law Commission Act of 1973 became law and a permanent law revision commission was established.

The Association is a member of the International Bar Association and regularly sends delegations to the meetings of that Association which take place in different parts of the world every two years. The Association has taken a keen interest in creating opportunities for Black students to serve articles of clerkship so as to qualify as attorneys. It has constituted its secretariat in Pretoria as a clearing house to find openings for Black clerks and to bring clerks and principals together. The wide sphere of the activities of the Association appears from the fact that it has sixteen standing committees while the profession is also represented on five official bodies. In addition to the standing committees the Association appoints ad hoc committees to study and report on particular problems as they arise from time to time. The Association has, over a period of many years, organized national law conferences at intervals of two or three years. The last conference was held in Durban in April 1981, the theme of the conference being consumer protection. The Association publishes *De Rebus* – the South African Attorneys' Journal, a monthly publication which concentrates on articles and issues which are of interest to attorneys. The Association also performs a number of functions in the field of public relations and legal education, e g the publication of brochures and papers, liaison with the press, arranging lectures and seminars, maintaining relations with overseas professional bodies and the establishment of practical training schools for articled clerks in South Africa.

Illustration acknowledgments

Balkema, AA: 43, 44, 45, 46 *(drostdye)*, 157 (court plan),
Cape Archives: 39 (minutes), 118 (documents)
De Rebus – the SA attorney's journal: 126–133 (chief justices), 160 (court buildings), 169 (Van Zyl)
Die Vaderland, Johannesburg: 111, 113 (cartoons)
Elsevier, Amsterdam: 1 (Rome)
Feenstra, R, Leyden: 12 (Codex Florentinus), 20 (Digest)
Giunti Marzocco, Florence: 2 (Twelve Tables)
Iconographisch Bureau: 23 (Damhouder), 24 (Grotius), 25 (Merula), 28 (Noodt), 29 (Van den Sande), 30 (Voet, Huber, Voorda, Van Leeuwen), 31 (Scheltinga, Van der Keessel, Van Bijnkershoek)
Lydenburg Municipality: 96 (magistrate's office, magistrate's court)
Musée de l'Armée, Paris: 51 (Napoleon)
National Cultural, History and Open-air Museum, Pretoria: 35 (Russouw), 37 (slaves), 48 (first British occupation), 53 (second British occupation), 55 (Eastern Province, 57 (Cape Legislative Assembly), 59 (prominent Cape residents), 67 (magistrate's office), 68 (Boshof), 69 (Froneman), 70 (Brand, Hoffman), 75 (Steyn), 76 (Raadsaal), 77 (Fischer), 80 (Isandhlwana), 81 (Rorke's Drift), 84 (Victoria), 94 (Pietermaritzburg), 98 (Bar), 99 (Coster), 100 (Leyds), 101 (Palace of Justice), 102 (Lawley), 103 (Kruger), 107 (political figures), 108 (conference), 109 (Hertzog), 110 (Malan), 111 (cartoon), 112 (Strijdom, Verwoerd), 113 (cartoon)
National Portrait Gallery, London: 119 (Mansfield), 122 (Halsbury)
Nuntius, Pretoria: 147, 148, 152, 153, 156, 159, 162, 163, 165
Phot Bibl Nat, Paris: 18 (Accursius, Baldus), 19 (Bartolus), 32 (Pothier)
Rijksmuseum, Amsterdam: 36 (Steelmasters' Guild)
SA Law Journal: 74 (Buchanan), 75 (Gregorowski), 77 (Maasdorp), 78 (Van den Heever), 87 (Cloete), 88 (Mason, Gallway), 89 (Tatham), 90 (Bale), 123 (Burton)
South African Library: 61 (Bell, Ayliff), 103 (Solomon)
Staatliche Museen Preuzzischer Kulturbesitz, Berlin: 120 (Von Savigny)
Van Schaik, Pretoria: 173 (Malherbe)
Westbrook, W: 54 (Elim)

Bibliography

Anon "The Honourable Mr Justice Dove-Wilson, KC" 1905 *Natal Law Quarterly Review* 1

Anon "The Hon A W Mason" 1916 *SALJ* 1

Anon "Sir Henry Connor" 1919 *SALJ* 223

Bird J *The Annals of Natal* 1495–1845 Cape Town: Struik (1965)

Bodenstein H D J "Our Universities and the Training of our Jurists" 1919 *SALJ* 358

Botha C Graham "Criminal Procedure at the Cape during the 17th and 18th centuries" 1915 *SALJ* 319

Botha C Graham "The Early Inferior Courts of Justice at the Cape" 1921 *SALJ* 406

Brookes E H and C de B Webb *A History of Natal* Pietermaritzburg: University of Natal Press (1965)

Broome F N *Not the Whole Truth* Pietermaritzburg: University of Natal Press (1962)

Cameron Edwin and Dirk van Zyl Smit "The Administration of Justice, Law Reform and Jurisprudence" 1979 *Annual Survey of South African Law* 538

Cowen D V "The History of the Faculty of Law in the University of Cape Town, 1859–1959" 1959 *Acta Juridica* 1

De Villiers Melius "Legal Education in South Africa" 1918 *SALJ* 155

De Villiers Melius "Random Reminiscences of the Orange Free State Bench" 1920 *SALJ* 398

Dugard J *Legal Aid in South Africa* Durban: Faculty of Law, University of Natal (1974)

Du Toit Niconette "Ons regserfenis: Melius de Villiers (1849–1938)" 1978 *DRP* 417

Ferreira J C *Strafprosesreg in die Laer Howe* Cape Town: Juta (1979)

F St L S "Honourable Sir W W Burton" 1935 *SALJ* 257

Greyvenstein G P "Die Prokureursorde van die Oranje-Vrystaat" 1978 *DR* 74

Hahlo H R and J C de Wet "The Legal Training of Advocates, Attorneys and Public Servants" 1959 *SALJ* 310

Hahlo H R and E Kahn *The Union of South Africa: The Development of its Laws and Constitution* London: Stevens Cape Town: Juta (1960)

Hahlo H R and E Kahn *The South African Legal System and its Background* Cape Town: Juta (1968)

Hermesdorf B H D *Schets der Uitwendige Geschiedenis van het Romeins Recht* Nijmegen: Dekker & Van de Vegt (1970)

Hoppenstein A S "Fusion – The Answer to the High Cost of Litigation" 1959 *SALJ* 296

Hosten W J A B Edwards Carmen Nathan and Francis Bosman *Introduction to South African Law and Legal Theory* Durban: Butterworths (1977)

H S C "A Note on the Extended Jurisdiction of Resident Magistrates" 1885 *Cape Law Journal* 283

Kaser M "Zur Methode der römischen Rechtsfindung" *Nachrichten der Akademie der Wissenschaften in Göttingen* Phil-Hist klasse (1) Göttingen: Vandenhoeck Ruprecht (1962)

Kaser M *Das römische Privatrecht* 1 München: Beck (1971)

Kunkel W *Römische Rechtsgeschichte: Eine Einführung* Köln-Wien: Böhlau (1972)

Maitland F W *Selected Essays* Cambridge: Cambridge University Press (1936)

Mostert A W "The Divided Bar: A Possible Solution" 1978 *DRP* 531

Nowers W A and C A Brink *Inventaris van die Argief van die Griffier van die Hooggeregshof van Suid-Afrika Oranje-Vrystaat Provinsiale Afdeling* (unpublished)

Pollock Frederick "Judicial Caution and Valour" 1929 *Law Quarterly Review* 293

Pont D "Die Opleiding van die Juris in Suid-Afrika" 1961 *Acta Juridica* 58

Pound Roscoe *Interpretations of Legal History* Cambridge: Cambridge University Press (1923)

RCS "Mr Justice Fischer" 1930 *SALJ* 1

Roberts A A *A South African Legal Bibliography* Pretoria: Wallachs (1942)

Sampson D H "Legal Education in Canada (1) Ontario" 1976 *DRP* 380

Sampson D H "Legal Education in Australia" 1977 *DRP* 629

Scholtz G D *Die Geskiedenis van die Regspleging in die Oranje-Vrystaat 1854–1876* MA thesis undated

Schulz F *History of Roman Legal Science* Oxford: Clarendon Press (1946)

Simons H J "The Status of Customary Unions" 1961 *Acta Juridica* 17

Söllner A *Römische Rechtsgeschichte, eine Einführung* Freiburg: Rombach (1971)

Spectator "News and Views" 1971 *DRP* 373

Spruit J E *Enchiridium, Overzicht van de Geschiedenis van het Romeins Privaatrecht* Deventer: Kluwer (1975)

Thomas J A C *Textbook of Roman Law* Amsterdam – New York – Oxford: North-Holland Publishing Co (1976)

Thompson L M "Constitutionalism in the South African Republics" 1954 *Butterworths South African Law Review* 49

Thompson L M *The Unification of South Africa 1902–1910* Oxford: Clarendon Press (1960)

Van Blommestein F *Professional Practice for Attorneys* Cape Town: Juta (1965)

Van Niekerk B v D ". . . Hanged by the Neck until you are dead" 1969 *SALJ* 457

Van Warmelo P *Die Oorsprong en Betekenis van die Romeinse Reg* Pretoria: Van Schaik (1978)

Van Wyk A H in *Legal Aid in South Africa* Durban: Faculty of Law, University of Natal (1974)

Van Zyl C H "A School of Law" 1889 *Cape Law Journal* 247

Van Zyl C H *Judicial Practice* Cape Town: Juta (1921, 1923)

VerLoren van Themaat J P "Die Regstelsel en Staatsregtelike Instellings van die Oranje-Vrystaatse Republiek" 1954 *THRHR* 142

Visagie G G *Regspleging en Reg aan die Kaap van 1652 tot 1806* Cape Town: Juta (1969)

Walker E A *The Great Trek* London: Black (1970)

Wilson M and Thompson L *The Oxford History of South Africa* London: Oxford University Press (1969)

Index

Bold numbers refer to illustrations

Bold numbers refer to illustrations

Bold numbers refer to illustrations

Bold numbers refer to illustrations

Bold numbers refer to illustrations

Bold numbers refer to illustrations

Bold numbers refer to illustrations

Bold numbers refer to illustrations

Bold numbers refer to illustrations

Bold numbers refer to illustrations

Cornelis de Cretser fiscael van
fort de goede Hoope aen Cabo
de Boa Esperança &a. ex offitio eijsr
ca. aenclaeger
contra

Anthonij Andriesz van Slane gewesen
soldaet ten dienste van de Nederlantse
geoctroijeerde Oost Indische Compe
op t'schip 't Huijs te Swieten en
nu ged.e gevanghen gedaeghde

De dato 22 maert ao. 1668

Seijde dat den ged.e en gevanghen gedaeghde, als een
overgegeven moortdadich mensch, sich soo verre
heeft comen te vergrijpen, dat alle den Eedt waer
mede aende Compe verbonden is vergetende,
sich dat hij als een mede moordenaer en maecker, door
aensprekinge van eene Jochim Cornelisz aengenomen
en met eede beloofft heeft, om met alle de schippers
oppenhoofden, mede lotgenoten, van tselven te vermoorden, en alsoo 't groote schip
Huijs Swieten af te loopen, nemaer om dat t'selve te
bequamer uijt te voeren, heeft aen eene Hans
Roddingh, alias Camboon, daer ooch toe versocht en
bewogen, verlangende alsoo met hun drien nevens
noch eene Michiel Cloppenburch (die op de reijse
overleden is) in stilte en behendicheijt, een
getall van de in de twintich sodanige schelmen.
met woorden getalt gesamentlijck geresolveert waren
(na dat ongeveer 14 dagen in zee waren geweest) te
gelijck de Capiteijn en de Constabels camer af te loopen,

de selve